'Out of Africa'

An investigation into the earliest occupation of the Old World

Marco Langbroek

BAR International Series 1244
2004

Published in 2016 by
BAR Publishing, Oxford

BAR International Series 1244

'Out of Africa'

ISBN 978 1 84171 604 6

© M Langbroek and the Publisher 2004

Author e-mail: marco.langbroek@wanadoo.nl

Author website: http://home.wanadoo.nl/marco.langbroek

BAR Publishing is the trading name of British Archaeological Reports (Oxford) Ltd.
British Archaeological Reports was first incorporated in 1974 to publish the BAR
Series, International and British. In 1992 Hadrian Books Ltd became part of the BAR
group. This volume was originally published by Archaeopress in conjunction with
British Archaeological Reports (Oxford) Ltd / Hadrian Books Ltd, the Series principal
publisher, in 2004. This present volume is published by BAR Publishing, 2016.

Printed in England

BAR
PUBLISHING

BAR titles are available from:

BAR Publishing
122 Banbury Rd, Oxford, OX2 7BP, UK
EMAIL   info@barpublishing.com
PHONE   +44 (0)1865 310431
FAX   +44 (0)1865 316916
www.barpublishing.com

Aan W.:

" 'Geen gekke bekken nou, Otje' zei hij kortaf, pinnig.
'Voelde je je toen door mij verraden? Dat wil ik weten!'.

'Verráden, Chrissie? Ai nou, wie is verraden? Jij bent
gegaan en ik ben gebleven. Zo is het leven, such is life,
zegt de Engelsman. Verraden? Wie zegt dat Chrissie?' "

F. Springer: *Bandoeng-Bandung (1993)*

Dedicated to:

Dirk Langbroek
(my father)

5 September 1932 – 3 November 2002

Why should I cry for you?
Why would you want me to?
What would it mean to say
I loved you in my fashion

Sting: *Why should I cry for you*
(from the album '*The Soul Cages*')

and to:

Marie Eugène François Thomas Dubois

Contents

List of illustrations:

Preface

*"This book is the first I have ever written.
I did not know it would be such a work."*

These words were written (or rather: dictated, as he had lost several of his fingers) around 1950-1951 by the French Alpinist Maurice Herzog [1]. They are the opening sentences of his book 'The Anapurna Expedition', a book which details his heroic and successful – and in aspects dramatic – attempt in the summer of 1950 to be the first to conquer a mountain of over 8000 metres. Dramatic, because he did so at the expense of several of his as well as of his comrade Louis Lachenal's toes and fingers and, while he was severely injured, had to suffer a dreadful journey back to the civilized world, carried over barren, remote mountain passes and through the jungle by his sherpas, with *ad hoc* surgery under very primitive conditions carried out on him by the expedition medic, Dr Jacques Oudot.

Herzog's words are rather apt for describing my feelings concerning this *BAR* volume, which is an adapted version of the dissertation on which I obtained my PhD degree at Leiden University in 2003. Writing a work actually has much in common with climbing a mountain. There is careful planning involved, a clear purpose and determination, very critical decision making along the journey, there is a necessary level of skill involved, it involves the endurance of hardships, and it takes considerable personal investment in terms of energy and dedication. Moreover, it brings you to a personal summit – at least, if you make it to the end. Just as conquering a mountain is not completed until the alpinist has successfully descended and reached the civilized world again (it is not enough to reach the top: one has to come back and be able to tell about it), a Ph.D. research is not completed until the results have been properly written up and approved of. As with climbing a serious mountain, completing the effort, when the body and mind are exhausted, is the most difficult, demanding part of the endeavour – and as often happens with climbing a mountain as well, disaster did strike from unexpected quarters during the final part of my particular descend.

Brief history of this monograph

While Herzog and his team very consciously set out to climb the 8075 metre high Anapurna and while I set out with a Ph.D. degree and a better understanding of the earliest occupation of Eurasia as my goals, the early hominins which found their ways into Eurasia some 1 million years ago probably were less driven by clear intentions and goals. This work is an inquiry into the events and processes which pushed and/or pulled them, out of Africa, into Eurasia. It involves a critical look at the chronology of early human dispersal, and several looks at opportunities and constraints provided by the environments these early humans entered. It tries to get some grip on how they coped with these constraints and opportunities. As for the exact 'why', we will probably never know. But at a very basic level, there is a rather down-to-earth answer possible. At some point in evolution, coping with an increasing variability in food availability on the developing African savanna made early humans reach a point of possessing the tactical capacities fit for other environments as well. Having reached that point, it probably was just inevitable that they dispersed. We do not know whether these early humans had purpose, but it is not likely that the dispersion of early humans into Eurasia was a case of purpose – it did not need purpose, only opportunity. This is the difference between occupying Eurasia on the one hand, and climbing a mountain, or writing a Ph.D. work, on the other.

The foundation of this work was laid in 1997, when I started to develop an interest in the hominin occupation of southeast Asia at the Brunhes-Matuyama boundary. The reason for this interest was the possibility of contemporaneity of hominin occupation with a large cataclysmic event: the impact of an asteroid in southeast Asia 0.8 Ma ago (see appendix 1). This was just a small issue of private interest at that time, not quite clearly connected to my studies in Palaeolithic Archaeology at Leiden University, and more the result of a strange engagement between my studies in archaeology and my private interest in the field of 'meteoritics'.

As the focus expanded to include the whole issue of "earliest occupations", it was decided that this should become my MA thesis, on which I graduated in September of 1998 and for which I was awarded the W.A. van Es prize that same year. Part of my thesis work eventually led to a small publication in the *Journal of Human Evolution* (Langbroek and Roebroeks 2000). With this publication, I entered the uneasy world of 'debating early occupations'. While I enjoyed building the models that are part of this work, I must admit I have never liked the seemingly endless debates regarding the chronology of early human occupations outside Africa. It was necessary to enter these debates however, in order to provide a basis for a model assessment of events which led to the early occupation of Eurasia. In my view, the only value of chronological debates is when they explicitly serve to arrive at a solid theoretical framework regarding the process behind the occupation. They are a burden which comes with the job of trying to make sense

---

1. M. Herzog: *De Annapurna Expeditie. De eerste top van 8000 m in de Himalaja bedwongen.* Scheltens & Giltay, Amsterdam (1952?). Quote translated from Dutch by the author.

of the earliest occupation of Eurasia, and the evolution of early hominin behaviour in Africa before and around that time.

Following my graduation, the realization had come that the study had the potential to be expanded into a Ph.D. research. Leftover funds of the NWO Pionier Project "Changing Views on Ice Age Foragers" (principal investigator Wil Roebroeks) financed one year of work. NWO then granted additional funding for another 1.5 years. In retrospect, these 2.5 years were not too much of a luxury: *"I did not know it would be such a work"*.

Acknowledgments

Climbing a mountain and writing a Ph.D. dissertation is a personal endeavour. However, just as Herzog had the support of his fellow expedition members and the many sherpas carrying supplies, preparing base camps, fixing climbing ropes, and supplying words of comfort, I had the support of several people, both in the Faculty of Archaeology at Leiden University and elsewhere, carrying scientific supplies, preparing scientific base camps, fastening scientific climbing ropes, and providing words of comfort. I want to thank my family, a few of my faculty colleagues, and my friends for their support, and several of the following persons in particular, in random order: the members of my PhD committee for their comments and suggestions; Alexander Verpoorte and Boudewijn Voormolen for many discussions and for setting out with me on the adventure of our joint Colmont field project in 2001; Raymond Corbey for sharing several enjoyable dinners with this "apeman" during which we pondered the riddles of handaxes without solving them; Thijs van Kolfschoten for much appreciated encouragement, support and valued feedback and discussion on issues of biochronology; Jan Kolen (now at the Free University, Amsterdam) for stimulating discussions on early hominin subsistence strategies in the days of my MA thesis work; Prof. Robin Dennell (Sheffield) for discussing ideas on grasslands and hominids in 1997-1998 in the context of my MA research, and for supplying several relevant publications; Prof. Naama Goren-Inbar (Jerusalem) for her hospitality and for showing me the artefacts from 'Ubeidiya and Gesher Benot Ya'agov during my visit to Jerusalem in April 2000, as well as for discussions and much appreciated comments on my work; and Prof. Youping Wang (Beijing), Prof. S. Matsu'ura (Tokyo), Prof. M. Hyodo (Kobe), Dr. John de Vos (Naturalis, Leiden) and Dr. Susan Keates (Oxford) for the supply of relevant publications.

I want to thank Aniek Abbink (Leiden) for her support and education while I was still an MA student; and my fellow students of that time, especially Erik van Rossenberg, Marjolijn Kok, Boudewijn Voormolen and Josara de Lange (the latter being a source of quibble very dear to me: I know she will not agree, and that is stimulating) and a number of other people mentioned below. I thank the students which enrolled in my classes, workshops and fieldwork (especially Gerrit Dusseldorp, Yannick Henk, Phil Glauberman, and Eline van Asperen) for enjoyable hours and thoughtful discussions – certainly they made it worthwhile; and I want to thank Natasja de Bruijn (Glasgow), Erik Peters (Leiden), Maartje van Bruggen (Leiden), Karianne Winthagen (Maastricht) and Olga Yates (Voorschoten) for moral support at several times and occasions. This work would also not have been possible without the excellent way in which Els Koeneman and Erik van Rossenberg as librarians maintain the accessibility of the library of the Leiden Faculty of Archaeology.

I wish to offer a special word of thanks to Els Koeneman, for her important effort in the late summer and autumn of 2002, when serious attrition started to take its toll, and my father died. Her strong and continuing personal support brought me comfort and at times helped me to go on. A similar word of thanks should be extended to Machiel van der Sman. Without these two persons, this monograph would perhaps not have been completed.

The list of persons whom I want to acknowledge is now almost finished: but not without mentioning Prof. Frans Rietmeijer (dept. of Earth and Planetary Sciences, UNM, Albuquerque) whom at several times has shown an accute interest in my work and the progress of my work, which is much appreciated, and helped me both to combine the fields of meteoritics and archaeology, and to jointly explore research questions outside the field of archaeology. He has also shown to be a good friend, in the best sense of this word. Last but not least, I thank Kelly Fennema for the much appreciated and not to be underestimated work of correcting the manuscript text into acceptable English, and for keeping me up to scratch when this manuscript was about to be finished.

Just as this work was being prepared for formal acceptance by the external examiner, my father, Dirk Langbroek, died on November 3rd, 2002. I dedicate this monograph to him. "Ouwe", you no doubt would have been proud, without showing it.

Leiden, the Netherlands,
summer-autumn 2002 & February 2004

10

Introductory chapter

"Nebst vielen Ueberresten der auch schon anderwärts in den andesitischen Tuffen des Kendeng in den Residentschaft Madiun, Surakarta und Kediri angetroffenen Arten pleistocäner Säugetiere und Reptilien wurden in der Nähe von Trinil, im Bezirk Ngawi der erstgenannten Residentschaft, Knochen und ein Zahn eines grossen menschenähnlichen Säugers ausgegraben, der offenbar ein Glied, wie es die Entwicklungstheorie zwischen dem Menschen und seinen nächsten Verwandten unter den bekannten Säugetierarten voraussetzte, dargestellt"

Opening sentence of:
Pithecanthropus erectus, eine menschenaehnliche uebergangsform aus Java, by Eugène Dubois, 1894

In 1887, the Dutch anatomist Eugène Dubois, who had just given up a teaching position at Amsterdam University and had enrolled as an army surgeon, left everything he had except his wife, and travelled to what was then the Dutch East Indies (Theunissen 1985; Trinkaus and Shipman 1993; Shipman 2001). He did so in pursuit of a dream. In 1891 he found it, buried beneath a riverbank at Trinil, Java: the very first remains of *Pithecanthropus erectus* (now: *Homo erectus*). As we now know, the bones he found represent what might be one of the earliest human occupants of Eurasia, a representative of the first hominin species to leave the tropical grasslands of Africa and trade these in for other, perhaps more challenging environments.

But exactly when did early humans make their first steps out of Africa? The *erectus* fossils from Java recently stirred up controversy again. The subject of this ongoing controversy is the age of the earliest presence of hominins outside Africa: 'Out of Africa 1'. This controversy is playing both in East and Southeast Asia, and in Europe. In Europe, the debate is whether an initial occupation of Europe took place 0.5 million years (Ma) ago or 1.0-1.5 Ma ago. In Asia, the debate is whether the initial occupation of this region occurred 1.8-1.9 Ma ago or around 1.0 Ma ago, and the Javanese fossils take a primary place in the latter debate.

While the positions taken by various parties engaged in the debates are entrenched, the claims for an old occupation age are usually not accompanied by a clear frame of reference with regard to the colonization

process(es) which led to claimed early occupations. Similarly, assessments of the chronological picture of early hominin colonizations usually are made in order to back a claim for a site, and not to understand the process of colonization nor to critically assess the chronological pattern in the first place. Unlike for the earliest occupation of the Americas (e.g. Dincauze 1984), such a well-articulated, critical methodology for assessment is largely lacking. Where the debate concerning an early occupation of the Americas is one where the mainstream gives priority to caution and well-backed evidence, leading to a framework of solid evidence to be taken as a basis for further theory building, the debate concerning the earliest occupation of Eurasia seems to be one where suggestive possibilities appear to be given more credence than critical assessments. Hence, in the latter area the basis of theory building now seems to be a *suggestion* of occupation at a certain age: not a well-assessed certainty.

In this work, the aim is to arrive at a meaningful frame of reference for the earliest occupation of Eurasia. The basis for this endeavour, and the subject of the first part of this work, is a solid chronology of occupation founded on a critical assessment of the evidence. This chronology is then compared to that of various events in and aspects of the evolution of global and regional climates and ecologies, as well as various events in and aspects of hominin evolution itself. Archaeological and biological clues to changing behaviour in Africa and Eurasia over the timespan of 2.5-0.3 Ma are assessed against the background of changing climate and environments in the second part of this work. These form the background against which an attempt is made to provide a context of behavioural and cognitive evolution leading to these earliest colonizations. The primary goal of this discussion of the earliest occupation of Eurasia therefore is not to present the earliest dates with as many dots as possible in remote spots on the World map: the primary goal is to understand how, because of which factors of change, these spots on the World map got their dot.

Discussing the dating evidence

It must be noted that the only methodology suitable to settle research questions like 'the earliest occupation' is one that is specifically designed to identify and eradicate any claims that are spurious. Methodological approaches of this kind have been advanced by amongst others Dincauze (1984) for the Americas and by Cook *et al.* (1982), Roebroeks and Van Kolfschoten (1994, 1995),

Raynal *et al.* (1995a) and other scholars for Europe. A focus on the ambiguities may either result in revealing the spurious character of a claim, or in the case of a genuine early site may lead to a future refinement of observations and evidence that make the case stronger and acceptable for inclusion in a future updated version of the model.

Dating debates often primarily concern the technical aspects (e.g. laboratory procedures) of the chronological work caried out. Arguments range over the 'reliability' of a certain dating method and the chronological resolution obtained. Problems with geochronological dating in general as well as particular dating techniques are discussed in Aitken (1990). Usually, much less focus is on the field context of the dated materials, which however is at least as important (Dincauze 1984). While quoted standard deviations give some measure of the accuracy of the laboratory procedure to which the dated sample(s) has (have) been subjected, a small standard deviation does not necessarily indicate that the date(s) obtained is (are) very accurate with regard to the research question (the age of a fossil or artefact assemblage). Reworking of materials, sedimentary hiatuses or the formation of lag deposits can squeeze a large time-period into a small sedimentary unit or horizon, combining 'old' dates with much younger archaeological materials into one stratigraphic horizon or two closely associated stratigraphic horizons. Dates obtained by dating horizons situated 'just below' archaeological horizons are always suspect in this aspect.

Equally important is the context of the artefacts or fossils to which a date is to be attached. A well-established, unambiguous *in situ* provenance is a fundamental requirement. The taphonomic history of a fossil or artefact assemblage can have a large bearing on the assessment of their context of chronological evidence.

A particular issue to be raised in the context of dating debates is the question how warranted the reliability attached to a certain dating method is. Almost all dating methods, be they 'absolute' physical dating methods or 'relative' methods like biostratigraphy, have their own particular problems that can be a source of error (cf. Aitken 1990). In that sense, dating deposits can only be reliably done if several different dating methods are used to cross-check each other. This is an important thing to note with regard to many presumed 'early' sites in southern Europe and East Asia which rely heavily on magnetostratigraphy for their claimed dates. As evidenced by the dating problems surrounding the Italian site of Isernia (Roebroeks and Van Kolfschoten 1994, 1995), and the several re-definitions of the magnetostratigraphy at a number of sites (e.g. Sangiran in Indonesia, Yuanmou in China and the Orce basin sites in Spain, see next chapters), magnetos-tratigraphic research on its own is prone to error and ambiguity (see also Verosub (1983) for a critical discussion of geomagnetic 'reversals' at several sites which are not reversals). Problems with pedological phenomena influencing the magnetostratigraphy are not the only source of error: one important but often neglected source of confusion is the many small reversals occurring

within normal polarity chrons like for instance the Brunhes chron (Valet and Meynadier 1993; Aitken 1990; Verosub 1983), combined with the effects of depositional hiatuses, or large differences in depositional rates between different stratigraphic horizons in a profile.

In Europe, much importance has been attached recently to biostratigraphic confirmation of physical dating results (e.g. Roebroeks and Van Kolfschoten 1994, 1995). This works as long as a proper, reliable biostratigraphic framework exists for the given region (such as is the case for Europe and East Africa). For some regions (e.g. Southeast Asia) biostratigraphies are however only cursorily established, or suggested biostratigraphic seriations lack an unambiguous chronological tie (e.g. Swisher (1994) in reply to De Vos and Sondaar (1994)). Biostratigraphy is hence of less relevance to proper dating of deposits in such regions and should be looked at with caution. It should also be noted that it is difficult to draw a line between biostratigraphic results that put constraints on a proposed age for faunal bearing sediments and new dates for faunal bearing sediments that put constraints on the existing biostratigraphic framework.

This is not the place to outline all potential problems with different dating techniques. Yet, these problems are of relevance when discussing the dating evidence of a particular site. The reader is referred to the standard work on dating techniques by Aitken (1990) as a source of information on particular dating techniques and their problems.

Discussing sites and the presence of artefacts and fossil hominin remains

Legitimate issues of discussion in the context of assessing evidence for early occupations are the genuine artificiality of recovered lithics, their correct geologic context, and the correct identification of presumed hominin remains. Questions have been raised (and will be raised in this work) on the archaeological content of some 'early'sites. Geofacts (lithics flaked by natural agents, not by hominins) are still a major source of confusion, simply because they are sometimes very difficult to distinguish from true artefacts. There are no technological flake criteria which are unique to anthropogene flaking processes. Geological flaking processes can produce flaked lithics with sometimes very convincing technological attributes like bulbs of percussion, ripple marks, and 'retouch'. Quite often, only the geological context of the reported specimens holds clues to their artificial/geoficial character. Therefore, one primary requirement is that each reported artefact occurrence is discussed with the proper geologic and lithostratigraphic details. Descriptions of pieces without proper details on (or only a cursory description of) their context of recovery and geological setting cannot be accepted. Likewise, the lithic material itself should be well described. Especially when an apparently simple technology is concerned, a basic understanding of the taphonomy behind the assemblage is necessary. Without such a taphonomic understanding, claims by definition are weak.

Identifying hominin remains is a speciality not mastered by the author of this work, but it will be noted that several 'early hominin sites' discussed have their fossil content disputed by palaeo-anthropologists (e.g. Longgupo in China and Venta Micena in Spain – see the discussions in the next chapters).

List of criteria

Assessment of claims for early occupations will be made according to a checklist designed to eradicate ambiguities, leaving a residue of solid cases. The only acceptable claims for an 'early' occupation site are those claims that meet the following requirements:

The dating:

(1) The geological context of the dated samples must have been taken into account properly;

(2) Preferably, physical dates obtained should be supported by biostratigraphical arguments;

(3) Dates must have been obtained using samples in clear stratigraphical context with the archaeological finds;

(4) Any inconsistencies with other dating attempts should be discussed, and it should be well argued why the advocated dates are considered correct.

Dates claimed should ideally be based on multiple dating evidence; this involves both the employment of multiple dating techniques and multiple dating samples per technique. Constraints on a dating framework based on only one dated sample are to be treated with caution ("*one date is no date, for several reasons*" (Aitken 1990: 95)).

The lithic artefacts:

(5) Morphologically simple 'artefacts' should not represent a small sample of superficially judged 'best pieces' picked out of a large sample of broken rock.

Effectively, this translates to: morphologically simple 'artefacts' should ideally come from fine-grained sediments in order to be acceptable as such. This point relates to the fact that coarse grained-sediments are always

suspected to carry 'geofacts', lithics flaked by natural processes that mimic morphologically simple true artefacts. For morphologically 'simple' presumed 'artefacts' it is therefore necessary that:

(6) All lithic material (flaked and non-flaked) in the findlayer should be described; if present, the presence of 'non-artificial' lithics must be explained and a significant difference with the 'artificial' lithics must be demonstrated;

In all cases, it is important that:

(7) 'Artefacts' have a well-established stratigraphical context: surface finds are inappropriate.

In essence, the last two points raised translate to one important requirement:

● **The 'artefact' assemblage as well as the dated samples in their context should be subject to a critical discussion of the site taphonomy.**

Taphonomic arguments should have a stronger weight in the discussion than morphologic arguments. When morphologically 'simple' artefacts are concerned (flakes, 'flake tools', simple 'cores' or 'core tools'), *it should be realized that there is no unique set of technological criteria that exclusively points to an artificial origin of the lithic material.* In such a case technological and morphological criteria alone are not enough to identify the lithics as true artefacts, but site taphonomy is decisive. As pointed out earlier, only valid taphonomic arguments can rule out a geological flaking origin for such specimens.

Acheulean and 'mode 1': introducing the 'Movius line'

An important topic discussed in the second part of this work (the part concerned with 'behaviour' and evolution in hominin behavioural capacities), is the relation between environment and the co-existence of Acheulean technology and 'mode 1' technologies, both in Africa and in Eurasia. Acheulean assemblages are assemblages with a substantial component of elaborate bifacial tools like handaxes, picks and cleavers. In the African 'Acheulean', these are primarily made on large flakes and often of basalt or similar igneous rock. In Europe, these are most often made of flint nodules, and cleavers do not attain a prominent part in the Acheulean of that area. Usually, 'Acheulean' assemblages also contain smaller amounts of various other tool types.

It should be noted, that different 'definitions' of what characterizes 'Acheulean' assemblages are in use. In Europe, usually the simple presence of handaxes is taken as the treshold for tagging an assemblage as 'Acheulean'. In Africa, at one time the definition, by Kleindienst, was that at least 40% of assemblage should consist of handaxes to classify it as Acheulean. Mary Leakey (1975) later opted for a distinction between 'Acheulean' and 'Developed Oldowan' based on the handaxe manufacturing technique: she choose to classify assemblages as 'Acheulean' when there is a presence of handaxes made on large flakes. In the current study, I have chosen to follow Mary Leakey's definition with regard to early Africa, and the wider 'European' definition with regard to the latter area.

The Acheulean first appears in the Early Palaeolithic of Africa, around 1.5 to 1.7 Ma (as will be discussed in chapter 3). The Acheulean technocomplex appears to be absent in East Asia from the time of the earliest occupation up to at least 0.2 Ma. Instead, relatively simple (from a technological perspective) core/flake industries occur in Eurasia. These are commonly designated as 'mode 1' industries (with the Acheulean being 'mode 2'), following a technological scheme by Clark (1977). It should be stressed that in Africa the two (Acheulean 'mode 2' and 'mode 1' core-flake assemblages, e.g. Oldowan and Developed Oldowan) appear side by side (see chapter 3), contemporaneous, from 1.5-1.7 Ma onwards. This is also the case in Northwestern Europe from the earliest occupation onwards.

The dichotomy between presence of 'mode 2' (Acheulean) in Africa and exclusive occurrence of 'mode 1' industries in the eastern part of Eurasia only, is known as the 'Movius line'. This 'line' actually is the dividing line between the geographical areas in question (see fig. 10). It was given its name by Hallam Movius, who in the earlier part of the 20th century turned this apparent dichotomy into a major research issue (Movius 1944, 1948).

The concept of a dichotomy between the Acheulean in the West and 'mode 1' in the East has survived several critical attacks (e.g. Yi and Clark 1983). In her review, Schick (1994) has pointed out that although Movius' characterization of East Asian archaeological assemblages as 'chopper-choppingtool complexes' is no longer tenable given the strong flake component in Asian assemblages as revealed by modern research, the absence of Acheulean industries in East Asia is still a point to uphold (*contra* Yi and Clark 1983). East Asian bifacial tools (1) are very rare in number of occurrences; (2) unlike in Acheulean assemblages of Africa and Europe, usually constitute only a very small part of the total site assemblage in the rare case that they are present; (3) are almost invariably crude, often trihedral pieces only; (4) almost all are from surface collections; (5) those few that come from a dated context (e.g. Dincun, China), so far are all very young (no older than 0.2 Ma). This also appears to be true for the often quoted Central Asian bifaces (see Shackley (1984)) and the Pacitanian bifacial industry from Java, Indonesia (see Bartstra 1983). A recent claim for abundant bifacial tools

in south China as early as 0.8 Ma ago, has given a new impetus to the debate. This claim is critically examined in chapter 2.1.

What generated the 'Movius line'?

Several hypothesis have been proposed to explain the dichotomy: Movius, amongst other people, sought to explain the apparently 'simple' character of the Asian Palaeolithic archaeological record, as compared to Africa and Europe, as evidence that Early Palaeolithic Asians were suffering from a cognitive evolutionary retardiation. Early Asian toolkits were 'simple' because early Asia was a cultural backwater. This one on one equation of the apparent character of stone tool kits and cognitive capacities is no longer supported by most palaeolithic scholars (Gamble 1993; Schick 1994).

Instead, other explanations have been put forward. Geoffrey Pope (Pope and Cronin 1984; Pope 1985) and Watanabe (1985) for example, have advanced the 'bamboo-karst hypothesis': the presence of suitable raw materials other than stone for tool manufacture, more specifically bamboo, in the Far East, would be the cause of the predominance of choppers and flakes and an absence of more elaborate stone tools. The flakes and chopping tools would be the 'tools to make the tools'. And of course, the bamboo tools used for subsistence tasks are not well preserved in the archaeological record. Pope and Watanabe's 'bamboo-karst' hypothesis is certainly one of the more sophisticated hypotheses recently advanced, and brings in view the influence of the environment on tool use and tool manufacture, a topic also explored – but from a different angle – in this work. However, there are some difficulties with the bamboo-karst hypothesis. Alternatives to stone were present in Africa and Europe too (note e.g. the bone handaxes from Fontana Rannucio in Italy, dating to about 0.45 Ma (Segre and Ascenzi 1984)), the Acheulean as well as bamboo are abundant in for example India, and the geographical position of the 'Movius line' is sometimes difficult to reconcile with the possibility of Pleistocene bamboo occurrences in the regions it crosses (Stringer 1990). Yet, the possibility of a strong bamboo component in (South-) East Asian palaeolithic toolkits should not be dismissed. The bamboo was there (as suggested by the widespread occurrence of bamboo-dependant *Ailuropoda* (Panda bear) in the Middle Pleistocene of southeast Asia: see Tougard *et al.* 1996) and is a suitable raw material. But so are bones and antler, but, apart from a few highly interesting occasions like Fontana Rannucio, regular use of bone and antler for tool manufacture is only properly documented for the Upper Palaeolithic (Gamble 1993; Stringer and Gamble 1993).

Toth and Schick (1993) have proposed that a quick dispersal combined with the limited linguistic capacities of early hominins are responsibe for the 'Movius line': the quick dispersal resulted in problems with locating suitable raw materials in the newly gained territories, with a temporary weaning of the Acheulean toolkit component as a result. As the hominins in question, due to their limited linguistic capacities, were not able to pass down the techniques to their offspring in the absence of practical teaching opportunities, Acheulean concepts were lost from the lithic traditions of the Far East. This hypothesis appears to be difficult to test, as it relies on the (unproven) assumption that hominins 1 Ma ago had only rudimentary communicative skills. In addition, it seems difficult to imagine that once out of Africa hominins were constantly on the move and did not allow themselves the time for reconnaissance of newly explored areas. This invokes the question how these hominins would have been able to survive at all if they did not allow themselves the time to get acquainted with important resource locations and distribution characteristics. It is unlikely that Early Pleistocene hominins were suffering from a Columbus-syndrome of 'find yourself the quickest way to the Far East'. Survival and reproduction, not colonization, would have been their primary concern. Speed in colonizing new territories would be determined by resource availability, not the other way round.

An explanation which has the attractiveness of being neat and simple recently gained some popularity but (as will be argued in this work) appears not consistent with the dating framework for the earliest hominin dispersions out of Africa. It is the idea that the Acheulean is absent in Asia simply because early hominins settled in Asia well before the Acheulean was 'invented' in Africa (Swisher et al. 1994; Larick and Ciochon 1996). This would mean: a dispersal of early hominins before the advent of the Acheulean in Africa at 1.5-1.7 Ma. This idea has recently gained popularity following the announcement of very early (Plio-Pleistocene) dates for some of the Indonesian erectus fossils (Swisher et al. 1994) and the controversial Longgupo Cave finds from China (Huang et al. 1995).

Apart from the debated point whether 'Out of Africa 1' really occurred as early as 1.8 Ma ago (the topic of part 1 of this work), which is a basic argument for making the hypothesis a valid proposal in the first place, the later and less debated occupation of parts of Eurasia by hominins which did introduce Acheulean technology, at about 0.8 Ma (Pakistan) to 0.5 Ma (Europe) ago, is left unexplained. This also makes one realise that what is usually discussed (and pictured) as 'the' Movius line, in reality was not a constant throughout the Pleistocene. Where exactly the line did run, changed repeatedly over time, as will become clear in chapters 2 to 4.

Uniformity and changing character of the Acheulean

A similar monolithic view as towards 'the' Movius line, is usually taken with regard to 'the' Acheulean. It is customary to lump together half a million years and/or thousands of miles between sites on different continents and regard the Acheulean of Olduvai Upper Bed II, the Masek Beds or Olorgesaillie as if identical to the

Acheulean of Boxgrove, Swanscombe or Cagny, representing the same phenomenon (e.g. Gamble 1999: 138). With respect to intra-site spatial patterning and typology, it might look like this, though it could be debatable for the latter (Wynn and Tierson 1990). But this is deceptive. Even ignoring clear technological differences, a closer look reveals that there is for example a difference in setting and occurrence between the Early African Acheulean of the period 1.5-1.0 Ma, and the European Acheulean from 0.5 Ma onwards. This aspect is explored in chapters 2 and 3, which delve into the Acheulean of Africa, and Europe.

That gross similarities can be deceptive if we do not understand well the trajectories which lead to observed archaeological patterns, is a point which might be appreciated after going through the detailed assessment of handaxe manufacture at the early European Acheulean site of Boxgrove provided in chapter 4.2. Boxgrove provides us with a rare detailed glimpse of how handaxes were made and employed, as part of a chain of activities on a palaeo-beach 0.5 Ma ago. It gives us a partial glimpse into technological and subsistence strategies, planning depth and capacities for displacement involved.

The chapter on Boxgrove provides a discussion on early hominin behaviour at a particular locality which is much more detailed than discussions on behaviour in the other chapters. This is the result of a difference in focus. Chapter 3.1 for example, is focused much more on behaviour over several parts of the African landscape. It is a broad look at subsistence on the African savanna, in which an attempt is made to arrive at meaningful explanations for observable patterns constructed from several fragmentary bits of information, fragmentary both in time and space. It leads us into the topic of possible seasonal and locational variations in subsistence activities, and the strategies behind them. The chapter on Boxgrove on the other hand is concerned with complexities in the planning of fabrication and employment of a certain tool form (handaxes) in a very specific locality during a relatively short timespan, which gives us some idea of the amount of versatility shown by the minds of these toolmakers. It takes advantage of the unique quality of site preservation, temporal integrity, detailed level of reporting, and spatial extension of excavation activities at this site. Like the evidence from Schöningen in Germany (Thieme 1999), this provides a rare, detailed, unique window onto a restricted set of activities. This is helpful as it serves to get an understanding of the complexity of behaviour and tool use which had been reached by this time. It should serve as a reminder of how much we lack in understanding of behaviour for earlier periods, due to differences in preservation of the archaeological record. The latter question is not unimportant, as an increase in complexity of behaviour may be the reason why hominins spread into temperate Northwestern Europe at 0.5 Ma, as will be explained in chapters 3 and 4. Boxgrove (and the evidence for hunting at Schöningen) provides us with arguments about the existence of a certain level of complexity, although in aspects these remain ambiguous (see below and in chapter 4.2). The question now is, whether these really are the first occurrences at this complexity level, as suggested by some other changing aspects of the archaeological record at this time; or whether we just are not able to discern it for earlier periods due to the difficult character of the archaeological record itself.

Time scales, inference problems and accomodating short-term variability

This work discusses a large stretch of prehistory: over 2 million years of time, and the archaeological record of three continents. Such a vast spatio-temporal treatment

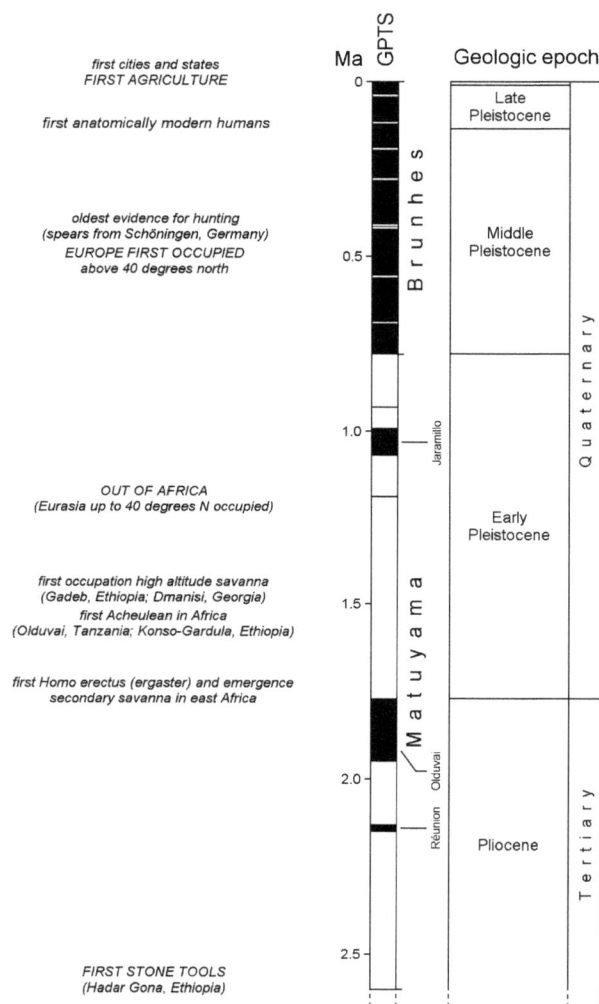

Figure 1: timeline, showing the chronological placement of chrons and subchrons of the Geomagnetic Polarity Time Scale (GPTS) and geological epochs to which frequent reference will be made in this work (Ma = million years. For sources on chronological boundaries, see main text). Some major events in the archaeological and palaeoanthropological records are indicated at left.

necessarily has to take a strong stance of generalization, at the expense of variation. This is not to ignore variation, both variation in time and in space. These certainly were in existence, as they are today (e.g. Sept (1986) with regard to variation in plant food occurrences in the riparian zones of the savanna environments of East Africa). But the topics on which this work is focusing benefit more from a focus on widely discernable, structural trends. With a fragmentary record like the Quaternary environmental record and Pleistocene archaeological record, one has to ascend to a level of analysis where short-term and small-scale variation is accomodated in larger structural patterns of development and change. Often one has to generalize from just a few widely scattered observations to a general broad picture, not by choice but by force. It is acknowledged that this is inherently dangerous but there are no clear alternatives. It would otherwise be impossible to assess structure at all and one would be left with just a meaningless collection of variation, with no anchor for theory building. Moreover, as Alexander Verpoorte has remarked: *"[T]he notion of spatio-temporal collapse is vulnerable to a regression* ad infinitum: *any scale of analysis seems to collapse a certain timespan, a spatial unit and a degree of variation, even at the level of the individual artefact"* (Verpoorte 2001: 21). Spatial-temporal collapse therefore being unavoidable, the amount of spatial-temporal collapse one is willing (and allowed) to permit depends on the research questions. Hence, in this work the focus is on broad generalized ecological patterns over time and space, and broad patterns in the archaeological record. Yet, the existence of variability is not completely ignored, it is taken into account and incorporated in the theoretical framework. For example, Potts concept of 'variability selection' (Potts 1998), which is much concerned with short-term variability in climate and ecology, is explicitly employed in chapter 3. The existence of variability is implicitly taken as a characteristic of many of the discussed ecological structures and archaeological records without being explicitly discussed.

The chapter on Boxgrove will provide an exception to this 'broad sweep', as I will attempt there to develop a fine-grained model of the use of Acheulean technology, taking advantage of the extremely fine-grained preservation of the archaeological record at this site, combined with the detailed level of research conducted at that site. This detailed look is useful as it provides a better appreciation of the landscape distribution patterns visible in the Acheulean of Europe, which appears to have a more 'hidden' structuring than that of Early Pleistocene Africa. As a surprising result, it will be noted that the structure of the Acheulean of Middle Pleistocene Europe looks similar to the structure of the Developed Oldowan of Early Pleistocene Africa. What the chapter with the Boxgrove analysis also points out, is how vexing the problem of going from observed patterns to ascertaining intentions behind it is. As the chapter shows, this is difficult to do (although the result is teasing) even when working with one of the best preserved sets of lithic archaeological data on the European early Acheulean in existence. As such, it is a useful exercise, and it points to a serious problem with regard to the archaeological reconstruction of (changing) levels of cognition in early hominins.

Chronology

Regular reference will be made to the geomagnetic polarity timescale (GPTS) in this work. The GPTS provides some useful timemarkers which are valid worldwide, such as the Brunhes-Matuyama boundary at 0.78 Ma (Baksi et al. 1992; Valet and Meynadier 1993; Tauxe et al. 1996), the Jaramillo subchron between 0.99 and 1.07 Ma (Valet and Meynadier 1993), and the Olduvai subchron between 1.78 and 1.96 Ma (McDougall et al. 1992). The Brunhes-Matuyama polarity reversal acts as the boundary between the Early and Middle Pleistocene. The upper Olduvai boundary acts as the boundary between the Pliocene and Pleistocene (Obradovich et al. 1982). Figure 1 provides a synthetic summary of the most important chronological units and events referred to in this work, in the form of a timeline.

A note on "savanna's"

In this work, a number of savanna types are discussed. With regard to the tropical savanna's of Africa, the major two types distinguished are "edaphic" grasslands, and "secondary" graslands, which are roughly equating to C_3-dominated and C_4-dominated grasslands (see the discussion and definitions in chapter 3.1). These two major types have different ecologies attached to them. That being said, I am well aware that my use of grassland characterizations, is a generalization of what in reality quite probably amounted to a heterogeneous set of environments (see e.g. Sept 1994). Yet, this generalization is inevitable, just as it is for some of the other topics discussed. As a note, I want to point out that whenever a "dry tropical grassland" or "dry tropical savanna" is mentioned, this is meant to be equivalent to a secondary grassland. "Tropical savanna" is a catch-all term used to denote the two major savanna types of the African continent as opposed to the temperate grasslands of Eurasia.

Spatio-temporal gaps in the archaeological record

This work is fully aware of the existence of spatio-temporal gaps in the archaeological (and geological) record. Hence, when the question is raised of "how did they get from sub-Saharan Africa to Israel at about 1.4 Ma ago?" (meaning: the route(s) taken), the answer simply is: "we do not know!". We don't have the data to tell us,

although we can make educated guesses about the specific route(s) taken. They *did* got from Africa to Israel, that we *do* know. 'Ubeidiya exemplifies this point, there is no way around this. A similar problem is evident with regard to the occupation of Indonesia, or the gap in knowledge about the earliest occupation of southeast Europe (Greece and neighbouring areas) when contrasted to Iberia and Northwest Europe. Presence in these "gaps on the route to", transient or not, can however be deduced from the established presence in the areas discussed (e.g. NW Europe, Israel), sometimes in combination with known issues about lack of (modern standard) research, or an unfavourable geological situation. In that sense, there is a difference compared to the discussion on the earliest presence in for example east Asia at 1.8 Ma. With regard to the construction of theory, the gap in knowledge in the former situation ("gaps in the route to") is less problematic than in the latter situation. Yet, these situations do remind us of the fragmentary, imperfect character of the archaeological, paleontological and geological records. Only research can solve these problems, if they can be solved: and signalling such gaps in knowledge therefore provides some interesting points for potential research agenda's. I have good hopes that, for example, the issue of "how did they get from sub-saharan Africa to Israel?" will be solved in the near future.

Chimps, tools and ancestors: under the hood of Pandora's box

This work is concerned with the earliest occupation of Eurasia by hominins. A last point to be raised is a very serious one which around the time when the writing of this work was finished, was brought prominently to the fore by a paper in *Science* of May 24, 2002. This paper (Mercader et al. 2002), which followed earlier experiments with captive apes (e.g. Toth et al. 1993), reports on the excavation of a site with Chimpanzee-made stone tools.

The point, which is of very serious concern, is what exactly are to be considered traces of hominin occupation. This question raised is one on a level very different from the criteria for artefact recognition outlined earlier in this introductory chapter. The question raised here is whether the presence of unambiguous stone tools really points to hominin presence. The possibility should be kept in the back of the mind that it concerns *hominoid* presence. Some extant hominoids, more specifically Chimpanzees, use stone tools, not just in an experimental setup, but also as part of their natural repertoire of behaviour in the wild (McGrew 1992). While wild Chimpanzees do not consciously flake tools (but at least Bonobos or 'pygmy chimpanzee' can be learned to do so in captivity (Toth et al. 1993)), they produce flakes and flaked pieces as a byproduct of their activities with these stone hammer tools. While these products technologically, i.e. in the sense of flake characteristics and structural flaking sequences, do not attain the level of most of even the earliest archaeological sites (e.g. the 2.3 Ma old Oldowan site of Lokalalei 2c (Roche *et al.* 1999) in the East African Rift valley, or the 2.6 Ma Oldowan site of Gona (Semaw *et al.* 1997; Semaw 2000) in Ethiopia), they do mimic some of the cruder Oldowan assemblages (Mercader *et al.* 2002), e.g. that of 2.3 Ma old Lokalalei 1 (Kibunjia 1994; Kibunjia *et al.* 1992).

This realization opens an archaeological box of Pandora: could some early stone tool sites, both in Plio-Pleistocene Africa and in (Plio-) Pleistocene Eurasia, be the product of hominoids, not early hominins? Can we exclude that Pliocene or Pleistocene extinct hominoids were capable of producing stone tools which are more sophisticated than what an extant Chimpanzee is able to produce? In all reality, we cannot. Indeed, Dennell (1998) has argued that, since both humans and Chimpanzees have a capacity to use stone tools, the use of stone tools likely represents a shared trait deriving from a common ancestor. While I do not think the latter proposition to be correct, the serious possibility that fossil hominoids produced stone tools that match the sophistication of the early Oldowan assemblages, is one which causes headaches. Can we be sure that the presence of simple stone tools in Georgia, Pakistan, China or elsewhere, equates to an early hominin occupation? In the case of Georgia, we have skulls to answer the question, although the owners of these skulls need not necesarily have been the makers of the stone tools. But what if we lack fossil hominin remains? What if *Giganthopithecus*, or *Lufengpithecus*, or *Pongo*, made simple stone tools in Plio-Pleistocene China? Could we be misled into believing that this brings in evidence early

hominin occupation? Moreover, if we extend this nagging question to include Plio-Pleistocene Africa, could we be basing some of our ideas on capacities and cognition of early *Homo* on the handicraft of a fossil Chimp ancestor? While these questions of 'Who dunnit?" are not new (see Wood 1997) and for example pose a serious problem in connection with the presence of multiple hominin species in Plio-Pleistocene Africa (early *Homo* as well as Australopithecines: see chapter 3.1), the added dimension of possible stone tool production by hominoids, makes it a very disturbing problem with regard to traces of early occupation in Eurasia. The problem is not easy to solve. It works twofold: it serves to be even more suspicious of very simple flaked stones with a minimum level of workmanship (e.g. the supposed stone tools from Longgupo, where *Gigantopithecus* as well as a Pongid are part of the faunal assemblage (Huang *et al.* 1995 – see also chapter 1.2)). It also serves to introduce some uneasiness, as it represents a potential weakness in the building of colonization models, based (partly) on the presence of stone tools at a certain age. For the moment, I will consider any stone tool assemblage at the sophistication level of Lokalalei 2c (Roche *et al.* 1999) as representing a hominin rather than hominoid presence, the (weak) rationale for that judgement being that *extant* hominoid stone tool production does not reach that level, not even with training in captivity. With some relief, I also note that the earliest occupation dates for various regions advocated in this work, almost invariably are backed by fossils as well as tools, not just tools. For the moment, we can close this box of Pandora with a sigh of relief.

Part I

Claims for early occupations of Eurasia before 1.4 Ma

Several claims exist for Eurasian finds of hominin fossils and/or tools with a Plio-Pleistocene age between 1.5-2.0 Ma. In order to arrive at a solid chronology for the earliest occupation of Eurasia, Part I of this work takes a critical look at these claims.

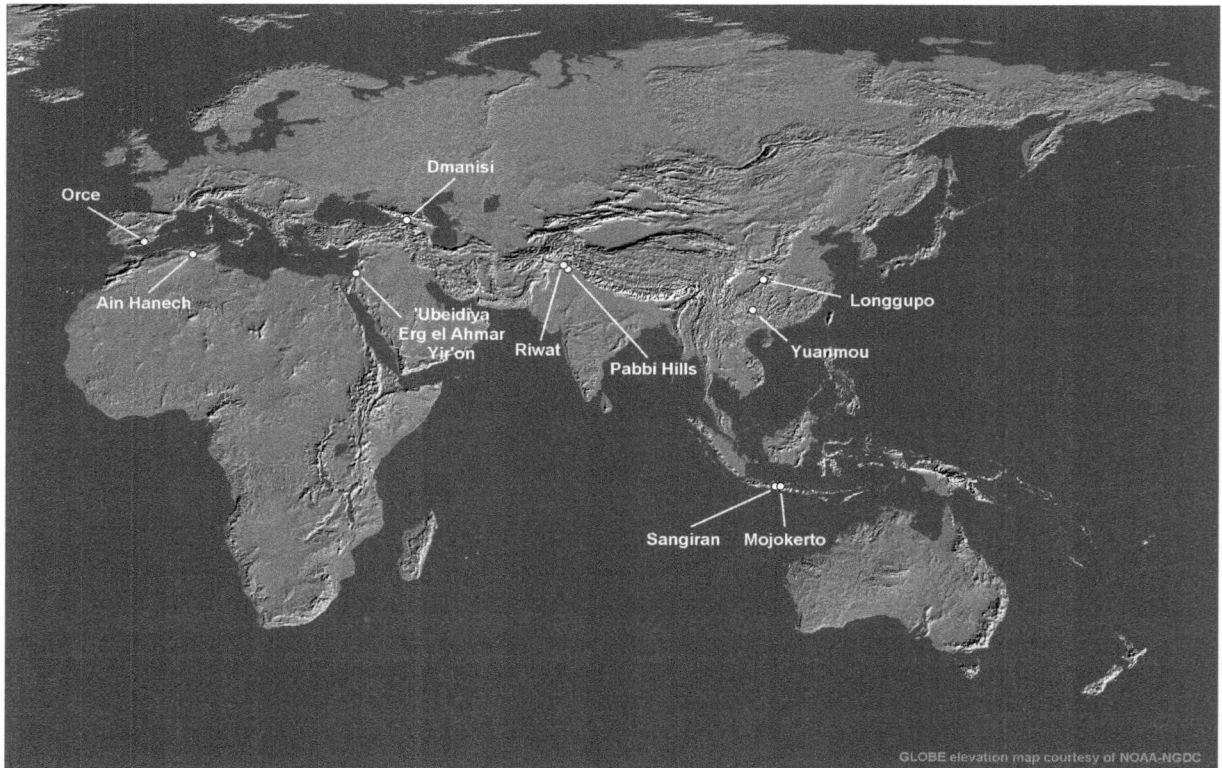

Figure 2:   Map of the Old World showing locations of discussed sites representing, or purported to represent, early occupations.

1.1 On the age of the Sangiran and Mojokerto (Java, Indonesia) hominin fossil bearing sediments [1]

1. This chapter is an expanded and updated version of a paper (Langbroek and Roebroeks 2000) published in the *Journal of Human Evolution*.

The age of the *Homo erectus* fossils from Sangiran, Trinil and Mojokerto in east and central Java, Indonesia, is a subject with a rich history of confusion and disagreement (see overviews and discussions in Orchiston and Siesser (1982), Pope and Cronin (1984) and Theunissen *et al.* (1990)). The debate surfaced prominently again during the last decade, after Swisher *et al.* (1994) published ^{40}Ar/^{39}Ar ages for Sangiran and Mojokerto which would place the earliest Javanese hominins at very early ages of 1.6 to 1.8 Ma. The validity of these ages has been strongly questioned (e.g. De Vos and Sondaar 1994; Langbroek and Roebroeks 2000; Hyodo *et al.* 2002), yet they are widely quoted, and used as evidence for an early Out of Africa in models of (genetic) dispersal (e.g. in Templeton 2002).

The Javanese hominin sites exhibit a very complex geology (see Watanabe and Kadar 1985). Moreover, almost none of the Javanese hominin fossils have been recovered under stratigraphically controlled conditions. Most, including those which feature high in the current debates, are finds of uncertain stratigraphic or even locational provenance (Jacob 1973; Pope and Cronin 1984; Itihara *et al.* 1985a, 1985c; Matsu'ura 1982, 1985; Larick *et al.* 2000; Sémah *et al.* 2000; for an amusing but disheartening sketch of how some of Von Koenigswald's fossils surfaced, see Theunissen *et al.* (1990: 45-47)). For a handful of the more recently discovered fossils as well as some of Von Koenigswald's specimens, find localities have been retraced and stratigraphic provenance assignments made by investigators with the help of the local collectors of the fossils. Some of these stratigraphic assignments are reinforced by a match of the fluorine content of these hominin fossils with that of mammal fossils recovered *in situ* (Matsu'ura 1982, 1985, 1986; Itihara *et al.* 1985a, 1985c, 1994). Yet some uncertainty pertains for all of the specimens. The fossils that have attained prime importance in the recent debates on the age of the earliest Javanese hominins are fossils S27 and S31 from Sangiran, and the Mojokerto child. All three are among those for which stratigraphic assignment remains troublesome, as will be outlined below. This should be well noted because Swisher *et al.* (1994) purport to date samples "*in direct association with the hominid find sites*" (Swisher *et al.* 1994: 1119; Swisher 1994).

Sangiran: basic geology

A basic geologic and lithostratigraphic framework for the Sangiran dome is detailed in Watanabe and Kadar (1985). A simplified lithostratigraphy is given in the accompanying diagram (fig. 3). Of relevance for this discussion are the Bapang and Sangiran Formations, also known as the Kabuh and Pucangan beds. The attempts to trace back the stratigraphic origins of several fossils by the joint Indonesian-Japanese team and the fluorine studies by Matsu'ura, suggest that the majority of the Sangiran hominin fossils derive from the Bapang (Kabuh) Formation, while some could derive from the uppermost part of the older Sangiran (Pucangan) Formation (Itihara *et al.* 1985a, 1985c; Matsu'ura 1982, 1985).

The Bapang (Kabuh) Formation consists of clays, silts, sands and gravels of fluvial origin displaying abundant occurrences of cross-bedding (see reports in Watanabe and Kadar (1985)). The top of the Sangiran (Pucangan) Formation consists of black clays and foraminiferal sands (sometimes showing cross-bedding (Kadar 1985: 223)) of lacustrine origin. The base of the sequence is formed by a lahar, a volcanic mudflow, designated as the Lower Lahar. This Lahar deposit predates on stratigraphical and palaeomagnetic grounds (see below) all the hominin fossils for which stratigraphic provenance inferences can be made. The foraminiferal sands in the upper Sangiran (Pucangan) Formation contain foraminifera of deep marine origin that however co-occur with freshwater molluscs. This, and the preservation state of the foraminifera, indicates that these foraminifera were reworked into the deposits (Kadar 1985: 223; Itihara *et al.* 1985c: 19-20; Itihara *et al.* 1994: 125). The sedimentary environment in the upper Sangiran (Pucangan) Formation gradually changed from marine and brackish-water to lacustrine/fluvial fresh-water, and the foraminiferal sands indicate that "*the uplifted hinterland of the basin was eroded to produce the allochtonous sediments*" (Itihara *et al.* 1985c: 20).

Within the Sangiran and Bapang Formations occur several tuff beds that to some extent can be used as marker tuffs (see fig. 3). The Bapang Formation has been divided by the Indonesian-Japanese team into four subunits separated by a 'lower', 'middle' and 'upper' tuf (for details, consult Watanabe and Kadar (1985)). A tektite horizon is present

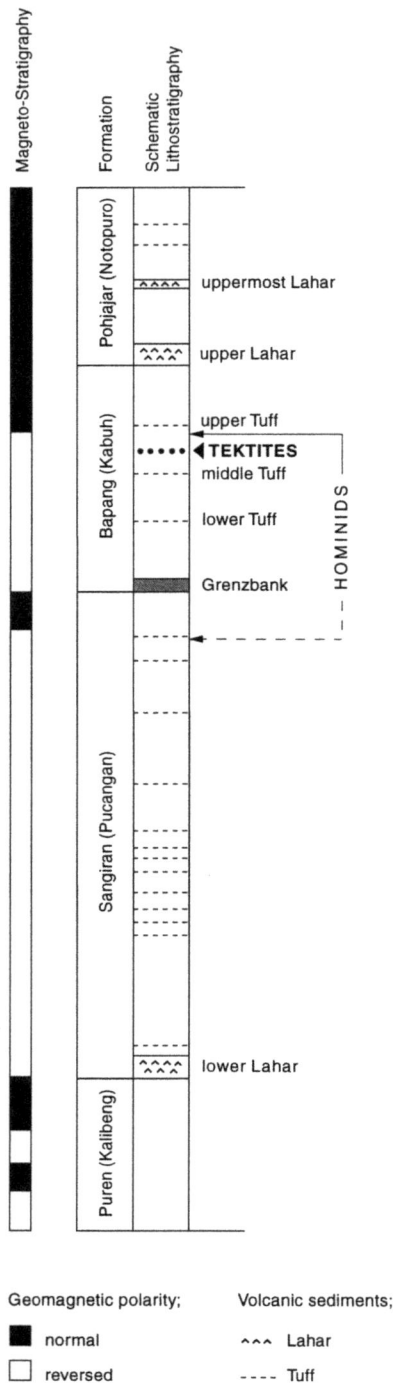

Figure 3: Schematic drawing of the Sangiran (Indonesia) lithostratigraphy (after Watanabe and Kadar, 1985). Shown are the major lithostratigraphic units, the tuff marker beds, the position of the tektite horizon, and an indication of the probable extend of the hominin fossil bearing part of the sequence. At left, the magnetostratigraphy as obtained for the Sangiran sequence by Hyodo *et al.* (1993) See the text for more details and an explication (drawing by Henk de Lorm).

between the Upper and the Middle tuffs in the Bapang Formation (Itihara *et al.* 1985b).

Sangiran chronostratigraphy (1): The ^{40}Ar/^{39}Ar ages for the Sangiran fossils by Swisher *et al.*

Paramount in the current dating controversy are fossils S27 and S31 from Sangiran, and the 'Mojokerto child' from Mojokerto. Swisher *et al.* (1994) attribute a provenance from "*the lower part of the Pucangan*" to S27 and S31 from Sangiran and associate these fossils with a weighted mean age of 1.66 ± 0.04 Ma using ^{40}Ar/^{39}Ar laser-incremental heating on hornblende separated from pumice recovered from "*a volcanic pumice-rich layer*" reportedly "*2 m above the horizon that yielded Meganthropus S27 and S31*" (Swisher *et al.* 1994: 1120). The reported "*direct association with the hominid find sites*" (Swisher *et al.* 1994: 1119) is however highly problematic and was recently put into context by Larick *et al.* (2000):

> "*The provenance issues of Kln-1978.07-GMUY (S27) and Kln-1979.07 ITB (Meganthropus II, S31) are disconcerting. Specimen S27 has no primary publication and S31, as treated among descriptive reports, has no real statement of provenance. Oral histories conflict as to where and how these fossils were discovered and how they got to their respective conserving institutions. [...] In the end, we have not been able to confirm the common notion that these two specimens share a findspot or provenance level in the Sangiran (Pucangan) formation*" (Larick *et al.* 2000: 748).

The association of the 1.66 Ma ^{40}Ar/^{39}Ar age with these fossils is therefore not as strong as purported by Swisher *et al.* Moreover, there is controversy about which stratigraphic level Swisher *et al.* dated. They assign their sample provenance to the lower part of the Pucangan (Sangiran) Formation. Larick *et al.* (2001, 2000) point out that most of the relevant exposed section at Jokotingkir is instead to be placed in the Bapang Formation, and that the Pucangan beds do not contain pumice except within the Lower Lahar, which forms the base of the sequence and on stratigraphic grounds is older than any of the fossils. At the purported Jokotingkir S27/S31 find locality, only two pumice-bearing levels appear to be present according to Larick *et al.*: a pumice-bearing lens in Bapang sediments, and the mentioned Lower Lahar, which crops out close by as the result of faulting (see map 6 in Watanabe and Kader (1985) and remarks in Sémah *et al.* 2000). Sémah *et al.* (1997, 2000), and Larick *et al.* (2000) point out that the 1.66 Ma age of Swisher *et al.* (1994) along with their sample provenance description would imply that Swisher *et al.* sampled the Lower Lahar. Sémah *et al.* obtained

^{40}Ar/^{39}Ar ages on amphiboles from the Lower Lahar at Puren and Cengklik of 1.66 ± 0.04 and 1.77 ± 0.08 Ma. The Swisher *et al.* date of 1.66 ± 0.04 Ma would fit in well with these. Palaeomagnetic investigations by Sémah *et al.* revealed that the Lower Lahar straddles a polarity transition from normal to reversed polarity, indicating in conjunction with the ^{40}Ar/^{39}Ar ages that it dates to the top of the Olduvai geomagnetic subchron. The Lahar deposit represents the first emergent landsurface in this area. The overlying clays of the Sangiran (Pucangan) Formation rest uncomformably on the deposit and post-date the Olduvai subchron (Sémah *et al.* 2000). According to Larick *et al.* (2000, 2001) the only other pumice-bearing level present at Jokotingkir besides the Lower Lahar, is a pumice-bearing lens within Bapang (Kabuh) sediments, not Sangiran (Pucangan) sediments, on which they obtained an ^{40}Ar/^{39}Ar age of 1.10 ± 0.07 Ma (Larick *et al.* 2001), clearly younger than the Swisher *et al.* age of 1.66 ± 0.04 Ma. Indeed, the occurrence of a pumice-rich layer as described by Swisher *et al.* in the Sangiran (Pucangan) sediments is also not immediately apparent in the lithological descriptions provided by the Indonesian-Japanese team, except for the Lower Lahar that forms the base of the formation (Watanabe and Kadar 1985; Yoshikawa and Suminto 1985).

While purportedly dating the lower reaches of the fossil bearing sediments at Sangiran, the 1.66 ± 0.04 Ma obtained by Swisher *et al.* (1994) can be judged to be irrelevant for the age of the fossils. The stratigraphic associations are unclear: most likely the ^{40}Ar/^{39}Ar age of 1.66 ± 0.04 Ma refers to a sample site within the Lower Lahar which predates the hominin fossils. The 1.7 Ma age therefore only has significance as a *terminus post quem*.

Sangiran chronostratigraphy (2): ^{40}Ar/^{39}Ar ages by Larick *et al.*

It would go too far in the context of this paper to address in detail all radiometric and relative dating attempts carried out on the fossil bearing sediment outcrops at Sangiran (*cf.* Orchiston and Siesser (1982) and Theunissen *et al.* (1990) for an outline), but the results have been notoriously contradictory and confusing. For the radiometric dates, Orchiston and Siesser (1982) have pointed out that much of the confusion finds its origin in the fact that almost all dates reported up to 1982 lacked adequate details about sampling provenance, and in addition many have not been published in full and often have no standard deviations quoted or their standard deviations not properly taken into account. Some of the more recent geochronological work at Sangiran suffers from similar problems. With regard to sampling provenance, the widely quoted Swisher *et al.* (1994) dates for example are problematic, as outlined

above. Positive exceptions are the dating work reported as part of the litho- and chronostratigraphic work by the joint Indonesian-Japanese research team CTA-41 (Watanabe and Kadar 1985) and the recent publication of ^{40}Ar/^{39}Ar datings by Larick *et al.* (2001).
The latter ^{40}Ar/^{39}Ar dates suggest that the whole hominin bearing section at Sangiran is older than 1.0 Ma, a similar conclusion as that reported (without full details) by Swisher (1997). Larick *et al.* provide an ^{40}Ar/^{39}Ar age of 1.02 ± 0.06 Ma for the Upper tuff in the upper part of the Bapang (Kabuh) Formation, a similar age of 0.98 ± 0.11, 1.05 ± 0.1, 1.02 ± 0.13 and 1.2 ± 0.2 Ma for levels just above the Middle tuff; an age of 1.27 ± 0.18 for the Middle tuff and similar ages of 1.24 ± 0.12, 1.33 ± 0.04, and 1.30 ± 0.12 between the Middle and the Lower tuff; and an age of 1.51 ± 0.05 for a level just above the 'Grenzbank', the Bapang/Sangiran (Kabuh/Pucangan) contact (see Larick *et al.* 2001). This would imply that the earliest Sangiran hominin fossils are ~1.5 Ma in age. Yet there are problems. The ^{40}Ar/^{39}Ar dates of both Larick *et al.* and Swisher *et al.* are contradicted by other dating evidence: magneto-stratigraphy, and the presence of tektites in the middle part of the Bapang (Kabuh) deposits.

Sangiran chronostratigraphy (3): age constraints from tektites and geomagnetic polarity

Magnetostratigraphic work has been carried out at Sangiran by Sémah (Sémah 1982; Sémah *et al.* 2000) and Hyodo *et al.* (1993). Both studies agree in that they yield a normal palaeomagnetic polarity for the upper part of the Bapang (Kabuh) Formation at Sangiran, as well as for the upper part of the Sangiran (Pucangan) Formation and upper part of the Puren (Kalibeng)/lowest part of the Sangiran (Pucangan) Formation. They also agree on a reversed palaeomagnetic polarity for most of the Sangiran (Pucangan) clays. They differ however in the polarity assignment for the middle and lower Bapang (Kabuh) Formation. While the study of Sémah yields a normal polarity, that of Hyodo *et al.* yields a reversed polarity. As a result, opinions differ on whether the normal polarity interval in the top of the Sangiran (Pucangan) clays, roughly from Tuff no. 11 in the upper Sangiran to the Grenzbank at the Sangiran-Bapang transition, represents the Jaramillo subchron (Hyodo *et al.* 1993) or the top of the Brunhes chron (Sémah 1982). Both studies assign the normal interval in the upper part of the Puren/lowest part of the Sangiran Formation (the upper part of which coincides with the Lower Lahar) to the Olduvai subchron. This appears consistent with ^{40}Ar/^{39}Ar dates of 1.66 ± 0.04 and 1.77 ± 0.08 Ma for the upper part of the Lower Lahar (Sémah *et al.* 2000). An age near the top of the Olduvai chron appears to be the typical age for lower Pucangan equivalent lahar deposits in east Java, which in many parts of east Java represent the first emergent landsurface. A similar age for example has been obtained on lahar deposits near Kedung Brubus. These lahar formations relate to the final formative phase of volcanic activity which played a role in the creation of this part of Java as a landsurface (see Bellon et al. 1989; Bandet et al. 1989).

The part of the Sangiran lithostratigraphic sequence on which the Sémah and Hyodo magneto-stratigraphies differ in opinion, is the lower part of the Bapang (Kabuh) Formation. Theunissen et al. (1990: 49) point out that this part of the sequence is dominated by "coarse clastic sediments with internal erosion contacts: a hazardous lithology for magnetostratigraphic research".

Notwithstanding this difference of opinion on the palaeomagnetic polarity of a part of the litho-stratigraphic sequence, the combination of the magnetostratigraphic properties and the presence of tektites in the middle part of the Bapang (Kabuh) Formation puts strong constraints on the upper and especially the lower boundaries of the hominin bearing sediments (see Leinders et al. 1985; Theunissen et al. 1990; Langbroek and Roebroeks 2000; Hyodo et al. 2002).

Tektites were found in situ in Bapang (Kabuh) deposits at Sangiran by the Indonesian-Japanese CTA-41 geologists (Itihara et al. 1985a, b, c). These tektites, natural silicate glass objects, occur all over southeast Asia and a part of Oceania, and are part of the Australasian strewnfield that finds its origin in the impact of a large asteroid 0.78 Ma ago. This impact occurred somewhere in Cambodia or Laos as suggested by the isotopic composition of the tektites and their distribution characteristics over southeast Asia (Blum et al. 1992; Glass 1993; Hartung and Koeberl 1994; Lee and Wei 2000). The tektites formed as molten rock from the impact site was thrown into the atmosphere, raining down over an area of 5×10^7 km^2 covering one tenth of the Earth's surface (see map in Glass et al. (1997)). The incidence of this large cosmic impact at a time when hominins already seem to have been present in Asia, although still not secured for the actual impact area (Olsen and Ciochon 1990; Ciochon and Olsen 1986), is interesting in the light of the ecological havoc it must have wrought over southeast Asia. This falls outside the scope of the present chapter, however. The possible implications are discussed in appendix 1.

The relevance for the current discussion is that the age of formation of the tektite strewnfield is extremely well known. K-Ar and fission-track dating of tektites from several southeast Asian and Australian localities points to an age near the Brunhes-Matuyama geomagnetic polarity reversal at 0.78 Ma (Izett and Obradovich 1992; Schneider et al. 1992; Lee and Wei 2000). This age is reinforced by the close association of the stratigraphic position of the microtektite strewnfield and the Brunhes-Matuyama

boundary in deep-sea sediment cores. From a detailed analysis of two cores (ODP sites 767 and 769 taken near the Philippines), Schneider, Kent and Mello (1992) concluded that the impact and strewnfield formation must have occurred during the later part of Oxygen Isotope Stage 20, an estimated 12 ka before the Brunhes-Matuyama polarity change, with an uncertainty of only a few thousands of years. A similar conclusion has been reached by Lee and Wei (2000) from analysis of two cores, MD972142 in the South China Sea and MD972143 in the West Philippine Sea. They provide an age estimate of 0.793 Ma for the impact.

When compared to the deep-sea cores stratigraphy, the tektite horizon at Sangiran stratigraphically fits well within the magnetostratigraphy of Hyodo et al. (1993) for Sangiran. The Sangiran tektite horizon is located just below a polarity reversal. This polarity reversal, the reversal from normal polarized sediments in the top of the Bapang (Kabuh) Formation to reversed sediments in the middle and lower parts of the Bapang (Kabuh) Formation, then must represent the Brunhes-Matuyama boundary and not the lower Jaramillo boundary. The implication of this is, that the normal polarization in the top of the Sangiran (Pucangan) Formation, between tuff 11 and the Grenzbank, is the Jaramillo subchron. The top of the normal polarization interval in the Lower Lahar then indeed would be the Olduvai chron. This interpretation would place the oldest hominin fossils in the sequence at the lower boundary of the Jaramillo subchron, i.e. slightly over 1.1 Ma ago. Most of the fossils would be younger than 1.0 Ma in this interpretation.

While Hyodo's magnetostratigraphy and the stratigraphic position of the tektites are consistent, their chronological implications are in contradiction with most of the ^{40}Ar/^{39}Ar ages obtained on the Bapang and upper Sangiran Formation sediments by Larick et al. (2001). The latter in themselves are in contradiction with fission-track ages on these same sediments (see Watanabe and Kadar 1985). With regard to radiometric dates, the evidence is clearly less consistent.

One possible reason for the problem with the radiometric dates is given by Bartstra (1983), who is of the opinion that:

"it is questionable whether the Kabuh beds in central Java contain fresh volcanic products. The Kabuh beds are a synorogenetic formation, build up of erosion products from the major anticlines...of South and Central Java (the Gunung Kidul and Kendeng respectively). During the formation of the Kabuh beds there was certainly not very much volcanic activity in Central Java, neither of the Lawu, nor of the Wilis...By far the greater part of the volcanic constituents of the Kabuh beds must therefore originate from older *formations; which means that K/Ar ages of the Kabuh deposits in Central Java are too high, and must be regarded with scepticism*" (Bartstra 1983: 425).

A similar point can be made for the upper part of the Sangiran (Pucangan) Formation, the base of the hominin bearing part of the sequence. The foraminiferal sands in the upper Sangiran (Pucangan) Formation contain foraminifera of deep marine origin that however co-occur with freshwater molluscs. This, and the preservation state of the foraminifera, indicates that these foraminifera were reworked into the deposits (Kadar 1985: 223; Itihara *et al.* 1985c: 19-20; Itihara *et al.* 1994: 125). As Itihara *et al.* (1985c: 20) remark, the sedimentary environment in the upper Sangiran (Pucangan) Formation gradually changed from marine and brackish-water to lacustrine/fluvial fresh-water, and the foraminiferal sands indicate that *"the uplifted hinterland of the basin was eroded to produce the allochtonous sediment"*. Then, the possibility should be taken seriously that this also accounts for the volcaniclastic facies of the upper Sangiran (Pucangan).

The presence of a tektite horizon between the Middle and the Upper Tuff in the Bapang (Kabuh) Formation, unambiguously shows that this part of the sequence cannot be older than 0.78 Ma. Yet it is associated with $^{40}Ar/^{39}Ar$ dates of 1.0 Ma (Larick *et al.* 2001). This again underlines that it appear to be the $^{40}Ar/^{39}Ar$ dates which are erroneous. If we consider that the stratigraphic level of the tektites is consistent with Hyodo's magnetostratigraphy, and that for at least a part of the sequence the $^{40}Ar/^{39}Ar$ dates *must* be too old as indicated by their mismatch with the tektites, the chronostratigraphic framework provided by Hyodo's magnetostratigraphic work is the only one which remains plausible. Hence, the conclusion must be that the earliest hominin fossils from Sangiran should be placed at about 1.1-1.2 Ma. This is an age similar to that of the earliest sites in China (see chapter 1.2).

Some words about the tektite provenance are in order, for this point recently has been put to question (Larick *et al.* 2001: 4871; and cited in Gibbons 2001: 628) in order to circumvent the problems they raise for acceptance of the $^{40}Ar/^{39}Ar$ chronology for Sangiran. Larick *et al.* address this question with a simple:

"The first programmed geological excavations in the dome claimed to find two tektites in Bapang sediments; one at Brangkal and the other at Pucung. However, detailed documentation was never provided" (Larick *et al.* 2001: 4871).

This remark is incorrect. The stratigraphic context of the Pucung tektite has been published in some detail in chapter 6, entitled "Pucung site", authored by F. Aziz, T.

Shibasaki and Suminto, on pages 87 to 90 of the CT-41 report (Watanabe and Kadar 1985). This chapter reports on the construction of a geological section (S59) at Pucung and describes it. With this chapter is provided a detailed section drawing of the step trench in question (not a schematised column, but a true section drawing) with the stratigraphic position of the tektite found clearly indicated in the section drawing and with additionally noted in the (brief) text: "*a tektite was discovered in a sand layer at step 3*". The section drawing is very detailed. I simply want to point out that the detail provided for the Pucung tektite find is far greater than has ever been published for any of the radiometric dating samples taken at Sangiran at whatever point in history; or for that matter, any of the Javanese hominin fossils themselves. Questioning this, questions everything from Sangiran published so far and would make the whole debate obsolete.

With regard to our tektite argument (Langbroek and Roebroeks 2000), Larick *et al.* (2001: 4871) in addition state:

"...in the last 10 years, programmed fieldwork has been carried out at multicomponent archaeological and paleontological sites at Ngebung, at Brangkal, Dayu and Ngledok, and at Sendangbusik. Although these more recent excavations have been intensive and meticulous throughout the lower and middle Bapang sequence (C1-C3), they have not recovered tektites"

This point is irrelevant, since the larger part of the indicated sequence, the mentioned lower Bapang (C1-2 in Larick *et al.*'s framework, see Larick *et al.* 2001: 4868) is well below the tektite horizon, as is the indicated part of the middle sequence (C3), or at least for the largest part: the tektites should be in C4 or near the C3-C4 contact.

Mojokerto

Similar problems as for Sangiran apply to the significance of the $^{40}Ar/^{39}Ar$ age of 1.81 ± 0.04 Ma (Swisher *et al.* 1994) proposed for the calvarium from Modjokerto (the "Mojokerto child" or P1, see Jacob 1973). The quoted age has been obtained on hornblende separated from pumice recovered from a conglomerate volcanic sandstone near what is believed to be the find locality of the Mojokerto calvarium (Swisher *et al.* 1994: 1119-1120). The significance of the $^{40}Ar/^{39}Ar$ age has been questioned (De Vos and Sondaar 1994).

The find locality and circumstances of recovery of the Mojokerto child calvarium are contested. Different localities, although in the same general area, have been pointed out on different occasions (see De Vos 1985;

Watanabe and Kadar 1985; Theunissen *et al.* 1990; Hyodo *et al.* 1993; Curtiss *et al.* 2000; Huffman 2001)). The find circumstances are likewise ambiguous, with the find being initially reported as a surface find, but then – following a dispute between Von Koenigswald and Dubois – as having been found at a depth of about 1 metre during the excavation of a *Leptobos* skull (see De Vos 1985; Theunissen *et al.* 1990).

Using pre-World War II photographs made by Von Koenigswald and De Terra extracted from various archives, Curtiss and Swisher (Curtiss *et al.* 2000; see also Huffman 2001) claim to have relocated the findspot (which, incidentally, is not the one sampled and published by Swisher *et al.* (1994)). Their exciting story reads like a detective novel. The starting point was a picture (published in De Terra 1943) taken during the visit which De Terra, Teilhard de Chardin, Movius and Von Koenigswald made to the assumed findspot in April 1938, two years after the find (De Terra 1943). On this occasion, an excavation pit was visible at the assumed spot and De Terra expressed surprise on the freshness of it:

"The excavation pit in which the skull had been found looked as fresh as though it had been dug only a few months prior to our visit. In reality it was three years old [this must be a mistake and should read 'two years' – ML] *and had during that time been exposed to tropical rains and strong surface wash"* (De Terra 1943: 442).

More pictures of this locality, including one that is presumably from an earlier visit by Von Koenigswald, were recently found in various archives (see Curtiss *et al.* 2000). These helped to relocate the spot in the field.

The question is, whether the locality to which Von Koenigswald took De Terra, Teilhard de Chardin and Movius in 1938, indeed is the locality where the skull was found. The skull was found by Handojo, a Geological Survey collector, and the true context of recovery of this find is highly uncertain, the story of recovery having changed several times. The find was first reported as a surface find, then as coming from a small excavation; and Handojo has pointed out different localities on different occasions as representing 'the' findspot. Unlike what appears to be suggested by Huffman (2001: 353), there were no other eyewitnesses. Duyfjes and Von Koenigswald did not visit the presumed Mojokerto findspot until several months after the find. How can one be sure that the locality to which Von Koenigswald guided De Terra's party is the correct one? His guidance was based on second-hand knowledge and there has been ambiguity about the Mojokerto skull recovery circumstances since the very beginning. The photographic evidence now brought up therefore in no way resolves the ambiguity which is central to the debate.

Was the skull a surface find or was it recovered stratigraphically *in situ* (De Vos 1985; Huffman 2001)? As mentioned, De Terra commented on the freshness of the excavation pit they encountered at the locality, pointing out that it *"looked as fresh as though it had been dug only a few months prior to our visit"* (De Terra 1943: 442). Maybe it was. It would be surprising if Von Koenigswald had not carried out further investigations at the spot pointed out to him by Handojo. I feel that too much has been made of the presence of an excavation pit two years after the discovery, and too much is being made of the photograph-aided relocation of this locality. These points do not solve the ambiguity which is the issue of previous debates (e.g. De Vos 1985; Theunissen *et al.* 1990).

Apart from the problems concerning the exact circumstances and locality of recovery of the fossil, the geological context of the site which produced the pumice sample yielding a $^{40}Ar/^{39}Ar$ age of 1.81 ± 0.04 Ma (Swisher *et al.* 1994) is debated, and this $^{40}Ar/^{39}Ar$ age again is contradicted by other dating evidence. De Vos and Sondaar (1994) pointed out that *"the pumice was taken from a conglomeratic volcanic sandstone which invites the interpretation that the pumice was likely reworked and redeposited"*. Geological mapping and palaeontological collecting has been carried out in the Mojokerto find area by Indonesian, French and Japanese geologists in the late 1970s and early 1980s (Sartono *et al.* 1981; Kumai *et al.* 1985). They describe the deposits as consisting of *"fluviatile facies which change downward into tuffaceous layers of secondary origin"* (Sartono *et al.* 1981: 94). Abundant cross-bedding is documented all over the lithostratigraphic section (Sartono *et al.* 1981, fig. 5).

Hyodo *et al.* (1993, 1992) carried out palaeomagnetic investigations in the Mojokerto area. They found a normal polarity for the sediments in the area where Swisher *et al.* obtained their dating sample. This normal polarity episode is preceded by sediments of reversed polarity in which the direction of the palaeopole shows a westward deflection. This same palaeomagnetic excursion has been found at Sangiran where it precedes the normal episode in the top of the Sangiran (Pucangan) Formation (Hyodo *et al.* 1992, 1993). The latter has been correlated with the Jaramillo subchron (see discussion earlier in this chapter) and by inference the normal polarity at Mojokerto should thus also be the Jaramillo subchron. As Hyodo *et al.* remark, the end of the sequence of westward deflections correlates in the sedimentary cycle of both sites with a shift from marine to lagoon sedimentation at Sangiran, and marine to fluvial sedimentation at Mojokerto: *"this coincidence seems to suggest a more or less simultanious occurrence of upheaval in the two areas"* (Hyodo *et al.* 1993: 177). The westward excursion has been estimated to have occurred between 1.5 and 1.7 Ma (Hyodo *et al.* 1992). This is reinforced by recent palaeomagnetic investigations of a 1700 metre drilling core from Osaka Bay, Japan, where a short excursion preceding the Jaramillo, and thought to be related to the Sangiran and Mojokerto excursion, can be pinned between dated tuff layers to an age of about 1.6 Ma (Biswas *et al.* 1999). The excursion is also present in the sequence at Yuanmou, China (Hyodo *et al.* 2002).

The relevant part of Java formed and emerged from the sea by a combination of tectonics and volcanic activity: originating from an arc of volcanoes along the axis of the emerging palaeo-Java island, lahars flowed into a shallow sea and sometimes formed land surfaces (Bellon *et al.* 1989; Bandet *et al.* 1989). This volcanic activity which created northeast Java took place in two major episodes that are K-Ar dated between the late middle Miocene and the late Pliocene, from about 11 Ma to 2-3 Ma (Bellon *et al.* 1989). At Gunung Butak near Kedung Brubus, a K-Ar age of 1.87 ± 0.04 Ma was obtained on volcanic samples recovered from a lahar breccia deposited on marine sediments that formed the first land surface in this area. Immediately above these lahar deposits occur the fluviatile deposits that contain the first fossil mammal remains (Bandet *et al.* 1989). The Lower Lahar at Sangiran likewise is dated to 1.8 Ma (see discussion earlier in this chapter) and is covered by shallow marine and lagoon clays.

The point is that the formative volcanic activity is likely to have occurred more or less simultaneously along the whole axis of the island as reconstructed by Bellon *et al.* (1989), and that the age of the final stage of this formative volcanic episode is equal to the ^{40}Ar/^{39}Ar age obtained on the volcaniclasts of Mojokerto by Swisher *et al.* (1994). Any sediments deposited by fluviatile action during the Pleistocene are likely to be erosively derived redepositions from this initial formative volcanic source deposit (but: see Huffman (2001) for a different opinion) This makes the ^{40}Ar/^{39}Ar age of 1.81 ± 0.04 obtained by Swisher *et al.*

(1994) for the Mojokerto fluviatile sediments that are believed to have yielded the Mojokerto hominin cranium at least suspect (here, we have to take to heart Bartstra's remark (1983: 425-426) that: "*the results of modern radiodating methods have to be regarded critically with a view to the geomorphic history of a particular region*"). The normal geomagnetic polarity that the site exhibits (Swisher *et al.* 1994: 1119-1120) could then indeed very well represent the Jaramillo chron.

Huffman (2001) in contrast argues that the Mojokerto sediments represent a quick depositional environment due to distant active volcanism. He feels that there has likely been not much time-depth between eruption and sedimentation of the volcanic constituents of the Mojokerto sediments. His reading of the geology in the Mojokerto area is that the sandstones represent sand depositions at river delta channels and/or a river delta front. The sediments in his opinion are derived from lahar mudflows down the edifice of distant volcanoes and represent a relatively short sedimentation span. If he is right, the normal polarity at the Swisher ^{40}Ar/^{39}Ar sampling site would then correlate to the Olduvai subchron, not the Jaramillo subchron (contra Hyodo *et al.* 1992, 1993, 2002). But Hyodo *et al.* (2002:39) maintain that there are no primary pumice deposits at Mojokerto. They therefore reject the old ages for the Javanese fossils, and maintain that East Asia and Southeast Asia were not occupied before 1.1 Ma (Hyodo *et al.* 2002).

It is clear that more work needs to be done in order to resolve the questions about the genesis of the Mojokerto sediments. But even this will not resolve the questions that pertain to the skull's provenance and its find circumstances. From the foregoing discussion it is clear that the Mojokerto infant skull does not make a reliable key fossil with regard to the question of when Java was first occupied by *Homo erectus.*

28

1.2   On Longgupo Cave and Yuanmou, China

Longgupo

A recent claim for hominin presence in east Asia well before 1.0 Ma comes from Longgupo Cave in Sichuan Province, China. Here, a rich fossil vertebrate assemblage was unearthed in 1985-1988, among which an incisor and a mandibular fragment both assigned to *Homo* sp. by the excavators. In addition, putative 'very primitive' stone tools have been described. Both the alleged hominin remains and the alleged stone tools are reported to come from localized clay facies that occur as approximately 2-3 metre wide longitudal channels along the cave walls. The centre of the cave consists of a gravel facies with clasts up of to 10 cm x 20 cm in size. Palaeomagnetic sampling of the localized clay facies suggests a series of normal and reversed polarities. The dental remains and putative stone tools come from sediments (level 7-8) with normal polarity which the excavators correlate to the Olduvai event, suggesting an age of about 1.8-1.9 Ma. In addition, one ESR determination on tooth enamel from a cervid premolar (recovered from the sediment infilling of the interior cavity of a mammalian long bone) about 3-4 metre higher in the cave infilling (level 4) results in a minimum age of 0.75 ± 0.09 Ma or a maximum age of 1.02 ± 0.12 Ma for this higher level, depending on an early or a linear uranium uptake history. Faunal remains from levels 2-12 combined, including *Nestoritherium*, suggest a Pliocene to early Pleistocene age according to Huang *et al.* (1995) and Wood and Turner (1995).

The dental evidence from Longgupo cave has turned out to be highly controversial among palaeontologists, while in addition doubts have been raised over the putative artefacts (e.g. Schwartz and Tattersall 1996; Dennell and Roebroeks 1996: 540). This author is not a hominin palaeontologist, but Wood and Turner, though supportive of the claims of the excavators, mention that the Longgupo remains "*are meagre pickings from a taxonomic point of view*" (Wood and Turner 1995: 240). Schwartz and Tattersall (1996: 201, emphasis added) state that: "*we believe that the morphology of the fossils indicates the presence of two* hominoids *whose specific taxonomic assignments* remain unclear". They note that the molars in the mandibular fragment share many characteristics with Middle Pleistocene orang-utan related fossil hominoid remains from Vietnam and hominoids in general, as opposed to being characteristic hominin features. To be fair, they also note that the isolated incisor "appears *to be hominin in morphology*" (Schwartz and Tattersall 1996: 201, emphasis added), but still they conclude that "*on the basis of the stone tools alone, one can make a case for the presence of hominids in China at whichever date (1 or 2 million*

years ago) is eventually confirmed. Morphologically, however, two different hominoids are represented at this site" (Schwartz and Tattersall 1996: 202). Other palaeontologist have expressed similar opinions (see Dennell and Roebroeks 1996: 540). Etler and Zhou (1998) recently argued the manibular fragment to have an ancestor/descendant relationship with *Lufengpithecus* and report that the isolated incisor "*is morphologically and metrically identical to a modern east Asian's and its association with the mandibular fragment must be viewed as a palimpsest*" (Etler and Zhou 1998).

In support of Dennell and Roebroeks (1996: 540; and contra Wood and Turner 1995; Schwartz and Tattersall 1996), the evidence in favour of an artefact status (as opposed to a *geofact* status) of the two putative 'stone tools' seems not convincing. Concerning the taphonomy of the Longgupo cave assemblage, the excavators note that the finds might result from accumulation in vertical karstic passages (which, as they note, are common in the karstic system to which Longgupo cave belongs), the faunal assemblage perhaps being "*the result of predation and falls*" (Huang *et al.* 1995: 275-276). The purported artefacts consist of a weathered cobble with some localized pitting on its surface (the pitting is also weathered), and a "flake", actually a naturally split and again heavily abraded and weathered cobble, with some alleged simple "retouching" (Huang *et al.* 1995). A number of other 'artefacts' have been published in Chinese (Hou *et al.* 1999). Judging from the published drawings and descriptions, the specimens fall within the range of naturally flaked pieces. In a taphonomic setting as described for Longgupo cave, flaking and battering is

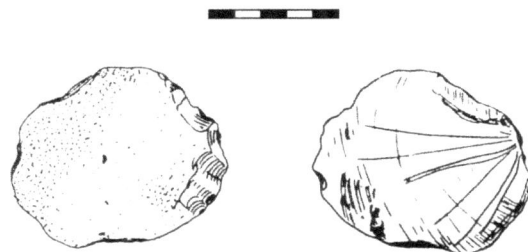

Figure 4: geofact collected by Clark in the Batoka Gorge, Africa (from Clark 1958; reproduced with permission).. Compare this drawing to the best Longgupo 'artefact' from Huang *et al.* (1995). Scale bar is in cm.

likely to occur when cobbles from the cave entrance fall down into the vertical passage onto the gravel infill of the cave system. Clark (1958) has collected and described such naturally flaked pieces from recent gravels at Batoka Gorge in Africa, which resulted from stones falling from the top of the gorge into the stream bed: in essence similar to pieces dropping into a vertical cave passage. The descriptions match the characteristics of the Longgupo specimens, indicating that they could very well have originated in this way (e.g. compare the similarity of the apparently 'retouched' naturally split cobble from Longgupo (Huang *et al.* 1995 figure 4b) with specimen #7 in fig. 1 of Clark (1958), reproduced with this chapter), although we should keep in mind the difference in raw material. In addition, the geologic and geomorphologic context of Longgupo cave might suggest that the cave deposits represent the trapped remnants of an eroded high energy deposit. In this aspect, the heavily weathered appearance of the two lithic specimens, including heavily weathered crest damage (text with fig. 4 in Huang *et al.* (1995)), should be taken into account. The circumstantial evidence cited by the excavators in favour of an artefact status for the pieces is weak in my opinion. The excavators state that the two pieces are "*twice the size of the normal deposit clasts*" (Huang *et al.* 1995: 277). However, this only applies to the narrow (2-3 metre diameter) very localized clay facies. The gravel infill in the central passage that forms the major part of the cave infilling contains clasts that can in fact be much larger (up to 10 x 20 cm: text with figure 2 of Huang *et al.* (1995)). If (partly or fully) derived from pieces falling into the cave, there is nothing against such pieces occasionally getting incorporated into the finer localized channel infillings, especially if one takes into consideration that falling pieces can bounce (it is for this reason that Wood and Turner's argument (1995: 239) that the specimens occur "*in finer sediment deposits that, as Gamble [1994] has pointed out, tend to categorize genuine archaeological assemblages as opposed to naturally bashed stones*" does not hold. Moreover, I am convinced that Gamble (1994) actually was thinking of open air sites in the cited comment). Equally, the "exotic" petrological composition of the pieces says little in favour of an artefact status, for "exotic" clearly is a relative thing in this particular case. As the excavators note, potential (secondary) sources for the raw materials are located in fluviatile sediments near Longgupo even today (Huang *et al.* 1995: 277-278). It cannot be excluded that these are remnants of deposits that were more widespread in the past, erosion clearly having played a role in the area around Longgupo. Karstic features such as Longgupo Cave can act as traps for the preservation of relics of such an eroded deposit. A similar phenomenon has acted at La Belle Roche in Belgium, where geofacts derived from a once extant but now, apart from some localized relics, eroded *cailloutis* were trapped, along with

faunal remains, in the karstic features of the site (Roebroeks 1986).

Thus, the artefact status of the Longgupo lithics remains unestablished in my view. Far from being positively the first artefacts in East Asia, they are *incertofacts* at best. In problematic situations like this, where the question of artificiality has large consequences for the general picture of Old World early hominin dispersal as it stands so far, the 'burden of proof' strongly rests on the shoulders of the excavators (Dincauze 1984; Roebroeks 1994; Roebroeks and Van Kolfschoten 1994, 1995). In my opinion, the "artefacts" of Longgupo do not convincingly pass the test so far.

Summarizing the above, serious controversy about the hominin status of the dental remains as well as the artefact status of the 'stone tools' surround the Longgupo Cave finds. New excavational activities at this site should provide more diagnostic fossil evidence before being acceptable.

In addition, and not unimportant, the site certainly needs more substantial dating. As Wood and Turner (1995: 239) note, the ESR age on the basis of an early uranium uptake of 0.75 ± 0.09 Ma for level 4 would mean that "*it could be argued that the normal magnetic event associated with the material is therefore likely to be Jaramillo*". They however add that "*the associated mammalian fauna is really too archaic and points instead to the earlier Olduvai event*". This could be true, but it should be noted that the faunal assemblage described seems to come (according to the report) from a wide range of levels (the middle zone, levels 2-12 (Huang *et al.* 1995: 275)) including levels several metres below the strata which yielded the dental remains (and in addition, contra Wood and Turner (1995), the unusual provenance of the dated cervid premolar points to some degree of reworking in the faunal sample). It becomes crucial to know whether the mammalian fossils that exclusively point to a terminal Pliocene-earliest Pleistocene age indeed come from the same levels (levels 7-8) as the dental remains and are, by chance, not restricted to the levels below. The argument by Etler and Zhou (1998) that the morphology of the isolated incisor from the believed "Plio-Pleistocene" deposits is indistinguishable from that of a modern Asian's incisor, indicating that the deposit with faunal remains represents a palimpsest of old and young materials, should also be a reason for caution. Note that the ESR age which is certainly not terminal Pliocene comes from this same broad range in levels. This exemplifies the possible pitfall, and leads to the inevitable conclusion that the current dating evidence is inconsistent (yet, Wood and Turner (1995: 239) characterize the elements of the dating evidence as "*none of them contradictory*"!). At least it can be argued that it lacks the proper resolution to support the case made by Huang *et al.*

(1995) and needs reconsideration. At this stage, this site cannot be a basis for a successful challenge of established dating frameworks.

Yuanmou

An older claim for Plio-Pleistocene hominin presence in China is Yuanmou, where two hominin incisors were found. However, the provenance of the two fossils appears to be unclear (Pope 1985), and the sediments from which they are believed to come have now been dated to the early Brunhes, following reassesment of the palaeomagnetic and lithostratigraphic sequence at Yuanmou (Hyodo *et al.* 2002; Urabe *et al.* 2001). Reassessment was based on renewed magneto-stratigraphic research, in which a succession of major reversals throughout the lithostratigraphic sequence was mapped, and these together with intra-Brunhes minor reversals, excursion events and the first appearance of *Equus* were put in sequence with the Geomagnetic Polarity Time Scale. In this chronological reassessment of the lithostratigraphic sequence, prominent changes in sedimentary regime match well with the ages of major climatological changes. In this sequence, the supposed find level of the hominin fossils is situated in normally polarized sediments, correlated to the early Brunhes (Hyodo *et al.* 2002). The Yuanmou incisors thus appear to be Middle Pleistocene. According to the critical assessment by Hyodo *et al.* (2002), there is no evidence for hominins in east and southeast Asia before 1.1 Ma.

32

1.3   On Riwat and the Pabbi Hills (Pakistan): a dilemma of interpretation

In 1983, members of the British Archaeological Mission to Pakistan discovered possible quartzite artefacts in Pliocene conglomerates of the Upper Siwalik Formation near Riwat, Pakistan (Dennell *et al*. 1988a, 1988b; Dennell 1989; Dennell *et al*. 1994). The debate has primarily focused on the artificiality of the lithic materials and the validity of the geological context of the finds (e.g. Hemingway and Stapert 1989). In general, the Riwat finds seem to be thoroughly ignored in contemporary literature on Plio-Pleistocene Asian hominids.

The dating arguments

The artefacts, consisting of quartzite flakes and flaked pieces including a large 'core tool' (flaked cobble), were discovered eroding from, but still firmly embedded in, a gritstone conglomerate outcrop (the 'core tool' mentioned had to be chiselled out of the conglomerate surface) exposed at the base of a deep erosion gully cutting through Upper Siwalik sediments. They therefore have a good stratigraphic context. The artefact-bearing outcrop occurs below 70 metres of overlaying sediment. The gritstone conglomerate and the sediments above it are part of the folded sediments of the Soan syncline and there is little doubt that these strata are indeed of Pliocene age. The folding of the syncline is inferred to have taken place around 1.9-2.1 Ma: the planed off surface of the folded strata are overlain by horizontally bedded, unfolded sediments that include a tuff dated by fission-track to 1.6 ± 0.18 Ma: since the sediment deposits that contain the tuff have a normal geomagnetic polarity, this suggests that they date to the Olduvai geomagnetic subchron, 1.67-1.87 Ma (Dennell *et al*. 1988a, 1994). The folded sediments at the Riwat find locality show a reversed geomagnetic polarity (that, by inference, must represent pre-Olduvai times) except for the basalmost part stratigraphically just below the find horizon, which is provisionally correlated with the 2.0 Ma Réunion-event. All this can be taken to indicate a minimum age of 1.9 Ma for the artefact bearing horizon (Dennell *et al*. 1988a). The excavators explicitly leave open the possibility that the basal normal polarized episode represents an older subchron than Réunion, which would imply that the possible artefacts could be considerably older than 1.9 Ma (Dennell priv. com.; Dennell 1998), for they believe that a considerable hiatus exists between the artefact bearing sediments and the post-Siwalik horizontal ash-bearing sediment sequence on top of it (Dennell *et al*. 1994: 153). Indeed, arguments have now been advanced

which indicate a possible age up to 2.5 Ma (Dennell 1998). The 1.9 Ma *minimum* age however, is a more safe and solid date to go with.

The recovered lithics

The possible artefacts are low in number, and since they derive from coarse conglomeratic sediments which are probably the result of a high-energy fluvial regime, this warrants caution because of the possibility of geologic flaking (see also Hemingway and Stapert (1989)). This point has been very well taken by the excavators, who have argued extensively why these specimens should be interpreted as artefacts and not geofacts (Dennell *et al*. 1988a, 1988b; Dennell 1989 (contra Hemingway and Stapert 1989); Dennell *et al*. 1994). The excavators have thoroughly addressed all key-features identified in Dincauze's (1984: 305) methodology for establishing the artificiality of the pieces. For example, they have explicitly addressed the character of the full suite of flaked rock from the locality (Dennell *et al*. 1988a; Dennell 1989), and presented that in the context of its matrix, the non-flaked part of the conglomerate in which they occur (Dennell 1989; Dennell *et al*. 1994), by detailed documenting of flaking and fracturing of clasts in the conglomerates. Flaked pieces and flakes are actually rare in the Riwat conglomeratic horizon. For example, after finding a probable artificial flake in the conglomeratic horizon some 50 metres from the earlier 1983 locality that yielded the initial artefact discoveries, Dennell and Hurcombe recorded all quartzite clasts larger than 2 cm in a 40 metre section, amounting to 1264 pieces. Of these, only one (besides the purported artefact mentioned) had been fractured (but not flaked). At the 1983 find locality, inspection of several tens of square metres of conglomerate resulted in only 24 flaked pieces (including the artefacts) out of an estimated 2000 clasts (Dennell 1989). Using a number of technological criteria (number of flakes removed; number of flakes with clear bulbs of percussion; number of directions in which flakes were removed; cortical area as a percentage of the original surface) and a subjective evaluation of the total characteristics of the piece, these 24 fractured lithics were rated on a scale from 0 to 5, with 0 denoting a piece indistinguishable from naturally flaked pieces, and 5 convincing for potentially being flaked by hominids. From the 24 pieces, 6 were rated category 4 or 5, 8 category 3, the rest category 1 or 2. The category 4/5 specimens have only small percentages of cortex, a high number of dorsal scars (up to 8) that are usually well defined, show clear negative bulbs of percussion and ripple scars, and they have been flaked from more than one widely divergent direction. The large 'core tool' R001 for example had 7 mostly large flakes detached from 5 different directions, while R014 had 7 flakes removed from 2 different directions (Dennell *et al.* 1988a). Given the low incidence of flaked pieces among the clast population of the conglomerate, and the differentiation apparent within the small population of flaked pieces, it seems inconceivable that extensively flaked pieces such as R001 and R014 and the other four category 4/5 pieces are the result of geological flaking processes. The specimens are not heavily rolled: the flake scars on the specimens all appear quite fresh, and although their fluvial sedimentary context points out that they are not in their original context of discard (i.e. they are to some extent transported by natural agents), transport has presumably not been extensive. In addition, tracing the artefact bearing horizon at Riwat over 5 kilometres, pieces regarded as hominid struck were all localized to within 100 metres of each other (Dennell 1989). In this case, the specimens interpreted to be artificial are clearly *not* a small limited selection of 'best' pieces from a very large array of geologically flaked stones. This invokes a dilemma.

A dilemma of interpretation

The dilemma invoked by the Riwat finds is that they do not come from fine-grained sediments, but from coarse fluviatile sediments, and they are almost certainly not in primary deposition (as is acknowledged by the excavators (Dennell 1989)). On the other hand, even with the finds coming from coarse-grained high energy deposits, there are nevertheless suggestions that the Riwat finds are genuine artefacts. The outstanding documentation of clast population characteristics, flaking incidence, and experimental determinations of the fracturing characteristics of the raw materials, all suggest that the extensively flaked specimens recovered are out of place in the natural clast population of the Riwat deposits, i.e. they are unlikely to be the result of natural flaking processes. It is for this reason that the evidence from Riwat should not be rejected. While from a very problematic type of context, my judgement is that it nevertheless concerns genuine artefacts with an age of at least 1.9 Ma. That in fact it is not surprising to find artefacts of this age in Pakistan, will be pointed out in chapter 3.1.

The Pabbi Hills

Another claim for a Plio-Pleistocene artefact occurrence by the same team of investigators concerns the Pabbi Hills, also in Pakistan (Dennell *et al.* 1993, 1994; Hurcombe and Dennell 1989). Here, morphologically simple artefacts are found as surface finds that *appear* to erode from 0.9-2.5 Ma old deposits. Some 290 specimens were collected during three field seasons. Apart from one still questionable case in which a piece of flaked rock was excavated from only 15 cm below the surface (Dennell *et al.* 1993), the fact that they do come from the Plio-Pleistocene strata from which they appear to erode cannot be established with certainty for any of these pieces. The taphonomic history of the single excavated piece is not clear, and its low recovery depth in combination with reportedly severe erosion phenomena in the Hills (Hurcombe and Dennell 1989) warrants caution. Given that these are surface finds without an unambiguously established stratigraphical provenance (as acknowledged by the investigators) and taphonomic history, the finds cannot be included in the framework of evidence for the current model. They could be older than 1.0 Ma but at the moment cannot be argued to be necessarily so.

1.4   On 'Ubeidiya (Israel) and Dmanisi (Georgia)

More acceptable evidence for an Earliest Pleistocene occupation outside the African continent comes from West Asia. The sites of 'Ubeidiya (Israel) and Dmanisi (Georgia) have received previous critical treatment of the dating evidence and, although retaining some uncertainty in their exact age, can with some confidence be judged to be at least 1.0 Ma and perhaps up to 1.4 ('Ubeidiya) or even 1.6 (Dmanisi) Ma old (cf. Bar-Yosef 1994, 1999; Dennell and Roebroeks 1996).

'Ubeidiya

In the Near East, the well-known Israelian site of 'Ubeidiya (Bar-Yosef and Goren-Inbar 1993) just south of the Sea of Galilee in the Jordan Valley provides good evidence for hominid presence during the Early Pleistocene. A combination of radiometric dates and faunal zonation brackets this site in the timespan of 1.0-1.4 Ma, with the older date being the most likely. The 'Ubeidiya Formation is underlain by the 3.1 Ma dated Cover basalt, and overlain by the 0.8 Ma dated Yarmuk basalt (Tchernov 1989, 1992; Bar-Yosef and Goren-Inbar 1993; Bar-Yosef 1994, 1995, 1999; Guérin et al. 1996), and has a reversed palaeomagnetic polarity. The fauna from the site is described as Late Villafranchian with some Gallerian elements, and can be characterized as a mixture of African and Eurasian species. It fits best between the faunas of Il Tasso and Farenta in Italy, and looks younger than those from Senéze and Le Coupet in France. Correlations with African sites indicate that it is older than Ternifine and perhaps similar in age to Ain Hanech (the age of which however is still floating, see chapter 1.5) and Olduvai Upper Bed II (Bar-Yosef and Goren-Inbar 1993; Bar-Yosef 1999).

The Plio-Pleistocene fauna of Betlehem in the southern Levant points to a palaeo-environment that strongly resembles the African-type tropical savanna grasslands (Tchernov 1992). A fauna with similar affinities to African dry savanna fauna's, backed by isotope studies suggesting dominance of C4 type vegetation, has recently been published for An Nafud in the northern part of Saudi Arabia (Thomas et al. 1998). At the Plio-Pleistocene boundary, the Levant and neighbouring Arabia could therefore be argued to be in unity with Africa in an environmental sense. The slightly later 'Ubeidiya fauna however, bears a stronger Eurasian stamp, although species of east African origin are present.

The site, best described as a palaeolithic landscape, consists of a series of rich archaeological layers that occur in lacustrine and alluvial deposits. Some sites represent a lakeshore context, others channelbank contexts and alluvial fans of drainage lines draining into the lake. Tectonic processes relating to the Afro-Syrian rift formation have created an anticline which folded the layers, and at present the once horizontally stratified layers occur as vertical stratification. Depending on their exact stratigraphic position, the archaeological materials in the site are partly *in situ*, partly derived from redeposition as artefacts from the surrounding hills washed into the fluviatile and alluvial lakeshore and floodplain deposits: some find layers are situated in fluvial and lacustrine silts and clays, others in coarser fluviatile gravel layers.

The earliest layers of the site contain an assemblage dominated by flakes, flake tools, choppers, and polyhedrons mainly made of flint and spheroids predominantly made of limestone. They resemble a Developed Oldowan B industry. Bifaces are insignificant in numbers but present (Bar-Yosef and Goren-Inbar 1993; Bar-Yosef and Shea 1999). Contrary to some older or secondary literature, the lower part of the archaeological sequence is certainly not 'Oldowan'. Bifaces (handaxes, picks) do appear in larger numbers in some of the younger layers, and are predominantly made of basalt (75.4%, with 93.3% of the handaxes), with a few on flint and limestone (Bar-Yosef and Goren-Inbar 1993; Bar-Yosef 1994, 1999). The bifaces, of which a fair number (61) have been recovered in most notably layer K30, are large, heavy, thick and very sturdy and morphologically (in terms of size, shape, raw materials) resemble those from Olduvai Bed II sites such as EF-HR (see Leakey 1971) to a high degree. They are rather unstandardized (see descriptions in Bar-Yosef and Goren-Inbar 1993). The surface flaking often consists of only a few large, rough and deep scars. The difference with the Olduvai Bed II Acheulean is in the manufacturing technique: all 'Ubeidiya handaxes (and indeed virtually the full biface sample) except 4 are made from cobbles instead of on large flakes, while the Early Acheulean handaxes from Olduvai Bed II are made on large flakes derived from boulder cores (Leakey 1971, 1975). In Olduvai, cobble-made bifaces are a feature of the Developed Oldowan. Apart from the bifaces, the heavier tool component consists of many limestone spheroids (sometimes of respectable size), with layer K29 being particularly rich in these, as well as a large number of 'chopping tools' and several heavy duty scrapers. The small tool fraction is dominated by notches and small retouched pieces (light duty scrapers) and includes some awls. The lack of bifaces in the earliest layers compared to the upper layers can be due to sample size, or the environmental shifts that occur in time through the sedimentary deposits at 'Ubeidiya, rather than the presence of two cultural groups of hominins. Bar-Yosef and Goren Inbar (1993) considered no evidence present for a relationship between assemblage type and local environment for 'Ubeidiya. However, layer K30, the only true Early Acheulean site rich in bifaces, and acknowledged to be deviating from the rest of the assemblage (Bar-Yosef and Goren-Inbar 1993: 201), is also exemplary in being located in a stream channel context. This corresponds with the model presented in chapter 3.2 for the early Acheulean of Africa, in which Developed Oldowan spreads over a wide array of local environments (including those where Acheulean is present), while contemporary Acheulean sites (*s.s.*) are restricted to a drainage line context. In this model, Developed Oldowan and Acheulean (*s.s.*) are activity facies of one cultural system, and there is a connection between assemblage content and paleoenvironment. 'Ubeidiya falls within this pattern.

'Ubeidiya has yielded some very limited hominin remains, which cannot be clearly identified on the species level (Tobias 1966).

'Ubeidiya in its Middle Eastern context

So far 'Ubeidiya is the only site in the Near East convincingly dated to the Earliest Pleistocene. The absence of other contemporary sites in the region (only Dmanisi in Georgia, at some distance, is comparable in age) is related to the tectonic history of the area: this part of the Afro-Syrian rift is a subduction zone, and in only a few miraculous instances local folding has pushed up and exposed older (Early Pleistocene) layers (Bar-Yosef and Goren-Inbar 1993; Goren-Inbar priv. com.). As far as the southern part of the Near East is concerned, the absence of sites may perhaps be more due to a lack of dated sites than to a true lack of sites from this timespan. Several sites, including (possible early) Acheulean ones, are present in the southern Levant, the Arabian peninsula (e.g. Whalen and Pease 1992; Petraglia 2003) and the Middle East. But most of them remain undated (Petraglia 2003; Bar-Yosef 1994; Clark 1994).

Purportedly late Pliocene artefacts from the Erq el Ahmar Formation in the Jordan Valley have been reported (Verosub and Tchernov 1991; see also Bar-Yosef 1995), as well as purported artefacts from sediments believed to date to over 2.4 Ma at Yir'on in Israel (Ronen 1991; Brunnacker *et al.* 1989), but so far the claims cannot be substantiated on many of the points outlined in the introduction (e.g. proper stratigraphic context, true artificial character and

site formation history, provenance from fine-grained sediments) and therefore in this stage they cannot be incorporated into the evidence presented here.

One of the problems with the age assigned to the Erg el Ahmar finds (Verosub and Tchernov 1991) is that the boundary between the 'Ubeidiya Formation and the Erg el Ahmar Formation is ill defined (see also Bar-Yosef 1999). Some of the Yir'on specimens (see Ronen 1991, figure 3) are doubtful pieces. An inspection of several casts of Yir'on finds (artefacts nos. 1, 2, 6, 7 and 8 in figure 3 of Ronen 1991) shows notable discrepancies with the descriptions and drawings in Ronen's (1991) report; in general, their condition and morphology is worse than is apparent in the publication. Artefacts nos. 6 and 7 are heavily rolled and edge-damaged and are natural pieces (*geofacts*) in my opinion. Whilst according to the text of the report the large flake scar on artefact no. 7 "is in a mint condition" (Ronen 1991: 161), contrary to the "heavily worn" rest of the piece with "rounded edges", the casts show that the ridge at the distal end of the stepped flake scar is heavily battered with many edge removals, just as the other edges of the piece. Artefacts nos. 1 and 2 are heavily rolled with rounded edges. They would be morphologically acceptable if they had come from a fine-grained context, but they are suspect *incertofacts* given their gravel provenance. The "retouch" of both pieces is questionable, especially if their rolled condition and the heavily edge-damaged character of the other pieces is taken into account. Contrary to the report, some edge removals are present on the edges of the ventral side of piece no. 1 as well. The assemblage however does contain a quite convincing multi-platformed core, with a rather fresh appearance with sharp-edged and well-defined flake scars (artefact no. 8 in figure 3 of Ronen 1991). Given the discrepancies noted between the casts I inspected and the drawings and descriptions in Ronen 1991, it is difficult to judge the remainder of the depicted finds.

The three or four pieces which are morphologically most convincing, would all fit typicalay a younger age than the late Pliocene age assigned to them (i.e. the blade fragment (no. 2), the small bifacial piece (no. 5) and the core (no. 8)). It is not clear whether the sediments of the find location indeed equate to the sediments underlying the Yir'on basalt some distance away from the find locality. The Yir'on basalt is dated to 2.4 Ma (Ronen 1991).

In one of the following chapters it will be shown that the presence of Early Pleistocene or even Plio-Pleistocene sites in the Levant and the Middle East would not be against all expectations. Indeed, the existence of Plio-Pleistocene sites in the Levant is one of the predictions of the model advanced in the following chapters. But as yet, only 'Ubeidiya is acceptable as representing such a site. To a large extent, the Middle East remains a chronological blank spot on the map.

Dmanisi

One of the earliest sites to represent perhaps the first hominid dispersal outside the tropical grasslands (according to one view: but see below) could be Dmanisi in the Caucasian republic of Georgia. This site (Dzaparidze *et al.* 1989) has yielded a stone tool assemblage, faunal remains, and a hominid mandible, as well as recently two almost complete skulls and a footbone (Gabunia and Vekua 1995; Gabunia *et al.* 1999, 2000b) discovered in Pleistocene sediments under the basement of a medieval fortification. The mandible and skulls were found together with remains of sabertooth cats, hyaenids, and several mammalian species including palaearctic ones attesting (together with pollen records) to an environment of humid woodland in a more open alpine setting (Dzaparidze *et al.* 1989; Bar-Yosef 1994, 1995). Yet, there might be some equivocality in the palaeo-environment reconstructed for this site. For example, open grassland species like a very large form of ostrich and *Equus* are present, which could suggest affinities of the palaeo-environment with open savanna grassland conditions (Gabunia *et al.* 2000a; Van Kolfschoten priv. com.). The carnivore population points to a highly competitive ecological environment indeed suggesting open grassland conditions.

The age of the site is still debated and there appears to be room for more than one interpretation of the dating evidence. Recent discussions are coloured by the fact that this site has become, with reason, one of the spearhead sites of the 'long chronologists' and this is something strongly guiding interpretations of the dating evidence. No doubt this site is old compared to other Eurasian sites, but how old is still a matter of disagreement.

Morphologically, the hominid mandible shares many characteristics with the later *Homo erectus* specimens which would suggest an age not much older than 1.0 Ma (Braüer and Schultz 1996). On the other hand, the two recently recovered skulls appear to be archaic, with affinities with the early African erectine hominids, now by many palaeoanthropologists designated *Homo ergaster*, which in Africa span a time range of 1.8 to perhaps 1.4 Ma (Gabunia *et al.* 1999, 2000b).

The artefact assemblage from Dmanisi has been classified as a mode 1 assemblage with affinities with the 'Oldowan'. It consists of many flakes, some flake tools, polyhedrons and chopping tools (Dzaparidze *et al.* 1989; Ljubin and Bosinski 1995). One fragmentary artefact (Dzaparidze *et al.* 1989, fig. 38) has been bifacially flaked and could well be the medial part of a broken handaxe. This piece is generally ignored in recent discussions which, in order to further the old age advocated, stress the 'primitive' character of the stone tools and the purported affinities of the assemblage with the older Plio-Pleistocene African archaeological assemblages.

A date of 1.8 Ma (Gabunia and Vekua 1995) is often quoted for this site. This date was obtained by radiometric dating and palaeomagnetic sampling on a basalt *below* the archaeological deposits (the Masavera basalt) interpreted as dating to the Olduvai subchron. The excavators favoured an age of approximately 1.6-1.7 Ma (Dzaparidze *et al.* 1989). Recent investigations suggest that the fauna, artefacts and hominid remains occur in sedimentary infills of intrusive tunnels (possibly carnivore dens: see Tappen *et al.* (2002)) cut into the sediments directly overlying the Masavera basalt. The palaeomagnetic polarization of the basalt is normal and the basalt yields ^{40}Ar/^{39}Ar ages of 1.85 ± 0.01 Ma (Gabunia *et al.* 1999, 2000b) pointing to an age of formation during the Olduvai subchron. The (archaeologically sterile!) sedimentary Unit A (Gabunia *et al.* 2000b) overlying the basalt equally has a normal palaeomagnetic polarization, and given the non-eroded character of the basalt surface below it probably was deposited very shortly after the formation of the basalt itself. However, the sedimentary tunnel fills yielding the archaeology and hominid remains have a *reversed* geomagnetic polarity, favouring a younger, post-Olduvai, Matuyama age between 0.8-1.7 Ma. (Gabunia *et al.* 1999, 2000b). These tunnels and their fills are intrusive features into Unit A, with an unclear relationship to the sediments of Unit B1 which also contain artefacts. The contact between Units A and B is an "abrupt erosional surface" (Gabunia *et al.* 2000b: 1023) and this combined with the clear geomagnetic polarity difference indicates that both Unit B1 and the intrusive tunnel fills cut into Unit A are clearly *later* (and post-Olduvai) than the likely Olduvai Unit A sediments and the 1.85 ± 0.01 Ma Masavera basalt underlying Unit A.

The excavators of the site however believe these tunnel fills to date from very shortly after the deposition of the basalt and thus claim a 1.7 Ma date for the site (note that an argument in favour of this age assignment involving the uneroded character of the Masavera basalt surface (Andrews cited in Balter and Gibbons 2000: 949) has little relevance because the archaeological layers do not occur in direct contact with the basalt: of relevance instead is the Unit A-Unit B1 contact and the contacts between the Unit A sediments and the intrusive tunnel fills. These are clearly erosive). But given that there is, according to the reports, a clear erosional hiatus of unknown duration between the Olduvai age sediments and the sediments containing the archaeology and hominid fossils, such an age assignment to the upper Olduvai boundary can only be substantiated with biostratigraphic arguments. A point of concern then becomes whether the faunal assemblage recovered has real temporal integrity. It has been acknowledged now that the fauna and lithics from the archaeological levels represent a hydraulic jumble of materials washed into the tunnel cavities (Gabunia *et al.* 1999, 2000b). The bone assemblage has recently been suggested to be the result of

37

carnivore denning (Tappen *et al*. 2002). The sediment fill of the intrusive tunnels into Unit A reportedly appears to be a heterogeneous mixture of Unit A sediments and some elements also recovered from Unit B sediments (Gabunia *et al*. 2000b: 1023). No arguments are given to separate fossils possibly deriving from eroded Unit A sediments (Unit A fossils redeposited in the younger tunnel infills at the time when these later erosive features were cut into Unit A) from fossils of mammals that actually date to the time of the tunnel fill deposition − note that the likely Olduvai aged but archaeologically sterile Unit A sediments do contain mammal fossils: for example, it yielded a partial *Dicerorhinus etruscus etruscus* mandible (Gabunia *et al*. 2000b: 1024). "The fauna says Olduvai and the magnetics say Matuyama" (Swisher quoted in Balter and Gibbons 2000: 949). The question to be answered is whether the mammal species that point to an Olduvai age are not reworked fossils from the older (and indeed, likely Olduvai) Unit A sediments into which the tunnel fills containing the archaeology and hominid remains are intrusive. If the fauna also contains elements which *contradict* an Olduvai age, these should be given a strong weighting in the age assessment, for the reasons outlined above. At least the more fragmentary fossils recovered from Unit B1 display different stages of weathering, and sediment infills of some of the bone cavities differ from the sediments in which they were found (Gabunia *et al*. 1999: 464).

A conservative age estimate, comparable to 'Ubeidiya, of about 1.2-1.5 Ma for the site seems most reasonable (cf. Bar-Yosef 1994; Dennell and Roebroeks 1996). This would still suggest it to be the earliest occurrence outside the Afro-Levantine tropical savanna grassland area, followed by the Nihewan sites and perhaps Gongwangling (Lantian) in China (see chapter 2.1) dated to 1.1 Ma. That is, if we accept non-savanna conditions for Dmanisi. If the presence of ostrich and other open grassland species are taken to indicate an environment with strong affinities with the tropical grasslands, then this site could represent an extension of the tropical savanna grasslands typically, but perhaps incorrectly, associated with Early Pleistocene Africa. Occupation of similar alpine settings of high altitude savanna in East Africa seems to have started at a similar time as the conservative age estimate for Dmanisi, around 1.5 Ma (e.g. Gadeb high plains in Ethiopia (Clark and Kurashina 1979; Williams *et al*. 1979)), and in that sense Dmanisi at an age of perhaps 1.5 Ma would *not* be exceptional. It would represent a trend around 1.5 Ma during which both inside Africa and at the fringes of the then populated part of Afro-Asia (Africa and a part of west Asia), hominins start to fill in higher parts of the landscape which in ecological structure have close affinities with their original lowland savanna environment. This development can perhaps be seen as a prelude to the colonization of southern Eurasia which follows at around 1.2-1.1 Ma, and is the result of the same evolutionary processes with regard to cognition and behaviour which eventually made 'Out of Africa 1' possible (most notably, as will be outlined in chapter 2, the development of more tolerance towards seasonal environments).

Note added: As the manuscript of this work was just completed, the find of a new skull from Dmanisi was announced (Vekua *et al*. 2002). It discerns itself from the other fossils by apparently having a very small brain, leading to speculation about small-brained hominins being the first hominins to go Out of Africa (see Balter and Gibbons 2002).

1.5   Ain Hanech (North Africa)

The chronology of the first occupation of Northern Africa is still poorly established (see review in Clark (1992) and discussions of the Moroccan evidence in Raynal and Texier (1989) and Raynal et al. (1995b)). So far, there is only a provisional chronology for this area which is rich in palaeolithic sites most of which however remain poorly dated (Clark 1992).

In Morocco, the earliest hominid fossils as well as archaeological find assemblages have an age slightly in excess of the Brunhes-Matuyama boundary, i.e. dating to the latest Matuyama around 0.9 Ma. The oldest sites (e.g. Thomas-1 quarry sites) are dated by palaeomagnetic sampling and biostratigraphy (Raynal and Texier 1989; Raynal et al. 1995b, 2001), while some of the Middle Pleistocene Acheulean sites also have ESR dates (e.g. the Grotte des Rhinocéros, 476 ± 75 ka (Rhodes et al. 1994)). It should be noted that in Morocco the sites, including the earlier ones, have an artefact assemblage of Acheulean character, including a clear percentage of cleavers and bifaces. There seems to be an evolution of rougher 'Abbevilian' type bifaces in the older (terminal Early Pleistocene) sites to thin and relatively small bifaces in the younger (Middle Pleistocene) sites. Note that putative chopping tool/pebble tool complexes that were once thought to predate the Acheulean in this area are now deemed geofacts or recent artefacts from surface colluvial deposits according to recent research (Raynal and Texier 1989; Raynal et al. 1995b, 2001).

Other sites in this area are poorly dated. Ternifine (Algeria), with hominid remains which according to some (e.g. Dean and Delson 1995) are transitional from *Homo erectus* to *Homo heidelbergensis* has been assigned ages quoted as 0.6-1.0 Ma (Hublin 1985) and 0.7 Ma (Dean and Delson 1995). Based on the associated microfauna, it must be older than a palaeontological assemblage associated with Acheulean artefacts from the Grotte des Rhinocéros (Morocco) which has an ESR date of 476 ± 75 ka (Rhodes et al. 1994). Hominid remains from Salé (Morocco) are regarded as 0.4 Ma in age (Hublin 1985)).

Northern Africa: Ain Hanech (Algeria)

The atlantic Moroccan picture might stand out from the other regions in North Africa, in the sense that it appears to have a later initial occupation and that the Acheulean occurs from the start of this initial occupation. A perhaps different picture comes from Algeria, east of the Atlas

mountains, a picture that could be reminiscent of that seen in Asia (and perhaps southern Europe) below 40° N latitude discussed in the following chapters. Of primary interest for the current chapter is a reported Plio-Pleistocene artefact occurrence in Algeria. At Ain Hanech and nearby El-Kherba in Northeast Algeria (Sahnouni 1998; Sahnouni et al. 1996; Sahnouni and De Heinzelin 1998), the lower archaeological deposits appear to represent a non-Acheulean 'mode 1' industry of Oldowan affinities, while the Acheulean occurs only later in the sequence in the uppermost surface deposits which, according to the excavators, must be considerably younger (Sahnouni 1998; Sahnouni et al. 1996; Sahnouni and De Heinzelin 1998).

The described artefacts (flint and limestone flakes, flaked cobbles — polyhedrons and unifacial and bifacial choppers, subspheroids and two spheroids — and some unsystematically retouched pieces of flint, 2667 pieces in total) come from fine-grained sands and silts; all are reported to be extremely fresh in appearance (Sahnouni 1998; Sahnouni et al. 1997: 703; Sahnouni and De Heinzelin 1998)). Apart from some large flaked cobbles and tools, the vast majority of the material represents debitage, most of which (80% of the full assemblage from both sites) is waste smaller than 2 cm. Retouched tools, cores/core tools and flakes/flake fragments larger than 2 cm number only 431 at the 50 m^2 Ain Hanech excavation and 128 at the 12 m^2 El-Kherba excavation (Sahnouni 1998; Sahnouni and De Heinzelin 1998: 1095). This small sample size and the small excavated total surface areas should be taken into account considering the absence of bifacial tools and the placement of the assemblages in the 'Oldowan' rather than the Developed Oldowan or Acheulean.

The artefacts occur in sediments with a normal palaeomagnetic polarization overlain and underlain by reversed polarized sediments, and they are reportedly associated with a faunal assemblage of 'Villafranchian affinities' (Sahnouni et al. 1996; Sahnouni 1998; Arambourg 1949). The archaeological horizon itself yielded a fragmentary fauna in the recent excavation campaigns reported on by Sahnouni et al. (Sahnouni 1998; Sahnouni et al. 1996; Sahnouni and De Heinzelin 1998). *Equus tabeti, Hippopotamus* sp., Bovidae sp. and *Gazella* sp. have been identified (Sahnouni 1998; Sahnouni and De Heinzelin 1998). The biostratigraphic age assignment for the site employs the larger faunal list of Arambourg (1949), which however seems to be at least partly obtained from a lower level (Unit P) if I read Sahnouni (1998: 16-19) correctly, a point also noted by Clark (1992: 20-21), who notes that the fauna: *"could be derived from underlying fossiliferous horizons"*. This Unit P has a reversed polarity and therefore is evidently older than the normally polarized archaeological Unit T. In addition, some post-excavation mixing of faunal elements from Ain Hanech and the nearby Pliocene palaeontological site of Ain Boucherit is thought to have occurred in the Arambourg collection: Sahnouni (1998: 18) provides this as an explanation for the reported occurrence of *Hipparion* in the Arambourg faunal list for Ain Hanech. It should be noted that the fossil pig *Kolpochoerus*, one of the three species (the other ones are *Mammuthus meridionalis* and *Sivatherium*) thought to indicate a Plio-Pleistocene age for Ain Hanech (Arambourg collection), is now also known from much younger (around 1.0 Ma, latest Late Matuyama postdating the Jaramillo) deposits in level Th1-L1 of the Moroccan Casablanca sequence (Raynal *et al.* 2001).

From the mentioned biostratigraphical arguments, Sahnouni *et al.* and Sahnouni and De Heinzelin opt for an identification with the Olduvai subchron *"rather than the onset of the Brunhes chron"* (Sahnouni *et al.* 1996: 641-642; Sahnouni and De Heinzelin 1998: 1087) for the normal palaeomagnetic polarity sediments in which the artefacts occur. Indeed, the deposits must be older than the onset of the Brunhes chron. In my view, however, there are no real arguments to prefer the identification of the palaeomagnetically normal polarized artefact bearing sediments with the ~1.77 Ma Olduvai subchron over the possibility of an identification with the younger ~1.0-1.1 Ma Jaramillo subchron, which I prefer but is not discussed as a possibility by Sahnouni *et al.* The recent decrease in the last appearance date of *Kolpochoerus* in North Africa reported by Raynal *et al.* (2001) serves as a warning against a too strict application of biostratigraphical correlations over large distances based on very few indicative fossils. For such long-distance correlations (between North Africa and East Africa in the case of Ain Hanech) the kind of interregional faunal dispersal patterns and regional isolations for East and North Africa and the Levant as discussed by Tchernov (1992) become relevant. It should be noted that Raynal *et al.* (2001) recently considered the age of Ain Hanech (the faunal complex of Arambourg, presumably) to be close to 1.2 Ma, near the base of the Jaramillo indeed, as opposed to the 1.8 Ma Olduvai age assigned to Ain Hanech by Sahnouni *et al.* Moreover, it seems still possible that the archaeological horizon as indicated is younger than the faunal horizon excavated by Arambourg.

The Ain Hanech chronological evidence therefore does not fully meet the criteria of the checklist given in the introduction. The stratigraphic relations between the artefacts and faunal assemblage are not entirely clear as the Arambourg faunal list seems to represent a stratigraphic unit different from the artefact bearing unit, and the palaeomagnetic dating evidence can be interpreted in more than one way. Currently, the Grotte des Rhinocéros in Morocco with an ESR age of 476 ± 75 ka and, related to this, the Ternifine hominid remains which on biostratigraphical grounds are thought to be older (Rhodes *et al.* 1994) are the oldest sites in North Africa dated reliably, while even the 0.9-1.0 Ma dates proposed for the 'older' Casablanca area sites (e.g. the Thomas-1 quarry sites) are to be treated with caution since these are largely based on palaeomagnetic sampling (Raynal and Texier 1989; Raynal *et al.* 1995b, 2001).

The Ain Hanech and El-Kherba deposits represent a floodplain environment, with the archaeological horizons of Ain Hanech representing a low energy channel environment in an alluvial plain, and El-Kherba representing the muddy margins of a channel (Sahnouni 1998). The palaeoenvironment of Ain Hanech has been reconstructed as open and grassy and of a Mediterranean type, both based on the faunal evidence (e.g. presence of *Equus* and *Gazella*) and on Carbon isotope analysis. From the Carbon isotope content of two *Equus tabeti* molars, a dominance of C_3 vegetation has been reconstructed for the Ain Hanech environment (Sahnouni 1998). This is unlike the Pleistocene savanna environments of East and Southern Africa, where C_4 grasses were and are prominent starting with the increasing aridity and formation of secondary grasslands at about 1.8 Ma (for an explanation of C_3 and C_4 grasslands, see chapter 3.1). The C_3 dominated palaeoenvironment of Ain Hanech together with its faunal content suggest a more Mediterranean ecology, such as still present in the area today (Sahnouni 1998).

1.6   On the Orce basin (Spain)

Proposed Plio-Pleistocene ages for European sites have been and still are published (e.g. contributions to Bonifay and Vandermeersch (1991)). These claims were thoroughly discussed at the 1993 Tautavel Conference, an ESF Workshop dedicated to the establishment of a reliable chronology for the first occupation of Europe. The discussion dealt with at the workshop will not be repeated here in detail (cf. for these discussions: Roebroeks 1994; Roebroeks and Van Kolfschoten 1994, 1995). Suffice it to remark that the outcome of that conference was that none of the claims for purported 'Plio-Pleistocene' European sites made up to 1993 was to be regarded as acceptable. Sites before about 0.5 Ma were shown to be problematic in respect of either the artificial character of the recovered stone "tools" (e.g.: Le Vallonet, Prezletice, Stranská Skalá), or the chronological assignment (e.g. Isernia la Pineta) (Roebroeks and Van Kolfschoten 1994, 1995). For Northwest Europe this still holds, and probably will hold in the future (Roebroeks 1996, 2001). For Southern Europe new evidence presented after 1993 suggests that Southern Europe may have a different history of occupation (see Dennell and Roebroeks 1996).

The Orce basin (Guadix-Baza, Spain)

One once highly contentuous case of a purported Plio-Pleistocene hominid occupation in Europe which has produced firmer evidence in several recent publications is the evidence from the vicinity of Orce in the Spanish Guadix-Baza basin (Gibert et al. 1994, 1998a, 1998b; Tixier et al. 1995; Turq et al. 1996; Navarro et al. 1997; Agusti et al. 1999; Oms et al. 2000). The evidence concerns genuine archaeological deposits: the Barranco del Leon and Fuente Nueva-3 sites contain undoubtedly genuine artefacts recovered from fine-grained sediments deposited in a low energy saline lake environment. In addition a highly contentuous case has been put forward (and keeps being restated) for possible hominin remains at the Venta Micena site (Gibert et al. 1998a), which according to some workers (now including those who originally identified them as 'Homo') are however Equus, not Homo (Palmqvist 1997; Moyà-Solà and Köhler 1997). Problems with the Guadix-Baza basin sites revolved around the chronology of the deposits (cf. Roe 1995; Dennell and Roebroeks 1996). Until recently the dating evidence appeared ambiguous, and in the past contradictory interpretations have been published within just a few months of each other by members of the same research team.

Difficulties in correlating strata between different sections in the Orce area are apparent (contra Gibert et al. (1998b); and a point acknowledged by Oms et al. (2000)), and as a result some palaeontological and archaeological sites in the Orce basin are assigned to different stratigraphic units in different publications. For example, Orce-6 is assigned to the ensemble vert by Tixier et al. (1995: fig. 2), but to the niveau noir by Gibert et al. (1998b: fig. 4), a shift of two stratigraphic units upward. This makes very clear that the correlations between different sections are not as clear cut as presented by e.g. Gibert et al. (1998b).

The artefacts of Fuente Nueva-3 (see Gibert et al. 1998b) were initially assigned a date just following the end of the Olduvai event (i.e., a Plio-Pleistocene age of 1.7 Ma), based on a presumed geomagnetically normal polarized horizon in the nearby FN-1 section correlated stratigraphically to a level only a few metres below the FN-3 artefact bearing levels (Gibert et al. 1994; Tixier et al. 1995). A renewed geomagnetic study of the FN-1 section suggested the normal polarity episode to be nonexistent (Navarro et al. 1997), and following this the archaeological FN-3 levels were assigned a somewhat younger pre-Jaramillo/post-Olduvai Matuyama age, both on the basis of the palaeomagnetism and faunal correlations with other sites. The validity of these palaeomagnetic datings was largely dependent on the validity of the correlation between the stratigraphy of the artefact bearing Fuente Nueva FN-3 section and the stratigraphy of the FN-1 section, the one which had been palaeomagnetically investigated (see Navarro et al. (1997) for details on Fuente Nueva-3 and -1). Moreover, some palaeontologists did and do see problems in matching the age estimates with the biostratigraphic evidence (cf. Dennell and Roebroeks 1996). To add to the confusion and doubts, the presence of a normally polarized horizon below the archaeological levels was reiterated by Gibert et al. (1998b) just a few months after Navarro et al. (1997) rejected it! Recently, new palaeomagnetic investigations of the artefact bearing FN-3 and Barranco del Leon sections themselves however established that these have a reversed polarization throughout the sections with no signs of normal episodes (Oms et al. 2000).

Following the new palaeomagnetic investigations and a new synthesis of the faunal evidence (Agusti et al. 1999; Oms et al. 2000), the original 'Plio-Pleistocene' age for FN-3 and Barranco del Leon was revised upward. The palaeomagnetic evidence suggests that both sites are to be placed in the upper part of the Matuyama chron; either between the upper Jaramillo and basal Brunhes (upper Early Pleistocene), or between the lower Jaramillo and upper Olduvai (lower Early Pleistocene). The faunal evidence puts further constraints on the datings. Barranco del Leon contains *Castillomys crusafonti* that is already absent in Atapuerca TD and in the probably latest Matuyama deposits of the Cúllar section (see Agusti *et al.* 1999). According to Oms *et al.* (2000), *Allophaiomys bourgondiae* from FN-3 is a more primitive species than *Microtus nivaloides* from both the French palaeontological site of Le Vallonet (dated to the Jaramillo) and the Spanish archaeological site of Atapuerca TD-6 (claimed to date to the latest post-Jaramillo Matuyama, and discussed later). This would indicate that FN-3 has to be placed in the lower Early Pleistocene, between the lower Jaramillo and upper Olduvai. Regional correlations (Agusti *et al.* 1999) suggest a clear post-Olduvai age. Given faunal similarities with the nearby palaeontological site of Venta Micena, which is biostratigraphically correlated with Dmanisi and 'Ubeidiya, an age between 1.0-1.5 Ma is suggested. Taking this somewhat conservatively, this suggests that FN-3 is at least 1.1 Ma old and may have a similar age as the earliest acceptable sites in the eastern part of Eurasia (China), i.e. about 1.2 Ma (see chapter 1.2). It is now up to those palaeontologists who still express doubts to put forward arguments which seriously challenge this age assignment.

Part II

Claims for early occupations of Eurasia between 1.4-0.5 Ma

Several claims exist for Eurasian finds of hominin fossils and/or tools with an Early Pleistocene age between 1.4-0.5 Ma, the latter age being the age for the earliest occupation of Europe as proposed by the 'short chronologists' (Roebroeks and van Kolfschoten 1994), the earlier age as advocated, with caution, by Dennell and Roebroeks (1996). Part II of this dissertation carries on a similar critical look on claims for evidence for occupations as employed in part I.

44

2.1   The Far East: China and central Asia

Starting probably near the younger side of the 1.5-1.0 Ma interval, hominins appear to disperse into previously unexploited environments. Hominin presence is no longer restricted to the dry tropical grasslands of Africa and the southwest of west Asia: hominins now enter the temperate environments of eastern China and the subtropical areas of Southeast Asia, followed by central Eurasia, Northwest Africa and perhaps southern Europe.

It should be stressed that East Asia did not possess a clear C_4 type grassland environment during the Quaternary (see chapter 3.1 for an overview of different grassland types including a discussion of C_4 and C_3 type habitats). In fact, evidence from Lingtai on the Chinese loess plateau suggests that C_4 type grasses, which in any case never were dominant in this part of the world, were in serious decline from about 3-2 Ma onward (Ding and Yang 2000). Hominin expansion into this part of Eurasia therefore appears to have little to do with an hypothetical expansion of a tropical C_4 dominated grassland habitat. Geographical expansion of a hominin species (*Homo erectus*), such as occurs at around 1.2 Ma, who initially occupied tropical C_4 habitats therefore suggests an evolutionary cause, namely a developing tolerance to other than C_4 type environments.
One of the earliest sites to represent such a first hominin dispersal outside the tropical savanna and an adaptation to environments different from the dry tropical savanna grasslands might be Dmanisi in Georgia, as discussed in chapters 1.4 and 3.1. Perhaps the oldest sites following Dmanisi are the Gongwangling hominin site and the archaeological Nihewan basin sites in China.

The early occupation of China and adjacent areas

The age of the initial occupation of the Far East is not something on which there is agreement. The contentious evidence for Pliocene hominin presence at Longgupo cave in China has been discussed (and rejected) in chapter 1.2, as has been the evidence for Pliocene hominins at Yuanmou.
Several Chinese archaeological and hominid find localities with reported ages up to 1.1 Ma have been published, some of which deserve to be taken seriously. Yet, we should keep in mind that many early sites in China have only provisional dates based on limited dating evidence. Most notably, heavy reliance is placed on palaeomagnetic dating. Tiemei and Yunping (1988: 98) are of the opinion that *"the palaeomagnetic dates...should not be taken as conclusive, unless they will be cross-checked with radiometric dates"*.

In addition, some dating techniques used are controversial, e.g. dating by TL of aeolic sediments up to purportedly 1 Ma (Aitken 1995). Yet, some dating studies, certainly those where soil horizons can be tied in with the chronology of the well-researched Chinese loess sections (e.g. An and Ho 1989) appear to be thorough. Evidence for at least some sites indicates that eastern China was occupied by 1.0 Ma ago (see also Hyodo *et al.* 2002).

The Nihewan basin sites (Donggutuo, Xiaochangliang)

Two neighbouring archaeological sites that represent the earliest acceptable evidence as such from Asia are Donggutuo and Xiaochangliang in the Nihewan basin, west of Beijing. Both sites have yielded unequivocal artefacts along with faunal remains in fine-grained sediments (sands and silts) of low energetic fluvial character that represent ancient lakeside deposits (Schick *et al.* 1991; Schick 1994; Pope and Keates 1994). There is some disagreement about the Donggutuo deposits, which might be colluvial according to Pope and Keates (1994). The faunal assemblage from Xiaochangliang includes *Allophaiomys* cf. *pliocaenicus, Mimomys chinensis, Hyaena (Pachycrocuta) licenti, Palaeoloxodon* sp., *Hipparion* sp., *Proboscidipparian sinensis, Equus sanmeniensis, Coelodonta antiquitatis, Marctes* sp. *Cervus* sp. and *Gazella* sp. (Zhu *et al.* 2001).
The faunal assemblage from the Nihewan deposits point to a grassland environment (Pope and Keates 1994). Dating relies on a combination of palaeomagnetic sampling and biozonation. The biostratigraphical age is perhaps not entirely unequivocal given that the Northeast Asian biozonation is still provisional in some respects (e.g. Clark and Schick 1988; Pope and Keates 1994; Qiu and Qiu 1995), but the species recorded at the Nihewan sites point to an Early Pleistocene age (Schick *et al.* 1991; Pope and Keates 1994; Zhu *et al.* 2001). This matches the geomagnetic evidence from the sites. Based on palaeomagnetic sampling of the sediment exposures, which show a sequence of reversed and normal polarized sediments, Donggutuo probably just antedates the Jaramillo subchron. Xiaochangliang is situated 13.4 metres below the bottom of a normal polarized episode in the sediment sequence. This episode is interpreted as the Jaramillo subchron. From the sedimentation rate calculated from the sediment span between the top of the Olduvai and the bottom of the Jaramillo, the age of the artefact layer is estimated to be about 1.36 Ma (Zhu *et al.* 2001).
The stone tool assemblages of these sites consist of many

unmodified flakes (some with macroscopic use wear), a number of cores described as "casually flaked involving relatively few flaking blows" (Schick *et al.* 1991) and relatively few retouched flakes (Keates 1994). Tools consist of side scrapers, notches, and a few end scrapers and burins (Zhu *et al.* 2001). Most were made of chert and some of quartzite (Schick *et al.* 1991). A similar assemblage comes from fine sediments (fine sands, silts and clays) at Cenjiawan, also in the Nihewan basin. Stratigraphic and palaeomagnetic research suggests that this site is younger than Xiaochangliang and Donggutuo and dates to either the Jaramillo subchron or the early Brunhes chron (Schick *et al.* 1991).

The Gongwangling (Lantian) skull

Perhaps the earliest hominin fossil in east Asia is the Gongwangling (Lantian) *Homo erectus* cranium (Woo 1966), assigned an age of about 1.1 Ma (which can now be revised to 1.2 Ma – see Lu *et al.* 1999) based on the magnetostratigraphy of the site and palaeosol correlations with the Luochuan loess profile. The associated fauna points to a warm forested climate comparable to present-day southern China and to a (much) older age than the Zhoukoudian cave finds (An and Ho 1989) which are dated to about 0.55 Ma based on multiple dating evidence (Grün *et al.* 1997). Magnetostratigraphy places the Gongwangling find horizon in palaeomagnetically reversed sediments 5 metres beneath palaeomagnetically normal sediments that in turn are overlain by a sequence of reversed and normal polarized sediments. The normally polarized sediments a few metres above the find horizon are correlated with the Jaramillo subchron, a correlation that is backed by matching palaeosols in the profile with palaeosols in the well-dated Luochuan loess sections (An and Ho 1989) although this is perhaps not unambiguous. The Gongwangling find level according to this correlation is equivalent to level L15 in the Luochuan section. The S15 soil in the top of this level at Luochuan is now dated to 1.2 Ma (Lu *et al.* 1999). Still, caution should be exercized until the ages of the Lantian sections have been cross-checked by radiometric dates, e.g. ESR.

Several sites with ages spanning from latest Matuyama to early Brunhes are reported for China (Clark and Schick 1988; Schick and Dong 1993; Schick 1994; Keates 1994). One example is the Chenjiawo (Lantian) mandible (Woo 1964), not to be confused with the earlier Gongwangling (Lantian) skull. It is dated to the early Brunhes, by a combination of magnetostratigraphic research and soil horizon correlations. The find level is situated a few metres above the base of palaeomagnetically normal polarized sediments. The level of the mandible corresponds to a paleosol, which is correlated to paleosol S6 in the Luochuan section (An and Ho 1989). The latest dating

framework for Luochuan puts this paleosol at about 0.67-0.69 Ma (Lu *et al.* 1999). Pollen and fauna from the Chenjiawo site suggest a relatively warm and seasonally humid climate (An and Ho 1989).

Baise: an early 'Acheulean' occurrence at the Brunhes/Matuyama boundary in China?

A highly interesting site complex claimed to be dating to the Brunhes/Matuyama boundary at 0.8 Ma is the site complex from the Baise (Bose) basin, south China (Huang *et al.* 1990; Guo *et al.* 1996, 1997; Hou *et al.* 2000; Potts *et al.* 2000). This site complex also deserves attention in the context of chapter 3.1; this because the sites contain numerous Acheulean-like bifacial tools. The T4 (4th) terrace of the Youjiang river at Bose consists of a 7 to 10 metres thick deposit of laterites, with stone tools in the top, underlain by several metres of cobble conglomerate. The artefact layer is 0.2 to 1.0 metres thick and at or close to the surface. The artefacts are embedded in a silt or clay matrix (Potts *et al.* 2000).

While bifacial tools are known from east Asia, so far they appear(ed) to be rather 'young' elements in the archaeological record of Asia, the few dated assemblages having an age of <200 ka (Schick 1994; Hou *et al.* 2000). The 0.8 Ma age now proposed for Baise would make this a much older occurrence, and would make the occurrence of prominent bifacial tool assemblages in east Asia contemporary with the African early Acheulean, breaching the concept of the 'Movius line'.

The age proposed is based on the presence of tektites in direct stratigraphic association with the stone tools at Baise. These tektites are part of the large Australasian strewnfield which was created by a large asteroid impact 0.8 Ma ago (see chapter 1.1 and appendix 1), and represent the northernmost extension of this strewnfield. Indeed, direct fission track dating (Guo *et al.* 1996, 1997) and $^{40}Ar/^{39}Ar$ dating (Hou *et al.* 2000) of Baise tektites yields an age of 0.8 Ma, as is to be expected.

The mistake being made is that it is assumed that the tektites are in their original stratigraphic position. This can be seriously doubted (see also the comment by Koeberl and Glass (2000)). The stratigraphy as described for Baise (Hou *et al.* 2000; Huang *et al.* 1990) bears a strong resemblance to that described for the wide array of tektite localities spread over Northern Thailand, Laos and Cambodia investigated by Fiske *et al.* (1996, 1999). At these localities tektites occur in the top of a laterite horizon, overlain by unconsolidated (aeolic) sediments. Fiske *et al.* showed the tektite-bearing top of the laterite at many if not all of the tektite localities to be a lag deposit (signifying a palaeo-erosional surface). Their studies point to a genesis of these lag deposits due to a denudation process. The tektites and stone tools in the top of a similar laterite horizon at Baise might represent time-transgressive material accumulated on a similar palaeo-erosional surface. It is interesting to note that this stratigraphic situation, where tektites occur on a (buried) palaeo-erosional surface in the top of a laterite horizon, seems to be present over *a very wide area* encompassing North Thailand, Laos, Cambodia, and Vietnam (Fiske *et al*. 1999).

The problem with the Baise tektite and artefact co-occurrence is therefore not the possible fluvial reworking as suggested by Keates in her comment on Hou *et al*. (Keates 2000). It is unfortunate that the reply by Potts *et al*. (2000) is strongly focusing on rebutting the idea of fluvial reworking as suggested by Keates, while the real problem is with a possible genesis of the artefact and tektite bearing layer due to a process of paleo-deflation. It should be pointed out here that Late Pleistocene or younger bifacially worked stone tools are known from Asia, e.g. at Dincun in China and Chongok-ni in Korea (Schick 1994), and at Pacitan in Indonesia (Bartstra 1983). Forcefully pointing out the problems is that as Fiske *et al*. mention (Fiske *et al*. 1996, 1999), charcoal associated with tektites in a laterite horizon in Vietnam has yielded *Holocene* radiocarbon dates. A suggestion would be to run as a first test some AMS readings on the charcoal from Baise, to see whether they yield infinite or finite ages. Although infinite ages would not yet say anything about the true age of the stone tools, finite ages (like in Vietnam) would not only settle the proposed "impact generated forest fire" issue (Hou *et al*. 2000), but also the chronological implications of association of materials in this horizon.

The argument that tektites appear to be absent in the younger T1-3 terraces (Potts *et al*. 2000) does *not* counter the possibility that they occur on a palaeo-erosional surface in the T4 terrace. The tektites might be absent in the younger terraces because these terraces date from after the tektite deposition event, and the downcutting of the river that produced these terraces removed all tektites present. The absence of tools from these terraces is more peculiar, but so is that they are apparently absent on the older T5-7 terraces. Entertaining the possibility of

a Late Pleistocene age, preferential site location might offer an explanation. The surficial pitting and flow lines on the tektites described by Potts *et al*. in their reply to Keates (Potts *et al*. 2000), are common on all Indochinese tektites. They are caused by solution etching by soil acids – they are therefore post-depositional and have no real bearing on the discussion whether they are fluvially (or otherwise) redeposited or not. The combination of one pitted and one smooth surface on several of the tektites as described by Potts *et al*. (2000) could actually be seen as a surface modification, in favour of a scenario whereby these tektites spent part of their history on a once (or several times) denuded paleo-surface.

Central Asia

In central Asia, the Kuldara site (Tadzhikistan) is believed to be the oldest site in the region (Ranov *et al*. 1995). The site has only a provisional date that, if we confront the dating evidence with the checklist in the introductory chapter, is not unequivocal enough to be fully acceptable. The loess sections at the site have yielded flakes and choppers. Palaeomagnetism suggests that the oldest levels are just below the Brunhes-Matuyama boundary. The lowest artefact levels appear just below normal polarized sediments in reversed sediment, which in turn are underlain by normal polarized sediments lower in the section. The upper reverse-normal transition is interpreted as the Brunhes/Matuyama boundary. The normal episode lower in the section, underlying the artefact level, as the Jaramillo subchron. This indicates an age near 0.8 Ma, latest Matuyama, for the lowest artefact levels (Ranov 1991; Ranov *et al*. 1995). There are many other palaeolithic sites in central Asia (e.g. Shackley 1984; Clark and Schick 1988; Yi and Clarke 1983) but these largely remain undated or appear to have ages of 0.5 Ma and younger (Ranov 1991). With the current state of research, palaeolithic central Asia can best be regarded as a chronological blank area on the map for the period under consideration.

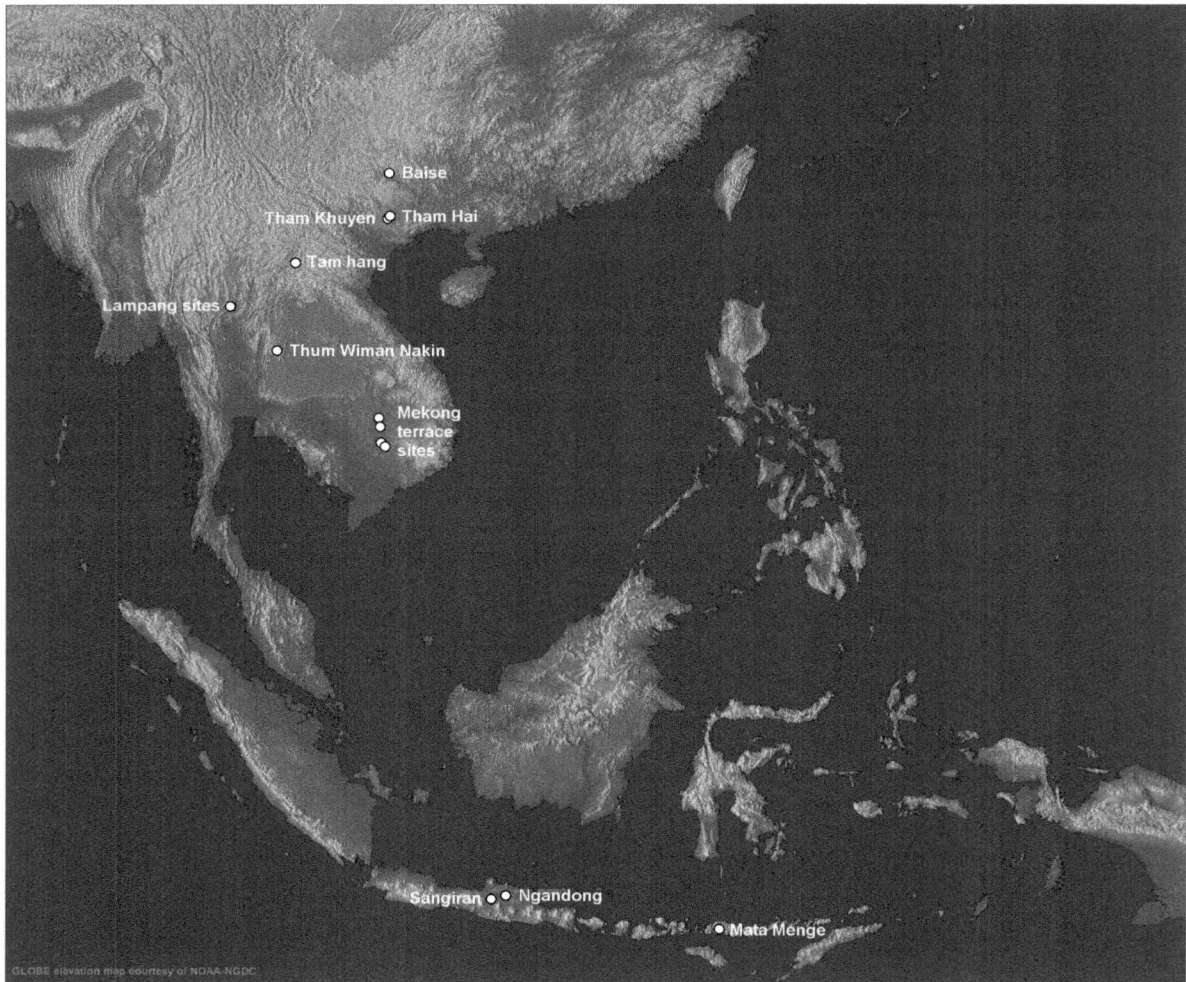

Figure 5: map showing discussed Southeast Asian sites

2.2   Southeast Asia

Both the topics of the age and the validity of fossil and artefact assemblages in mainland Southeast Asia (Indochina and the Malay peninsula) and island Southeast Asia (Indonesia and the Philippines) have a rich history of disagreement (e.g. Harrison 1975; Hutterer 1985; Theunissen *et al.* 1990; Pope and Cronin 1984; Pope and Keates 1994; Sémah *et al.* 1992; Bellwood 1987; Bartstra 1982, 1983, 1985; Bartstra and Basoeki 1989; Bartstra *et al.* 1988; Reynolds 1993; Albrecht and Moser 1996). There are problems with the provenance of many important finds, and the geomorphological and geological history of many regions puts severe constraints on archaeological and geochronological research (see also chapter 1.1). In addition, the post-colonial instability of parts of this region has severed international contacts that have only recently begun to recover (e.g. Ciochon and Olsen 1986; Olsen and Ciochon 1990). Chronologies are poorly established in this part of the world. Reliable biostratigraphies for the Early and early Middle Pleistocene do not exist, certainly not for island Southeast Asia that has seen a repeated sequence of flooding and exposure of the shallow continental shelf (the Sunda-shelf) during the Pleistocene (e.g. Bellwood 1987), leading to a difficult to entangle sequence of faunal dispersals over temporary land bridges, as well as faunal isolations, extinctions and endemism during insular conditions (e.g. Swisher (1994) in reply to De Vos and Sondaar (1994)). The geofact-problem is still paramount in this region (cf. Albrecht and Moser 1996), with many very problematic and highly questionable sites (e.g. the well-known and much discussed Kota Tampan 'site' on the Malay peninsula (Walker and Sieveking 1962; Harrison 1975; Pope and Keates 1994)) continuing to be fiercely advocated by their proponents and criticized by others.

Early and early Middle Pleistocene stone tools from mainland Southeast Asia?

Evidence from the Indochinese peninsula is highly contentious (e.g. Harrison 1975; Hutterer 1985; Pope and Keates 1994; Albrecht and Moser 1996). Malaysia, Burma and peninsular Thailand so far have not yielded fossil hominid remains predating the latest Pleistocene (Northern Thailand however has hominid remains attributed to the late Middle Pleistocene, see discussion on Indochina below), but several putative and contentious Middle and Early Pleistocene 'chopper' and 'flake-chopper' assemblages have been reported. Many of these seem to concern small samples of morphologically very simple flaked

cobbles consisting of superficially judged 'best' pieces picked out of a comparatively infinite large number of rejected flaked specimens. Especially with the geomorphological and geotaphonomical processes operational in tropical Asia (e.g. large river systems such as that of the Mekong and Irrawaddy, and severe erosion and torrential mudflows during the monsoon season), such 'artefact' occurrences are suspect. Albrecht and Moser (1996) have published cautionary tales about natural flaking processes and geofact occurrences in the Mekong and Irrawaddy river gravels. Presumed early 'artefact' assemblages from Southeast Asia invariably never comply with the standards of the checklist in the introductory chapter. One case of a reported but questionable 'lower palaeolithic artefact occurrence' concerns the finds from Ban Mae Tha in the Lampang Province of Northern Thailand described in Pope and Keates (1994) and Pope *et al.* (1986), and collected from alluvial plain gravels reported to be older than 0.73 Ma (a radiometric date obtained on an overlying basalt (Pope *et al.* 1986). Note that the artefacts reported in Pope *et al.* (1986) do not come from below the basalt but were collected from a locality where the basalt is absent, i.e. it could represent younger material deposited on an erosional surface. However, according to Pope and Keates (1994) specimens have been recovered in nearby localities from directly under the basalt). The morphologically very simple unifacially flaked 'choppers' (with only a few flaking negatives) and a 'nosed scraper' collected from the cobble deposits concern only a selection of pieces with a number which is infinitely small compared to the whole. This seems to be the general pattern of presumed 'sites' in this area. The investigators note that:

"*one important characteristic of the Northern Thai localities [...] is the* low density *of artifacts at any one locality or level*" (Pope and Keates 1994: 536, emphasis added); "*the excavation of the rockshelter of Kao Pah Nam has produced the same pattern of* low density *and absence of small flakes discerned at the open sites*" (Pope and Keates 1994: 540, emphasis added).

The 'Lannathaian' from Northern Thailand discussed by Pope and Keates (1994) exemplifies the problems:

"*Our own inspection of a portion of the specimens attributed to the Lannathaian convinces us that while some artifacts are present, a great number of them cannot be convincingly considered as anything but natural*" (Pope and Keates 1994: 540).

It is clear from these descriptions that the specimens considered 'artefacts' amount to only a few 'best' specimens picked out of a huge quantity of rejected flaked material. Confronting these 'sites' with the methodological checklist in the introductory chapter, it is clear that they are unacceptable as proof of hominine presence in Thailand near the Brunhes-Matuyama boundary. Albrecht and Moser (1996: 136), from their study of natural flaking processes and geofact occurrences in Southeast Asian river deposits, make the following statement, concerning the 'tools' from the Lampang Province:

"Einzelne Stücke oder eine kleine Auswahl aus grossen Fundkomplexen wie Schotterkörper oder Gesteins-schuttlagen sind ohne eine genaue Analyse der Zusammenhänge und Genese nicht geeignet, die urgeschichtliche Forschung hier weiterzubringen. Die als derzeits frühesten Artefakte des südostasiatischen Festlands deklarierten Gerölle aus der Lampang-Provinz in Nordthailand (K-Ar 0.6±0.2 und 0.8±0.3: Pope et al. 1986) zum Beispiel sind zudem selbst nach der Publikation kaum als menschliche Produkte zu betrachten. Erstaunlich ist die grosse Sicherheit, mit der die Autoren ohne Discussion selbst die Möglichkeit einer natürlichen Herkunft verneinen".

This short strong statement sums up the main problem concerning lithic studies of 'early Palaeolithic' artefact occurrences in this region.

Purported artefacts (resembling choppers, flakes and polyhedrons: but see Albrecht and Moser 1996) from the Mekong river terraces near Stung Treng in Cambodia have been assigned an early Middle Pleistocene age on the basis of associated tektites in the deposits (Olsen and Ciochon 1990). However, given the coarse fluviatile character of the deposits, it should not be assumed that the tektites are *in situ* and therefore the actual age of the deposits could be much younger. The *in situ* character of tektites has shown to be a problematic topic at many tektite yielding land localities in Indochina and elsewhere in the Australasian tektite strewnfield, with many cases of redeposition (Fudali 1993; Fiske *et al.* 1996), and I therefore do not advocate the use of tektites as a chronostratigraphic marker with a fixed age of 0.79 Ma as proposed by Olsen and Ciochon (1990). Fiske *et al.* (1996), from 'hands on' experience on Thai tektite localities, have urged caution *"as it is sometimes difficult to establish the in situ nature of tektites with certainty"* (Fiske *et al.* 1996: 40). Albrecht and Moser (1996: 136-137) have drawn attention to the mixing and redeposition of artefacts from several periods in the Mekong gravels. Embedded tektites therefore should only be taken to indicate that deposits post-date the Early to Middle Pleistocene transition, with the real possibility that the deposits in question can be considerably (up to several hundreds of thousands of years) younger, especially when

it concerns fluviatile or colluvial deposits or deflational surfaces. Concerning the possible artefacts from the Mekong river terraces, the problems with natural flaking agencies mentioned earlier should be taken into account. It is very likely that they concern geofacts, given the 'primitive' character of the pieces, their coarse lithological context and the great abundance of such geofacts elsewhere in the Mekong gravels (*cf.* Albrecht and Moser 1996). Both the dating arguments and the artefacts themselves therefore cannot be accepted when confronted with the checklist in the introductory chapter.

Middle Pleistocene hominin remains from Indochina

Several hominine sites exist in Northern Thailand, Laos and Vietnam (Ciochon and Olsen 1986; Olsen and Ciochon 1990). Most of these are insufficiently dated. The oldest sites, yielding *Homo erectus* (mainly dental remains), might be Tham Khuyen and Tham Hai in North Vietnam, near the Chinese border. On biostratigraphical grounds (which amount to correlations with the cave fissure faunas of *Stegodon-Ailuropoda* type in subtropical China) they are provisionally dated to about 0.4 Ma (Olsen and Ciochon 1990). For Tham Khuyen, this age assessment is corroborated by ESR and Uranium-series datings. ESR dates on mammal tooth enamel from the fossil-bearing units S1-S3 yield Early Uptake ages of 404 ± 51 ka. Calcite crystals from the overlying speleothem yield an U/Th age of 117 ± 30 ka (Ciochon *et al.* 1996). In the Tham Khuyen fauna, *Homo erectus* co-occurs with the primates *Giganthopithecus* and Orang Utan.

The skull remains from Tam Hang cave in Northern Laos are probably also Middle Pleistocene given the associated faunal remains (Olsen and Ciochon 1990). Cave deposits from Thum Wiman Nakin cave in Northern Thailand yielded faunal remains including one of the most southern occurrences of the panda bear *Ailuropoda melanoleuca baconi* (linking this fauna to that of the North Vietnamese fissure deposit faunas mentioned above) but also fragmented *Homo* sp. On the basis of the faunal assemblage, these are tentatively assigned a late Middle Pleistocene age. Absolute Uranium/Thorium dating attempts yielded a wide variety of ages ranging from 80 000 to 350 000 BP (Tougard *et al.* 1996). As Tougard *et al.* (1996) have pointed out, it is interesting to note the presence of *Ailuropoda* in Thailand during (or so it is believed) the late Middle to early Late Pleistocene. *Ailuropoda* is dependent on the presence of bamboo species that require more temperate conditions than exist in Indochina today, and from the distribution of Middle and Late Pleistocene *Ailuropoda* throughout Vietnam, Laos, Cambodia, southern China and northern Thailand and Burma as well as palaeobotanical evidence from Indonesia, it seems that such more temperate conditions were geographically much more extensive in that area during the Middle Pleistocene timespan than they are today, signifying that the area saw a noted increase in temperature in the Latest Pleistocene and Holocene (Tougard *et al.* 1996: 977-978). However, it must be kept in mind that species can change habitat preference over the course of time. Indeed, the common co-occurrence (if not an artefact of the excavation strategies) reported for *Pongo pygmaeus* (Orang Utan) and *Ailuropoda* (giant Panda) in Pleistocene Southeast Asian faunas might suggest this.

There is a conspicuous lack of faunal assemblages dating to the Early Pleistocene and Early/Middle Pleistocene transition from Indochina. Most assemblages found so far are believed to date from the second half of the Middle Pleistocene and later (Ginsburg *et al.* 1982). This seems to be a case of either selected prospection and sampling or geological inaccessibility of deposits from this timespan. It is possible that archaeological and palaeontological deposits dating to the Early/Middle Pleistocene transition are buried beneath a thick succession of fluvial sediments, e.g. from the Mekong river system. Perhaps, it is significant to note that almost all Indochinese occurrences of tektites (see chapter 1.1, the discussion of the Baise sites in the previous chapter, and appendix 1) appear to represent occurrences on an erosional surface that seems to be widespread in Indochina (Fiske *et al.* 1996). Perhaps a severe post-Matuyama erosion phase has wiped out faunal deposits from this timespan in a major part of Indochina.

Island Southeast Asia: Java (Indonesia)

The Indonesian island of Java occupies an important place in palaeoanthropology because of the hominine fossils recovered at Mojokerto, in the Sangiran dome area and along the Solo river. Problems about the age of these fossil hominine remains have already been discussed in chapter 1.1. In essence, the finds remain undated, though there are suggestions that the oldest fossils perhaps date to close to 1.2 Ma, an age similar to the oldest hominid fossils and archaeological find localities in China (see previous chapter).

Wallacea (I): Early Pleistocene stone tools from the Indonesian island of Flores?

Java, like Sumatra and Borneo, was connected to the mainland at several times during times of low sea levels (Bellwood 1987). For the parts of Indonesia which were never connected to the mainland of Asia, arguments for early stone tool occurrences dating as far back as the Brunhes-Matuyama geomagnetic transition have been advanced.

Morwood *et al.* (1998) have reported fission-track ages of Pleistocene sediments from Mata Menge and Boa Lesa on the Indonesian island of Flores. These sediments are reported to contain fossils of *Stegodon, Hooijeromis* and other animals, as well as flaked lithics interpreted as artefacts (Sondaar *et al.* 1994; Morwood *et al.* 1997, 1998, 1999). The fission-track dates bracket the age of the sediment deposits and their presumed artificial content between 0.88 ± 0.07 and 0.80 ± 0.07 Ma (Morwood *et al.* 1998), backing earlier preliminary palaeomagnetic dating results (Sondaar *et al.* 1994). The presence of flaked lithic material interpreted as artefacts in the Early/Middle Pleistocene sediments would suggest that hominines had reached the island of Flores and by inference were capable of crossing stretches of sea at least 20 km wide by this time (Sondaar *et al.* 1994; Morwood *et al.* 1997, 1998, 1999). Both the first hominid presence in Wallacea and the development of the capability to cross substantial stretches of water were hitherto believed to be of much more recent date (Bartstra *et al.* 1991).

The problem with the evidence from Flores is with the unambiguous identification of the flaked lithics as artificial. For an unambiguous identification of morphologically simple flaked lithic material (such as the lithic material from Flores) as artificial, it is not enough to demonstrate that the flaked lithic specimens described comply with a set of technological criteria such as presence of bulbs of percussion, dorsal flake scars, ripple-marks etcetera. It is well known that under certain conditions natural (geological) processes can produce flaked lithics (or *geofacts*) that possess all these characteristics and mimic true artefacts to a high degree (Clark 1958; Roebroeks and Van Kolfschoten 1994, 1995; Raynal *et al.* 1995a).

What must be demonstrated before accepting the described flaked lithic material as unambiguous artefacts is that they come from a context and have a taphonomic history which with certainty precludes that they are the result of natural flaking processes (Dincauze 1984; Roebroeks and Van Kolfschoten 1994, 1995; Raynal *et al.* 1995a). This has already been outlined in the introductory chapter. Let us restate these points: for this purpose, it is amongst others necessary:

(1) to give a detailed description of the lithology of the deposits from which they derive focusing on the demonstration that the character of the lithology excludes flaking possibilities by other than human agencies;

(2) to describe the full suite of lithic material contained within the sediments investigated;

(3) if a selection of pieces is made, to demonstrate a significant difference between the pieces selected and those excluded from the analysis and to account for the presence of the rejected specimens;

(4)   to subject to a critical assessment the proposition that human behaviour was the agent responsible for the assemblage. This last criterion involves a critical discussion of the taphonomy of the assemblage.

The evidence as recently presented by Morwood *et al.* (1997, 1998, 1999) does not appear to meet all demands necessary before accepting the proposition that Early Pleistocene hominids reached Flores. The lithic assemblage described concerns a selection of pieces. Only cursory drawings have been published so far, and these represent the 'best' pieces only (and are not quite convincing – e.g. compare the geofacts in Raynal *et al* 1995a). The 'artefacts' clearly concern a subsample of the total lithic inventory recovered, a large part of which is *rejected* as non-artefactual. In fact, at Mata Menge the 'artefacts' represent only 31% (14 out of reportedly some 45 recovered pieces, that is 1 in 3) of all lithic materials collected in the excavation: and a part of these 'artefacts' (4 out of 14) actually come from the surface or the topsoil and do not have provenance in the undisturbed layers. The presence and character of the 31 rejected pieces is not well explained, nor are they satisfactorily incorporated in a comprehensive taphonomic consideration of the whole assemblage.

Descriptions of the lithics in the deposits sound a bell of caution, because it seems that a full continuum from rounded pebbles through broken pebbles through flaked pebbles/flakes (both with and without striking platforms) is present, of which only a minor part resembling morphologically simple artefacts is considered artificial on technological criteria that in themselves are not indisputable proof of human flaking agencies. Even the presence of these basic technological characteristics appears to be questionable for some of the lithics. Sondaar *et al.* (1994: 1261) report that *some* of the 14 (Morwood *et al.* 1998) or 15 (Sondaar *et al.* 1994) lithics believed to be artefacts possess a striking platform. The 'artefacts' almost exclusively seem to come from the more coarse-grained part of the lithology only. This lithology in question is from a fluvial context. Additional taphonomic arguments are necessary, otherwise, these lithics should be classified as *incertofacts*, which cannot be a base for meaningful theory building.

The Mata Menge section shows a repetition of fining upwards sequences as described by Sondaar *et al.* (1994). According to Sondaar *et al.* (1994: 1261), *"flakes from the upper silty part of the [artifact bearing] layer have a very fresh appearance with sharp edges, whereas flakes from the lower sandy part show some rounding due to transport"*. This has a counterpart in the preservation of the bone material, which is reported to be *"rather fragmented in the lower sandy interval, while from the upper silty interval complete bones were recovered"* (Sondaar *et al.* 1994: 1261). It is clear from these descriptions that the depositional agent of both bone and lithics in the tuffaceous sandstone is similar, and that this agent is *natural*. Both bones and lithics in the sandstone appear to be *not* in primary context of deposition even though some show no visual signs of transport. The presumed artefacts seem to derive from the coarser grained flow structures only, not from the fine tuffs, which however do contain bone (Morwood *et al.* 1998). These observations, together with the presence of rounded (and sometimes broken) pebbles and rejected specimens as discussed above, imply that the flaked material could represent secondary deposits of materials winnowed from a geologically flaked deposit situated in a higher energy regime upstream, redeposited in an increasingly lower energy regime. Given the volcanic character of the lithology, this introduces the possibility it concerns *tephrofacts*, which are very difficult to differentiate from true artefacts once they are recovered outside their primary volcanic context (see Raynal *et al.* (1995a) for this problem in the context of the French *Massif Central*).

Note that the significant number of rejected specimens unambiguously points to natural flaking processes *having* played a role at Mata Menge. This warrants the caution expressed above.

Most of the Mata Menge 'artefacts' are of basalt, but a few are of chert. Chert pieces identified as 'artefacts' at Mata Menge come from the surface and topsoil part of the site (unit A – see Morwood *et al.* 1997, 1998), not from the deeper layers of unit B (Morwood *et al.* 1997, 1999). Hence, they are not 'in situ'. Interestingly, a number of chert pieces are also present in the top only of unit B, close to the contact with the topsoil, but all of these are judged to be not artificial by Morwood *et al.* (1997). Morwood *et al.* continue to say that chert is an unexpected class of material in this 'volcanic' environment and hence they claim the material represents anthropogenely introduced material and constitutes a strong argument for the artificiality of the pieces. This is an incorrect proposition since for example chalcedony, a non-volcanic rock, is also present in the Javanese volcaniclastic deposits. And anyway, the pieces in question were not recovered from the relevant 'in situ' part of the sequence. Moreover, Morwood *et al.* undermine their own argument by judging those pieces that do come from (the top only of) the relevant part of the deposits to be not unambiguously artificial, begging the taphonomic question how these chert pieces then became incorporated in these deposits.

Little significance can be attached to the reported possible 'use-wear' traces on the lithic material (Morwood *et al.* 1998), given their inferred taphonomic history and their coarse- grained lithological context. Likewise, the reported presence of plant remains in the sediments (Sondaar *et al.* 1994; Morwood *et al.* 1998) precludes assigning significance to the detection of possible plant residues on the lithics from Mata Menge (Morwood *et al.* 1998).

In addition to the Mata Menge materials, Morwood et al. (1999) report a few basalt 'artefacts' from Boa Lesa (also on Flores) associated with a fission-track age of 0.87 ± 0.07 Ma. Again, the finer grained tuffs apparently do not contain 'artefacts' here, while the coarser grained channel deposits do. At Mata Menge as well as at Boa Lesa the occurrence of 'artefacts' thus is related to channel action and deposits which contain natural clasts (and as pointed out, apparently natural clasts with various degrees of geological flaking) derived from somewhere else by fluvial action. My concern is that the 'artefacts' are just the top end of this spectrum, selected as 'artefacts'.

Pending resolution of the taphonomic questions pertaining to the full suite of lithics at Mata Menge, the palaeontological and geochronological research at Flores documents and dates a turnover in the Early Pleistocene island fauna for which several explanations are possible, but it does not establish the presence and seafaring capabilities of Early Pleistocene hominids with the degree of certainty necessary to make the evidence meaningful for unambiguous theory building.

Sondaar et al. (1994) claim that an apparent faunal turnover on Flores at the Early-Middle Pleistocene boundary is related to the purported arrival of Homo erectus. What the turnover amounts to is that a typical island fauna with the large tortoise Geochelone, a pygmy Stegodon, a giant rat and Komodo dragon, is 'replaced' by a fauna which lacks the tortoise and pygmy Stegodon, but newly includes a large Stegodon. We should note that the number of faunal elements is small by any means. Rather than the result of hunting to extinction by Homo erectus, it is perhaps more likely that the disappearance of the pygmy Stegodon and possibly Geochelone as well is related to an influx of new faunal elements, including the large Stegodon. The same seems to occur on Java, where Geochelone disappears when connections with the Asian mainland create a faunal influx (De Vos et al. 1994). The appearance of the large Stegodon on Flores following the Early/Middle Pleistocene transition shows that even if it is not a matter of incomplete sampling, it is not just island fauna disappearing but also continental fauna entering. The turnover at about 0.8 Ma could be seen as part of a new influx of animals during the peak of OIS 20, when sea levels were low, much of the Sunda shelf exposed, and animals from mainland Asia dispersed over it. Animals capable of swimming (like Stegodon) could very well reach Flores and replace island endemics like the pygmy Stegodon. I see no necessary reason to consider the actions of Homo erectus behind this, the more so because I see no firm evidence for the presence of this hominine.

Wallacea (II) and Sahul

In the Philippines, Sulawesi and Borneo, human fossils as well as stone tools do not occur before the terminal Pleistocene (approximately 40 000 BP) and some workers in this area believe that they must be associated with fully modern humans (Hutterer 1985; Bellwood 1987; Bartstra et al. 1991). Rejecting the Flores evidence, it appears that Wallacea has been settled rather late. The oldest age implicated is that provided by the first occupation of the Sahul continent (Australia and New Guinea). The Lake Mungo 3 skeleton is currently dated to 60 ka and as such represents the oldest evidence from Australia (Thorne et al. 1999; Grün et al. 2000). Recently claims for artefacts predating 100 ka at Jinmium in Northern Australia have been advanced (Fullagar et al. 1996) but the dates have been questioned on technical grounds (Spooner 1998) and were then replaced by much younger (10 ka) AMS and OSL ages (Roberts et al. 1998).

Summary: Southeast Asia during the Early and Middle Pleistocene

Summing up the above outline of Southeast Asian evidence, it is clear that this part of the world still lacks a proper chronology. Mainland Southeast Asia lacks evidence for an occupation before the second part of the Middle Pleistocene (roughly translating to about 0.4 Ma ago). The evidence from Java (Indonesia) is inconclusive. There is the suggestion of a possible occupation up to 1.2 Ma ago (see chapter 1.1) contemporaneous with the evidence from China. Evidence for hominid presence in Wallacea as far back as the Brunhes-Matuyama boundary is rejected.

At first sight (since hominids first had to pass through this area before entering the Sunda landmass), the lack of pre-Middle Pleistocene sites in mainland Southeast Asia would argue against an early 1.2 Ma occupation of Sunda. This argument may be flawed however. A conspicuous lack of faunal assemblages dating to the Early Pleistocene in mainland Southeast Asia suggests that this early period is underrepresented due to either an inadequate sampling of deposits from this time interval or inaccessibility of the deposits.

Let me stress that 'absence of evidence' is not necessarily 'evidence of absence'. In this part of the world, catastrophic volcanic activity and strong fluviatile action of a tropical character put severe limitations on the interpretability of either naturally or anthropogenely flaked stone assemblages (Bartstra 1982; Pope and Keates 1994). Large parts of the Sunda landmass are currently submerged and therefore inaccessible. This warrants caution not only with regard to alleged primitive stone cultures, but also with regard to the seeming 'absence' of evidence.

An interesting aspect to note concerning the palaeo-environment of Pleistocene Southeast Asia is the evidence (outlined above) that a large part of Middle Pleistocene Southeast Asia featured a more temperate climate than today (Tougard *et al*. 1996; *contra* Pope and Keates 1994). This is perhaps also indicated by the evidence for the existence of more arid open woodlands on Northeast Java during parts of the Pleistocene, perhaps the periods that the Sunda landmass was exposed due to glacial low sea levels, as indicated by the faunal remains from the Sangiran deposits and other palaeontological sites on Java (De Vos 1985; De Vos *et al*. 1994).

Some scholars picture much of Pleistocene Southeast Asia as a tropical rainforest environment, an environment which is quite challenging (Gamble 1993; Pope and Keates 1994). Pope (Pope and Cronin 1984; Pope 1985; Pope and Keates 1994) has argued for a barrier of tropical forest between mainland Asia and Sunda throughout the Pleistocene, in order to explain the absence of giraffoids, camelids and horses (known from Pleistocene Northern Asia) in the Pleistocene faunas of Java. But instead of tropical forest, a temperate bamboo forest over a large part of Pleistocene Indochina may have been the barrier. This type of environment does not seem to have prevented hominine occupation of the area at some point during the Pleistocene as evidenced by the fragmentary *Homo* remains from the Indochinese fissure deposits, but exactly when hominids started to occupy this environment is not clear with the current chronological problems. It stands to reason from the Chinese and Eurasian evidence however that this was not before 1.2 Ma (*contra* Larick and Ciochon 1996) and perhaps even well after that date.

2.3   Western Eurasia: Southern Europe

Considering the evidence for an occupation of temperate maritime China by 1.1 Ma, a similarly aged occupation of temperate western Eurasia should be expected. In chapter 1.6 the contentious evidence from Orce in Southern Europe has already been discussed. Another claim for an 'old' occupation of Southern Europe comes from Atapuerca in Spain, and a number of other sites (e.g. Ceprano in Italy) have been presented as possible evidence for an Early Pleistocene occupation date.

The earliest occupation of Europe

The evidence for the earliest occupation of Europe was thoroughly re-examined a few years ago. Early dates, even up to the Pliocene, can be found widespread in the literature (e.g. contributions to Bonifay and Vandermeersch (1991)). An in-depth examination of the evidence for the earliest occupation of Europe took place during a European Science Foundation Network Workshop in 1993, now known as the Tautavel conference. It was established during this workshop that there was no firm evidence for an occupation of Europe before 0.5 Ma ago (Roebroeks 1994; Roebroeks and Van Kolfschoten 1995). Putative earlier sites all come as assemblages of 'tools' of very simple and primitive character collected from coarse high-energy deposits, with in many cases a quite uneven ratio of accepted to rejected pieces (e.g. sites such as Kärlich A and B, Beroun and Mussov, Prezletice and Stránská Skála), or these sites produce 'artefacts' that lack convincing signs of hominine interference and come from deposits that also contain ample evidence for geological flaking (e.g. Le Vallonet). These artefacts therefore are now deemed as geofacts or at best *incertofacts* which cannot serve as reliable arguments for a pre-0.5 Ma occupation (Roebroeks and Van Kolfschoten 1995). The contrast with the post-0.5 Ma assemblages, which include many sites from fine-grained deposits with preserved knapping floors, is large. The rare few assemblages, more specifically Isernia la Pineta (Italy), that do come from fine sediments and have evidence for knapping floors and were believed to predate 0.5 Ma, have now been redated to the early Brunhes (Roebroeks and Van Kolfschoten 1994, 1995; Mussi 1995, 2001). Moreover, all European hominid fossils reported up to 1993 postdated 0.5 Ma (Roebroeks and Van Kolfschoten 1994, 1995; see also Cook *et al.* 1982). This situation only changed with the announcement of the Atapuerca TD-6 finds (Carbonell *et al.* 1995; Bermúdez de Castro *et al.* 1997).

For Europe above 40° latitude, this general picture of hominine absence before 0.5-0.6 Ma still stands up firmly. This part of the world has a very long and outstanding history of research, including over a century of very extensive sampling of a large number of very rich Plio-Pleistocene palaeontological occurrences. As has been argued, for Northwest and Central Europe the "absence of evidence" therefore can be equated with "evidence of absence" (Roebroeks 1996).

For Southern Europe, things could be different and new evidence has popped up since 1993. Many of this is still contentious. Four localities, two in Iberia and two in Italy, are paramount in the debate: Orce (Spain), Atapuerca (Spain), Monte Poggiolo (Italy) and Ceprano (Italy). Of these, Atapuerca is now generally regarded as a convincing claim for hominid occupation around the Brunhes-Matuyama transition at 0.78 Ma. As such it stands alone, for the other claims still leave considerable questions (Orce, Monte Poggiolo) or are downright dubious (Ceprano).

Atapuerca TD-6 (Spain)

Artefacts as well as hominine remains ('*Homo antecessor*' (Bermúdez de Castro *et al.* 1997)) were recently reported from the Spanish site of Atapuerca, Tranchera Dolina level 6 (Atapuerca TD-6). The find level has been assigned a late Matuyama age, >0.78 Ma, by a combination of palaeomagnetic sampling and biozonation (Carbonell *et al.* 1995; Parés and Pérez-González 1995). This age assignment has long been contentious but is now gaining acceptance.

The small assemblage (N=100) of lithics excavated from Atapuerca TD-6 level so far is of mode 1 affinities, with no bifacial technology, only small numbers of retouched flakes, only a small number of cores and core tools and a predominance of simple flakes (Carbonell *et al.* 1995), but given the small size of the assemblage and most notably the small surface area of the excavation, this character might be deceptive.

The fossils from TD-6 are, though fragmentary, undoubtedly hominine. It has recently been proposed that they represent a separate species, *Homo antecessor* (Bermúdez de Castro *et al.* 1997), which is distinct from both *Homo erectus* and *Homo heidelbergensis* and ancestral to all Middle Pleistocene European hominines, including *Homo heidelbergensis* and the Neanderthals.

Palaeomagnetic research shows that the artefact- and hominid fossil bearing TD-6 level is located in reversed polarized sediments consisting of mudstones and clays. A change to normal polarized sediments is one level up, in TD-7, aproximately 1 metre above the artefact and fossil yielding 'aurora-stratum'. This polarity change is interpreted as the Brunhes-Matuyama boundary (Parés and Pérez-Gonzáles 1995, 1999). Recently, a strong argument has been put forward (Parés and Pérez-Gonzáles 1999), contra a suggestion by Dennell and Roebroeks (1996), that the reversed episode could represent one of the short intra-Brunhes reversals. An interval of normal polarized sediments has also been located in level TD-1, at the base of the sequence below the artefact and fossil bearing TD-6. This is possibly the Jaramillo subchron at ~1 Ma (Parés and Pérez-Gonzáles 1999).

ESR and Uranium-series dates are available for levels TD-6, TD-8, TD-10 and TD-11 (Falguères et al. 1999). Level TD-6 yielded ages of 676 ± 101 ka (AT9604), 762 ± 114 ka (AT9602) and 770 ± 116 ka (AT9603). Level TD-8 yielded ages of 586 ± 88 ka (AT9604), 606 ± 91 ka (AT9605) and 615 ± 92 ka (AT9702). These ESR/U-series dates place the artefact and fossil bearing level TD-6 at or just above the Brunhes-Matuyama boundary.

The chronological placement of the microfauna is a subject of contention. It concerns a Biharian fauna typical of the end of the early Pleistocene and the beginning of the Middle Pleistocene (Guenca-Bescós et al. 1999: 370). Guenca-Bescós et al. opt for a placement in the Early Pleistocene. On the basis of the Arvicolids, the TD-6 fauna is considered more modern than the Jaramillo-aged faunas from Untermassfeldt and Les Valerots (Guenca-Bescós et al. 1999: 370).

The placement of the microfauna in the Early Pleistocene rather than the early part of the Middle Pleistocene has been criticized by Van Kolfschoten (1998). In his view, there are no firm arguments in the species present to support an age in the latest Matuyama instead of the early part of the Brunhes:

"There is [...] no indication for an Early Pleistocene age of the deposits as suggested by palaeomagnetic data. The smaller as well as the larger fauna are composed of species which occurred in Europe during the earlier part of the Middle Pleistocene and there are no species represented which are restricted to the early Pleistocene" (Van Kolfschoten 1998: 115).

Indeed, the ESR and U-series dating would not be incompatible with such an early Middle Pleistocene age. The only argument to opt for a latest Early Pleistocene instead is the reversed palaeomagnetic polarization of TD-6, with which two of the three ESR/U-series dates for TD-6 are compatible. If it was not for the palaeomagnetic characteristics of TD-6, the most parsimonious interpretation would be an age in the early Middle Pleistocene, *circa* 600-700 ka. This is slightly older than

Boxgrove (~550 ka), to some extent pushing back but not creating a strong breach in the age barrier of the 'short chronology' (Roebroeks and Van Kolfschoten 1995; Roebroeks and Dennell 1996). The palaeomagnetic characteristics of TD-6 push back the age another 100 ka to ~800 ka, but the fact remains that this age is not unambiguously corroborated by the other dating evidence, while some palaeontologists maintain that other dating methods (the microfauna) continue to speak against it.

The 'mode 1' character of the lithic assemblage from TD-6 seems to be used as an additional dating argument by the excavators, who mention that it points to the "pre-Acheulean period" (Carbonell et al. 1995: 827):

"The presence in the TD6 hominids of numerous primitive traits, together with the absence of hand axes, picks and cleavers, which allow inclusion of the lithic industry in the pre-Acheulean technology (Mode 1), suggest that the settlement of Western Europe probably occurred during the early Pleistocene" (Carbonell et al. 1995: 829).

This ties in with the typo-chronological ideas developed by two of the excavators and a Russian colleague as expressed in Ranov et al. (1995). However, 'mode 1' technology is not restricted to the Early Pleistocene, neither in Africa and Europe nor in Asia, and therefore cannot be used in a typo-chronological way (see also Villa 2001). Middle Pleistocene but 'mode 1' (Oldowan) occurrences in Africa are for example known from the Middle Awash Valley in Ethiopia, where they have been dated to less than 0.64 Ma (Clark et al. 1994). Numerous 'mode 1' assemblages are known from Middle Pleistocene Europe, e.g. the well-known 'Clactonian' assemblages from Great Britain at sites such as Clacton and Barnham, and mode 1 assemblages from High Lodge and Swanscombe which are contemporary with Acheulean occurrences (Swanscombe for example has both 'Clactonian' and Acheulean assemblages that are more or less contemporary) (Roberts et al. 1995). There are numerous mode 1 assemblages elsewhere in Europe, such as Vértesszölös in Hungary (Svoboda 1987), and even some of the 0.25 Ma Maastricht Belvédère sites, e.g. sites F and H (Roebroeks 1988; Langbroek 1998), to name only a few.

A mode 1 assemblage therefore does not necessarily point to an Early Pleistocene age for Atapuerca TD-6. Moreover, the assemblage size for Atapuerca TD-6 is small (about 100 artefacts) and the absence of mode 2 therefore could be a matter of sample bias. It should be noted that at one time handaxes were actually reported from Atapuerca TD-6 (Atapuerca Excavation Team 1992), but these are now said to have no clear provenance.

If the site and some of the other sites mentioned in this chapter and in chapter 1.6 are indeed from the Early

Pleistocene, significantly predating 0.5 Ma, it in fact would appear that all early Southern European sites have a mode 1 assemblage, similar to the Asian sites from 1.2 Ma onwards (see chapter 2.1). But we should be careful not to convert this possible pattern (if it exists at all, given the chronological and sample size problems with the Southern European sites mentioned!) into a typo-chronological scheme in which all 'primitive' mode 1 assemblages are automatically considered 'old'.

Monte Poggiolo

The problems around the earliest occupation of Italy have been discussed in detail by Mussi in the ESF Workshop proceedings, and in her book on earliest Italy (Mussi 1995, 2001), and recently by Villa (2001). I will give only a short summary here and refer to Mussi (especially Mussi 2001) for more elaborate discussions. The earliest site claimed for Italy is Monte Poggiolo (Peretto 1992), which has yielded an industry with choppers, notches and denticulates, scrapers, debitage, tested pieces and two handaxes (which are surface finds). The findspot represents a deltaic environment close to a former seashore. Pollen and Gastropod remains suggest a cool and cold climate (Mussi 2001).

It is the dating of the site which is problematic. The marine clays which underlie the archaeological levels are dated to 1.5-1.3 Ma, based amongst others on ESR dating. The overlying sands which contain the archaeological levels have yielded one single palaeomagnetic reading, which is reverse. This could indicate a late Matuyama age. It could also represent one of the intra-Brunhes reversals.

The sands which contain the archaeological levels are considered to correlate to marine sands, the *Sabbie Gialle*, at Monte Vescovado, some 1.5 km from Monte Poggiolo, and at San Biagio, some 6 km from Monte Poggiolo. This correlation is not accepted by everyone (see Villa 2001). The base of the *Sabbie Gialle* at Monte Vescovado is thought to be no younger than 1.2-1.1 Ma, based on malacological data and ESR. Higher in the sequence, a normal palaeomagnetic episode correlated to the Jaramillo subchron has been found, as well as the base of normal polarized sediments correlated to the Brunhes normal chron (Gagnepain *et al.* 1992). An ESR age of 1.29 ± 0.53 Ma has been obtained on quartzite grains from the *Sabbie Gialle* at Monte Vescovado, and of 0.72 ± 0.21 Ma at San Biagio (Yokoyama *et al.* 1992). This could be taken to indicate that Monte Poggiolo dates to between 0.7 and 1.3 Ma (cf. Peretto 1992). Yet, these dates stem from indirect and not unequivocal correlations of the archaeological layers with strata elsewhere, as explained above. Moreover, even if the *Sabbie Gialle* is one regional unit, it shows a wide age range at different localities, with the ESR

age at San Biagio being only half that of the ESR age at Monte Vescovado. From the limited number of dated sample points, the true extent of this age range is by no means well defined.

The Ceprano skullcap

Another highly contentious 'early' site in Italy, is Ceprano in Latium, where a hominine skullcap was found in 1994 and attributed to *Homo erectus* (Ascenzi *et al.* 1996; Manzi *et al.* 2001). As with Monte Poggiolo, the problem lies with the proposed indirect correlations of geological strata, which are correlations over considerable distance. As Mussi (2001: 45) remarks, these lithostratigraphic correlations of sites over a wide region have been modified several times in the past. Villa (2001: 122) notes that the long-distance correlations in the area are not based on detailed mapping and lack stratigraphic details. A level overlying the findlayer at Ceprano is correlated to strata at the early Acheulean site of Fontana Ranuccio, over 30 km distant from Ceprano, with an ^{40}Ar-^{39}Ar age of 0.458 ± 0.006 Ma. Levels under the find horizon at Ceprano are correllated with strata at Castro dei Volsci which are believed to be over 0.8 Ma (Ascenzi *et al.* 1996). From these correlations, Ascenzi *et al.* propose an age of 0.7 Ma or even 0.8-0.9 Ma (Manzi *et al.* 2001) for the Ceprano skull. But all that can be said, even if the proposed correlations are valid, is that the age of the fossil is between 0.46 and 0.8 Ma and the fossil thus would have a *minimum* age of *0.46 Ma*. Pleading for an older age of ~0.8 Ma for the Ceprano fossil bearing deposit solely rests on the absence of leucitic-augitic components in the colluvial/marshy sediments which yielded the fossil (see also Mussi 2001), which is taken to indicate that deposition predates the onset of a volcanic phase in the area which is believed to have started at 0.7 Ma. This is a dangerous kind of argument by inference. In addition, the odd taphonomic phenomenon of provenance of a strongly fossilized skullcap from clays which are for the rest completely barren of any preserved macro- or microfossils (Ascenzi *et al.* 1996: 412-415), warrants caution. To quote Mussi (2001: 34) with regard to Ceprano: "*The date of the calvarium is far from assessed*".

When was Europe first occupied?

In summary, only Atapuerca provides acceptable evidence for an occupation of southern Europe at the Brunhes-Matuyama boundary. Orce (see chapter 1.6), and Monte Poggiolo could push this date back further, yet at the moment the dating of these sites leaves too much to be desired to be acceptable. Even the Atapuerca dates are still debated. For Europe north of the Alps and Pyrenees, the well-argued verdict by Roebroeks and Van Kolfschoten (1994, 1995) is still valid: there does not appear to be firm evidence for an occupation prior to the latest Cromerian in the early Middle Pleistocene, about 0.5 Ma. There is an ill-founded trend in the current literature discussing 'long 'and 'short' chronologies, which seeks to re-introduce sites like Le Vallonet 'via the back door' as valid early sites north of the Alps/Pyrenees following the acceptance of an early age for Atapuerca TD-6. However, acceptance of the evidence for Atapuerca in no way can be employed insupport of the validity of these sites. They were rejected on grounds other than their age: they were rejected because of doubts about the artificial character of their content and these doubts still stand up firmly (see Roebroeks 2001: 441-442). This is a point which should be well taken, for the signalled phenomenon in the literature threatens to cloud objective discussion on the age and process of the earliest occupation of Europe.

Chapter 2.4   Summary of parts I and II: when did the first 'Out of Africa' happen?

In the preceding chapters, a list of claims for early occupations of Eurasia has been discussed. The relevance of assessing these claims is that it provides a chronological picture of early hominin dispersal from Africa to Eurasia, which is based on a critical assessment in which validity of the evidence is the primary concern. As outlined in the introduction, the methodology aims at arriving at a *solid* chronology based on indisputable evidence, rather than a 'could be'. This is necessary for meaningful theory building. The next step will be to interpret the chronological patterning found. In the following chapters, the aim is to construct a model of colonization – or rather: colonizations – which can serve as a theoretical framework for the early occupation of Eurasia. By looking at environmental contexts, climatological and ecological aspects of environment and diachrone developments therein, as well as at complexity of archaeological signatures (and changes therein), and at evidence for subsistence and deducted minimum levels of cognition, the chronological picture can be transformed into a model of the evolution of hominin capacities. Moreover, it will be argued that these evolutionary developments in early *Homo* find their cause in the forces of climatic and ecological change in Africa during the Plio-Pleistocene. As will be argued, these changes selected for a new breed of flexible hominins. The colonization of Eurasia hence is a byproduct of change in Africa. We therefore have to look to Africa, not just Eurasia, if we want to understand the driving forces behind the primary occupation of Eurasia.

The basic picture emerging from the chronological assessment of the previous chapters is that claims for hominin presence outside Africa, plus a part of west Asia before 1.5 Ma, are lacking true substance. The evidence leaves too much to be desired. This verdict concerns the early occupation of Indonesia, the evidence from Longgupo and Yuanmou in China, and Orce in Spain. Dmanisi in Georgia clearly is a valid case of early hominins in Eurasia. However, the 1.7 Ma age so often quoted for this site might be a slight overestimate. But even at a cautious 1.5 Ma, Dmanisi indisputably is one of the earliest traces of hominins outside Africa. It is perhaps only surpassed in age by the evidence from Riwat, Pakistan. Riwat ecologically may represent occupation of an African-like grassland environment, an extreme eastern representation of the continuum of 'African' ecology into a part of west Asia during the Plio-Pleistocene (this will be further discussed in chapter 3.1).

Dmanisi, with a high altitude savanna environment, can be argued, as pointed out in chapter 1.4, to represent a phenomenon which is also visible within Africa around 1.5 Ma: an opportunistic infilling and first occupation of environments with an ecological structure close to that of the African low savanna. This happens both within Africa and in the directly bordering areas of west Asia (the Dmanisi site belonging to the latter category. In Africa itself, the occupation of the Gadeb high plain savanna in Ethiopia at 1.5 Ma represents a similar phenomenon). It signals an increasing hominin flexibility to cope with different environmental structures, and as such represents a prelude to the first colonization of Eurasia.

From 1.5-1.3 Ma onwards, there are well-argued cases for hominin presence in parts of Eurasia up to latitude 40° North. Apart from the already mentioned Dmanisi evidence, it concerns 'Ubeidiya in Israel at about 1.4 Ma, the Nihewan basin sites in China at about 1.2-1.3 Ma, and Gongwangling in China at about 1.2 Ma. The age of the first Indonesian hominins quite likely also falls into this age range of slightly over 1 Ma. Orce in Spain could belong to this first colonization event too, but leaves some questions pertaining. This occupation represents the first true 'Out of Africa', with for the Chinese examples occupation of temperate environments clearly dissimilar in ecological structure to the African tropical grasslands. 'Ubeidiya and Dmanisi are special cases, since their ecology is still close, though not entirely similar, to the African ecological realm.

In southern Europe, Atapuerca TD-6 in Iberia provides evidence for an occupation at the Brunhes-Matuyama boundary, at about 0.8 Ma. This is slightly younger than the earliest occupation of China and arguably Indonesia. The Orce Basin sites in Iberia might push the age barrier even further back, if the current claims hold, to an age similar to the early Chinese sites. Yet, the occupation of (southern) Europe appears to have been a marginal event. Claims for early sites in Italy (Monte Poggiolo, Ceprano) are not well substantiated as far as anything over 0.6-0.5 Ma (Isernia la Pineta) is concerned. And it remains an event restricted to the Mediterranean margin of Europe. Europe north of the Pyrenees was not occupied until 0.5 Ma ago.

Although the number of sites is small, it appears that throughout Eurasia there is a northern limit of 40° latitude North to this first Early Pleistocene hominin dispersal. A possible reason as to why Early Pleistocene hominins did not cross the 40° Northern latitude barrier will be explored in chapter 3.2.

In order to put the observations with regard to the ~1.2 Ma 'Out of Africa 1' into context, we have to digress to the Plio-Pleistocene of Africa first. The roots of 'Out of Africa 1' are in developments taking place in Africa, not Eurasia, during the period of 2.5 to 1.5 Ma. These developments, and how they lead to 'Out of Africa 1', are the subject of the next chapters. In this context, possible causes behind the enigmatic phenomenon of the 'Movius line' will be explored as well.

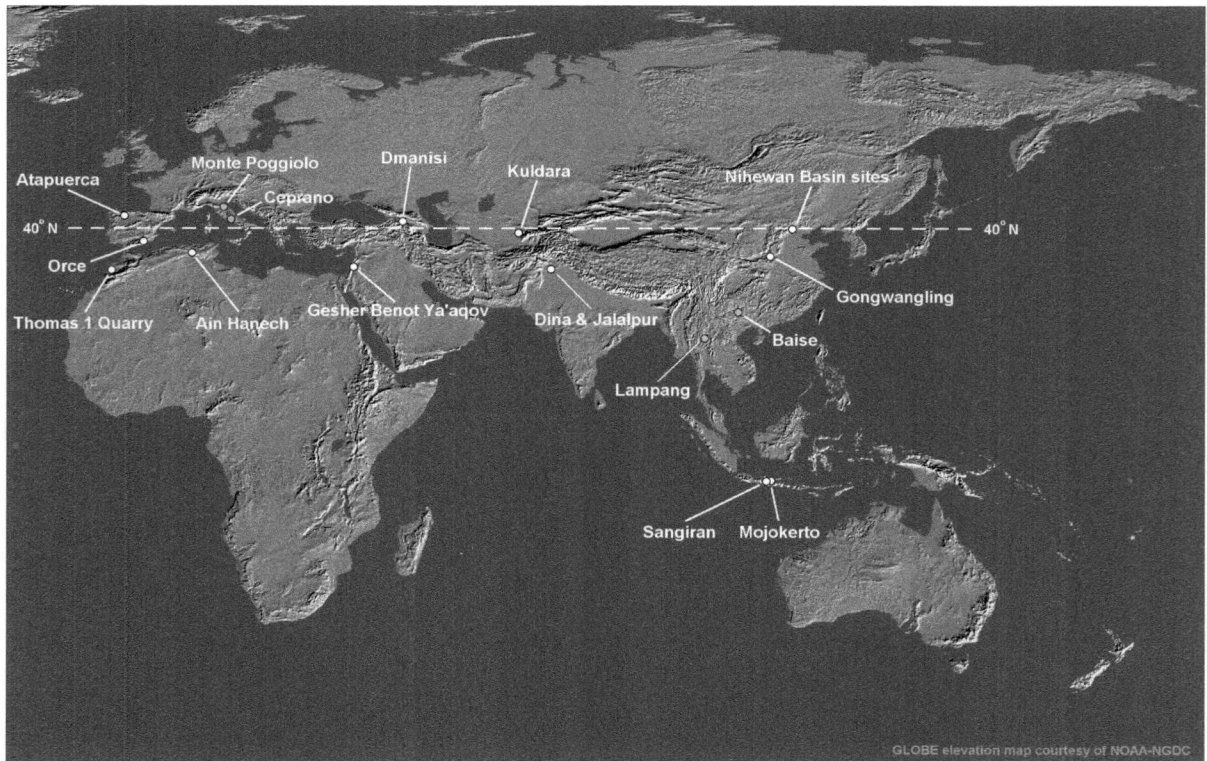

Figure 6: map showing discussed key sites and the inferred extent of 'Out of Africa 1', with the approximate 40 degrees Northern latitude upper limit of occupation throughout Eurasia indicated. Sites marked with a grey dot are doubtful

Part III

The roots of 'Out of Africa I'; Africa before 1 Ma, the source area

In order to understand 'Out of Africa I', a first dispersal of hominins into parts of Eurasia occurring around 1.3 Ma, it is necessary to look at the interplay between climatic developments, changing ecological structures, and related behavioural change in Africa before 1.0 Ma. As part of this discussion, a behavioural model will be proposed with regard to the emergence of the Acheulean technocomplex, including the Developed Oldowan. From this model, an explanation is generated for the Early Pleistocene "Movius line" phenomenon.

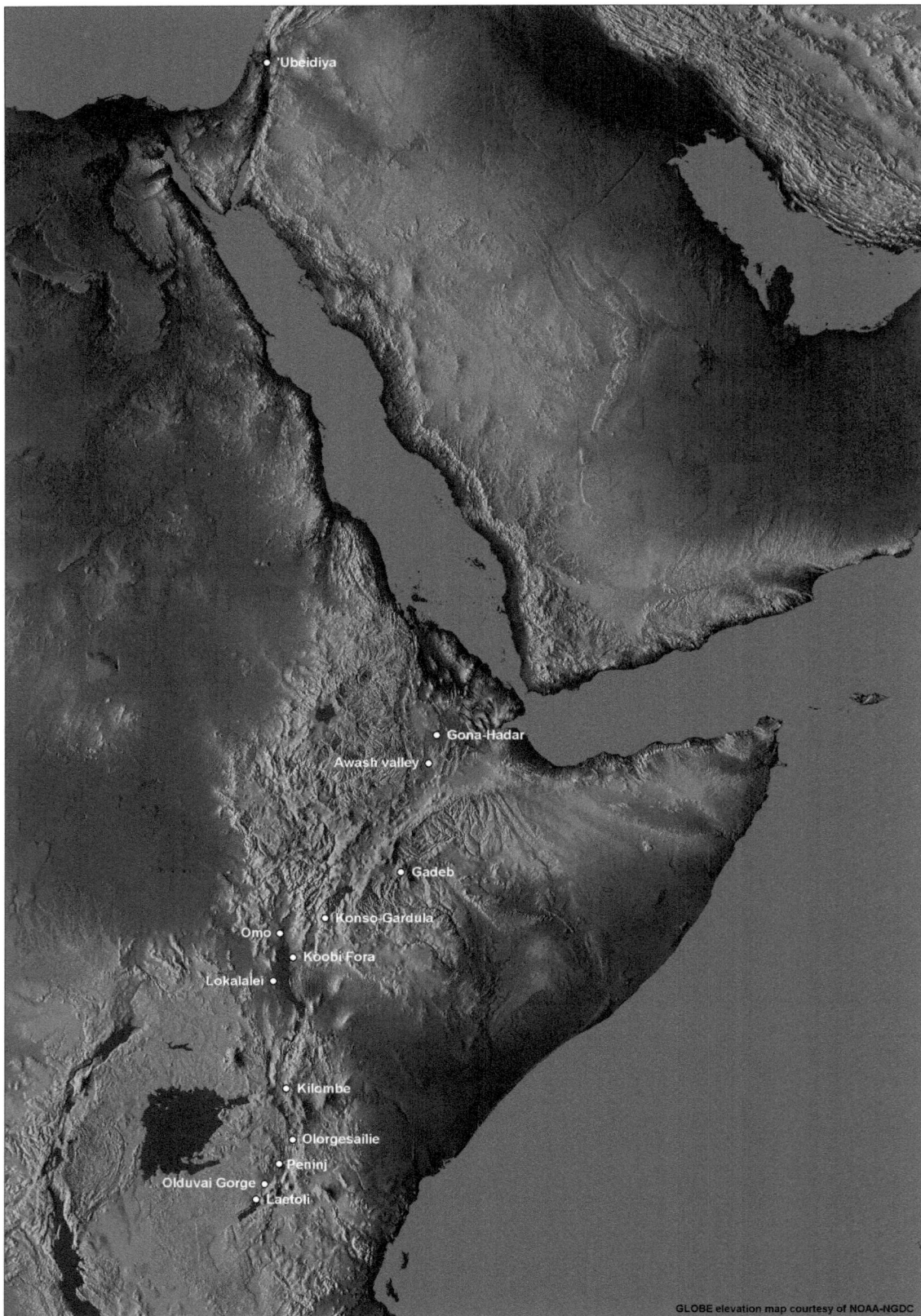

Figure 7: Map showing principal Eastern African archaeological and palaeoanthropological sites.

Chapter 3.1   Inside Africa

Grasslands feature high in discussions on hominin evolution. Not too long ago, it was thought that the emergence of savanna grasslands had been vital for the development of key hominin features such as bipedality and the use of stone tools. Recent palaeoecological studies have shown that this is a flawed picture. The emergence of open grasslands in Africa significantly post-dates the emergence of bipedality in hominins, and post-dates the first use of stone tools (e.g. Kingston *et al.* 1994; Spencer 1997; Reed 1997). Yet, there still appear to be relationships between the emergence of (open) grassland and some important aspects of Plio-Pleistocene hominin evolution and behavioural change. These will be discussed in this chapter.

C$_3$ and C$_4$ grasslands, edaphic and secondary grasslands

The presence of grasslands can be deduced from several types of palaeo-environmental data (Retallack 2001). These include palaeontological data, e.g. on the presence and dietary adaptations of bovids (e.g. Spencer 1997), pedological data, and palynological data (e.g. Hoorn *et al.* 2000). Recently, analyses of stable isotopes from palaeosol carbonates have developed into an important tool for the reconstruction of grassland existence and character (e.g. Kingston *et al.* 1994; Quade and Cerling 1995).

An important distinction to be made is the difference between so-called C$_3$ and C$_4$ dominated grasslands, which are differentiated in stable isotope studies by their different δ^{13}C values (see Quade and Cerling 1995). These different isotope signatures for C$_3$ and C$_4$ plants relate to different ways of photosynthesis. Nearly all trees and shrubs, and grasses which favour a cool growing season (temperate grassland grasses), are recognizable by having a C$_3$-type isotopic signature. Grasses which grow under conditions of negligible temperature variation but significant seasonal variation in precipitation, such as those of the African secondary savanna, and just a few shrubs have a C$_4$-type isotope signature. A dominance of C$_4$ vegetation thus points to an open, warm, monsoonal environment (Kingston *et al.* 1994; Quade and Cerling 1995). It is the signature of the open dry savanna with marked dry and wet seasons. This type of tropical grassland such as occurs today in for example the east African Rift Valley is also designated as 'secondary savanna' (Spencer 1997). It is characterized by large stretches of open grassland, some scattered trees, and is

transected by gallery forests along drainage lines. These grasslands feature a characteristic seasonal cycle of herbivores (see below), which together with fire are important factors in maintaining its open character.

It is not the only type of grassland possible in the tropics. A second (and 'older') type of grassland is known as 'edaphic' grassland. This type of grassland comes into existence as a result of waterlogging, and consists of a broken landscape of wooded terrain mixed with wet patchy pieces of grassland (Spencer 1997). The ecology of such edaphic grasslands is different from that of secondary grasslands. Edaphic grasslands have a C$_3$-type isotopic signature.

There are significant differences in ecological structure and richness/availability of resources between temperate grasslands, tropical edaphic grasslands and open 'secondary' tropical grasslands (see Marean 1997) which will be investigated in more detail below. Important differences between edaphic and secondary grassland flora and fauna with regard to this study on early hominin subsistence include differences in carnivore behaviour (e.g. Domínguez-Rodrigo 1999, 2001) and edible plant richness and distribution (Marean 1997).

The emergence of the African savanna

During the Miocene to mid-Pliocene, tropical West and East Africa was considerably warmer and more humid than today, with abundant annually wet rainforests and closed woodlands in the lowlands (DeMenocal 1995). Heterogeneity existed over a large geographic scale, with some geographic areas, from stable carbonate isotope evidence, being less humid and more open perhaps than others (Kingston *et al.* 1994). Around 2.8 Ma, a trend of periodically cooler and drier, more seasonal conditions set in in Africa (DeMenocal 1995), creating a mosaic of open woodlands with patches of wet edaphic grassland around pockets of forest in East Africa. Following a slight return to more humid conditions around 2.0 Ma (Bromage and Schrenk 1995), a trend of strong seasonal variation in precipitation and increasing aridity emerged around 1.7 Ma (DeMenocal 1995), creating the large-scale emergence of dry secondary C$_4$ type grasslands (Kingston *et al.*, 1994; Spencer 1997) with riparian forest along drainage lines in East Africa. Along the extent of the Rift Valley, this initiated the stereotypical 'Serengeti'-type African savanna featuring vast stretches of open dry grassland transected by riparian woodlands with a seasonal cycle of migratory grazers.

Emergence of the secondary savanna

Both in east Africa and west Asia, the process of C_4 grassland emergence is probably related to intensifying monsoon patterns due to uplift of the Tibet-Qinghai plateau (DeMenocal 1995; Quade and Cerling 1995; Hoorn *et al.* 2000; Freeman and Colarusso 2001). In East Africa, the development of these secondary grasslands might have been partly pushed by volcanic events in addition to climate change (Spencer 1997). Interestingly, there are indications from palynological, paleontological and most notably stable isotope data that in west Asia (the sub-Himalayas) the emergence of semi-arid C_4 dominated grasslands with seasonal precipitation and large herbivores entirely dependent on grazing C_4 grasses might have preceded considerabbly C_4 grassland emergence in east Africa (Kingston *et al.* 1994; Quade and Cerling 1995; Hoorn *et al.* 2000; Freeman and Colarusso 2001). By contrast, the Mediterranean during the Late Pliocene and Early Pleistocene remained dominated by C_3 type vegetation (Quade and Cerling 1995; see also Leone *et al.* 2000; Sahnouni 1998).

Savanna development and hominin evolution and biogeography

Pliocene and Early Pleistocene hominin evolution and biogeography must be seen in the light of these climatic and ecological developments (e.g., Bromage and Schrenk 1995). *Ardipithecus* (White *et al.* 1994, 1995), the new *Kenyanthropus* (Leakey *et al.* 2001) and early *Australopithecinae* (Leakey *et al.* 1995; Ward *et al.* 1999) inhabited wooded, wet environments (WoldeGabriel *et al.* 1994, 2001). Later *Australopithecinae* and earliest *Homo* (s.l.) inhabited slightly more open, but still wooded, habitats including edaphic grasslands (Reed 1997). *Homo ergaster* (a synonym for African *erectus*) is the first hominid to include the emerging dry secondary grassland savanna around 1.8 Ma into its habitat (Reed 1997; Spencer 1997), at a time that the contemporaneous robust *Australopithecinae* seem to have preferred the edaphic grassland-woodland habitats. Just prior to this, robust *Australopithecinae* and early *Homo* frequently appear to share a habitat (Reed 1997). This is underlined by isotopic evidence for similarities in their dietary range (Lee-Thorp *et al.* 2000; Sillen *et al.* 1998), and the fact that both appear at about a similar time in South Africa, after having developed in and been endemic to East Africa for some time (Bromage and Schrenk 1995). It is tempting to regard the robust *Australopithecinae* as the specialized end result of an early adaptation towards a slightly more open mixed woodland-edaphic grassland habitat, exploited in a broad generalized all-year-round way. *Homo ergaster* may be the descendant from an evolutionary line that adapted to more open, mosaic environments relatively late in time. This evolutionary line may have found a niche in an adaptation to exploitation of the emergent seasonal resources within the mixed edaphic grassland-woodland habitat, unlike the all-year-round exploitation of resources by robust *Australopithecinae* and their direct ancestors, and perhaps to non-seasonal resources that were not accessible to *Australopithecinae*. This trait then became a selective advantage when the profound aridification around 1.8 Ma set in which created the dry and (by comparison) highly seasonal secondary grasslands. Although it certainly cannot excuded that the robust *Australopithecinae* also used tools (see Wood (1997) and Susman (1991): the more so with the current evidence for bone tools used for termite digging by robust *Australopithecinae* from South Africa (Backwell and d'Errico 2001)), stone tool use by early *Homo* and its immediate forerunners could have been one of the adaptational instruments involved. The oldest stone tools are currently dated to 2.6 Ma at Gona, Ethiopia (Semaw *et al.* 1997; Semaw 2000).

Bromage and Schrenk (1995; Bromage *et al.* 1995) have suggested that the appearance in southern Africa of both early *Homo* and robust *Australopithecinae* at around 2.0 Ma was a symptom of the expansion of their habitats away from the equator when the climate temporarily returned to more warm and humid conditions. As a result, forest expanded at equatorial latitudes and woodland and grassland (savanna) biomes shifted latitudinally away from the equator, as indicated by faunal dispersals between eastern and southern Africa happening around this time. While this brought robust *Australopithecinae* and early *Homo* to southern Africa (and brought about the demise of *Australopithecus africanus* adapted to more wooded environments), this may also have facilitated a similar dispersal towards the north, as indeed indicated by faunal dispersals into the Levant (Tchernov 1992). During the latest Pliocene the southern Levantine mammal faunas, like those from Betlehem and the 'Erg-el-Ahmar, mainly consisted of open country species which indicate environmental similarities to an African savanna-like landscape (Tchernov 1992). With evidence for a similar 'African'-like Plio-Pleistocene C_4 grassland environment now emerging from paleontological and stable isotope data for the neighbouring part of Arabia (Thomas *et al.* 1998), as well as strong indications, from palaeontological, palynological and stable isotope data, for the presence of semi-arid savanna-like grasslands dominated by C_4 vegetation in the large floodplains of the Plio-Pleistocene Upper Siwalik Formation of Pakistan and Nepal (Hussain *et al.* 1992; Quade and Cerling 1995; Hoorn *et al.* 2000; Freeman and Colarusso 2001), this biogeographic process with regard to hominins could have extended as far as the latter area (see also Dennell 1998). Evidence claimed for a possible 2 Ma early hominin occupation of Riwat and the Pabbi Hills in Pakistan (see chapter 1.3) must be seen in this circumstantial light, although we must beware of what Dincauze (1984: 293) calls a "probabilist fallacy". Yet, hominin presence here during the Plio-Pleistocene would be less of an anomaly, from an ecological viewpoint, than it might seem. It differs in that sense, from similar claims for an early occupation of south China and Southeast Asia, or Mediterranean Europe (see chapter 1.6). The claim for a 1.7 Ma occupation made for Dmanisi in Georgia (see chapter 1.4), like Riwat, would also be easier to reconcile with the above biogeographic model than do the south European, southeast Asian and Chinese claims for a Plio-Pleistocene occupation, although the African stamp on the Dmanisi fauna is actually rather limited (similarities with the African savanna are more with regard to indications for an open grassland with a strong carnivorous guild, see chapter 1.4), and I prefer a slightly different biogeographic model for this site which I will outline later. Likewise, early Pleistocene 'Ubeidiya contains some clear East African faunal elements like *Kolpochoerus olduvaiensis*, *Hippopotamus gorgops*, *Pelorovis oldowayensis* and *Crocuta crocuta* (Tchernov 1992) suggesting affinities, although with some dissimilarities, to Africa. Both sites signify a first cautious broadening of the ecological tolerance of early *Homo*.

Early *Homo* and adaptations to emerging seasonality in the African savanna

Three phenomena emerging in the archaeologic record between 2 and 1 Ma could be related to a process of adaptation to more seasonal conditions as these emerged in Africa at that time, selecting for seasonal resource exploitation strategies in the dry secondary grasslands and riparian habitats by *Homo erectus/ ergaster*. The first is the emergence of the Acheulean in Africa and neighbouring West Asia somewhere around 1.4-1.7 Ma (Asfaw *et al.* 1992; Clark 1994). The second is the occupation, starting around 1.5 Ma, of higher altitude savanna habitats within and at the fringe of the African realm, such as the Gadeb plateau in East Africa (Williams *et al.* 1979; Clark and Kuraschina 1979) and (and this is the biogeographic model I suggest for this site) Dmanisi in Georgia. The third is 'Out of Africa 1' the first proper dispersal of hominins out of the African savanna realm *sensu lato*, into Eurasia, somewhere after 1.3 Ma. In the model which will be advanced in the next chapters, it is these developments of adaptation to increasing seasonality and associated shifts in diet, behaviour, anatomy and cognitive level between 2.5 and 1 Ma, which provide the driving force behind 'Out of Africa 1'. With regard to the emergence of the Acheulean, which is often thought of as having enabled 'Out of Africa 1', I want to emphasize (in order to prevent misunderstanding) that in my view the emergence of the Acheulean and 'Out of Africa 1' are both *symptoms* of one and the same process: not cause and result. The early Acheulean in my model, as elaborated below, is a behavioural phenomenon strictly tied to the ecological structure of the African dry savanna as it emerged after 1.8 Ma. In this work, I will advance a model which employs this concept as an explanation for the 'Movius line problem', the apparent absence of the Acheulean technocomplex at the early Pleistocene sites of Eurasia.

The character of resources on the African savanna

The African savanna realm with dry secondary grasslands crossed by riparian corridors, as it established itself following 1.8 Ma in eastern and southern Africa (Spencer 1997), offered aspects that were not present (or not present to such a degree) outside this realm. Some of the unique aspects of these African tropical grasslands have been outlined by Marean (1997) and are interesting with regard to both the Plio-Pleistocene hominin biogeographic restriction to these environments until the first 'Out of Africa' after 1.3 Ma, and the development and (following 'Out of Africa 1') the geographic restriction of the early Acheulean to these environments from 1.5 Ma until after 1.0 Ma.

Seasonality and availability of biomass and plant foods have a distinctly different character in the African grasslands compared to temperate and cold grasslands such as those of Pleistocene Eurasia (Marean 1997). The tropical grasslands of Africa are different from the temperate and cold Eurasian grasslands in their richness and diversity, not only in biomass but also in plant resources, as well as their predictability in time and space. Biomass is highly mobile both in temperate/cold grasslands and in dry tropical secondary grasslands, and in that sense the presence of a certain herbivore species is seasonal and unpredictable in both, but tropical grasslands have the advantage that, as Marean (1997) points out:

"The migrations in tropical African grasslands typically involve a succession of animals spread over several months, facilitating niche separation and accommodating the high diversity of migratory species. Successions of this type are present in both secondary and edaphic grassland ecosystems. These successions begin with one species that can tolerate the more fibrous tops of grass plants and then other species move in as their particular plant part is made available through the actions of the prior feeders. Succession systems increase the time that a region can support a migratory population and may thus increase the temporal availability of large herbivores in tropical grasslands relative to migration systems that lack successions" (Marean 1997: 193).

In other words: the succession in migratory herbivore presence, such as occurs in tropical secondary as well as edaphic grasslands, effectively creates a predictable presence of biomass that spans over the seasons, reducing seasonality. In addition, tropical grasslands also have a higher abundance of resident herbivores that roam patches of edaphic grassland and the riparian woodlands transecting secondary grasslands. The distribution of this food source is *"patchy but temporarily and spatially predictable and not seasonal"* (Marean 1997: 199). Indeed, scavengeable carcasses are present all year round in some African savanna environments or savanna habitats, though their number and yield varies with the seasons as well as with local environment (Blumenschine 1987; Tappen

1995; Domínguez-Rodrigo 1999, 2001). This predictability in time and space and much smaller seasonal variation in biomass present is the main character of tropical savanna grasslands, as opposed to the characteristics in availability of animal resources outside the African savanna realm. Outside the African savanna, resource availability was even more seasonal and moreover less predictable in time and space. Also with regard to plant food resources, the situation in tropical grasslands is much more favourable than that in temperate/cold grasslands (Marean 1997; see also Sept 1994). The tropical grasslands have a much larger abundance in plant foods with underground storage organs (e.g. tubers, bulbs) that in turn, though patchily available, are temporally and spatially predictable and not seasonable, being edible and available all year round though the nutritional value varies with the seasons. They are more abundant in the dry secondary C_4 grasslands than in edaphic grasslands. The riparian woodlands near streams would produce above ground plant food such as fruits, nuts and berries. The distribution of this type of plant food is very patchy and highly seasonal, but when they are available they are a very rich source and moreover, their occurrence is highly predictable in time and space (Marean 1997: 192-200; Sept 1994).

In summary, resources of the type of secondary grassland savanna with riparian corridors along water courses, that established itself in Africa from 1.8 Ma onwards, are seasonal but predictable in time and space. Part of the seasonality can be overcome by focusing on different resources in different seasons. This is the main difference with the seasonal environments of the Pleistocene temperate and cold latitudes of Eurasia. In such temperate grasslands and woodlands, the ecological distribution of particular resources was probably spatially more patchy and less rich, and seasonal dips in resources were more pronounced. Resources suitable to hominins were probably spatially less densely concentrated and less predictable, and therefore the minimum spatial foraging range needed to be larger. Combined with a more pronounced seasonal availability, hominins venturing outside the African savanna had to be markedly more flexible to sustain themselves. I will argue that this flexibility emerged, through a process of variability selection (Potts 1998), on the African savanna before the onset of 'Out of Africa 1', stimulated by the emerging seasonality of savanna resources after 2 Ma. It was this emerging flexibility with regard to seasonal exploitation of resources which made 'Out of Africa' possible.

Scavenging ecologies of the savannas

One of the possible savanna resources utilized by Plio-Pleistocene hominins, and one that has been suggested to have been involved in the evolution of larger brain sizes (Aiello and Wheeler 1995), as well as the emergence of stone tools (e.g. Semaw 2000) are scavengeable carcasses of mammals. The scavenging paradigm (Binford 1981,

1983; Shipman 1986) for early hominins is now well-entrenched within early man studies (e.g., Blumenschine 1987; Blumenschine and Cavallo 1992; see also discussion in Domínguez-Rodrigo 2002). Blumenschine (1987), Tappen (1995) and Domínguez-Rodrigo (1999, 2001) have made actualistic studies of scavenging opportunities in modern savanna habitats, mapping and documenting carcass densities, lifespans and yields within different sub-environments, and from this estimated scavenging opportunities in Plio-Pleistocene savanna habitats. Incorporating information and estimates about availability of other resources, Peters and Blumenschine (1995) constructed a model of seasonal landscape affordance under various climatic conditions for the palaeo-Olduvai basin. These studies have yielded valuable information and models on scavenging opportunity differences between various subhabitats in the African savanna as well as with regard to seasonal variations. These, together with nutritional considerations from studies by Speth (Speth 1987; Speth and Spielmann 1983) which emphasize seasonal variations in nutritional yield, will be employed in the now following model for scavenging and landuse with regard to the Oldowan and the early African Acheulean and Developed Oldowan. It should be noted that the actualistic studies in modern savanna habitats referred to are not one-on-one analogies for the situations in Plio-Pleistocene savanna habitats. They are however the best guides we currently have to the scavenging ecologies of these Plio-Pleistocene savannas, and some broad generalizations from these studies would appear to be transferable to the Plio-Pleistocene of the African Rift.

The studies referred to show a difference in scavenging ecology between wet edaphic grasslands and dry secondary grasslands (Tappen 1995; Domínguez-Rodrigo 1999, 2001). Scavenging in open habitats is only worthwhile in edaphic grasslands with slight seasonality and no biomass migrations (Domínguez-Rodrigo 1999, 2001). For the dry secondary grassland habitat *sensu lato*, by contrast scavenging opportunities are present on a seasonal basis in the closed riparian corridors crossing it (Domínguez-Rodrigo 1999, 2001; Blumenschine 1987) by virtue of seasonal migrations of biomass.

Patches of edaphic grassland before 2 Ma therefore may have yielded scavenging opportunities for *Australopithecinae* and early *Homo* on a non-seasonal basis (Tappen 1995), focusing on marrow and occasionally some limited scraps of meat. An Oldowan toolkit, mainly composed of core-choppers, hammerstones and flakes, would serve well for such a purpose, explaining perhaps the apparent technological stasis within this technocomplex between 2.5 and 1.8 Ma (see Semaw 2000), following its emergence. Carcass availability is usually scattered in this type of habitat, as indicated by the bone distribution study performed by Tappen (1995) in the edaphic grasslands of Virunga National Park in Zaire. If the Tappen study is taken as a proxy for carcass availability in Plio-Pleistocene edaphic grasslands, and the Oldowan tools are taken to be involved with direct carcass processing, then it would be in the line of expectation that Oldowan sites from the period of 2.5-1.8 Ma likewise are distributed rather continuously over the landscape, unlike the distribution of the (later) Acheulean sites following 1.5-1.7 Ma as they seem to be more closely tied to specific habitats of the landscape (which will be discussed later). The relatively high percentage of flake debitage in Oldowan sites (Semaw 2000) would either indicate that carcasses in this habitat did yield more than occasional scraps of flesh when hominins gained access to them (indeed, this seems to be suggested by Domínguez-Rodrigo (1999, 2002)), which is in theory testable by analyzing cutmark patterns on bones from Oldowan assemblages (see Domínguez-Rodrigo 2002, and note at the end of this chapter) or that carcass processing was not the only activity in which these stone tools served.

The edaphic grassland characteristics are profoundly different from those of the dry secondary grasslands which established themselves in (East and Southern) Africa after 1.8 Ma. Studies into scavenging opportunities provided by the dry secondary grasslands of the Serengeti by Blumenschine (1987) suggest that only scavenging in the closed riparian parts of this habitat is feasible, and only during specific seasons (Blumenschine 1987; Domínguez-Rodrigo 1999). This type of habitat, at least in contemporary East Africa, features the phenomenon of seasonal migrations of large herds of grazers, who graze dispersed on the open plains during the wet season and aggregate near water sources during the dry season. In the Plio-Pleistocene African Rift, this seasonal migration could have taken place along the riparian drainage lines between higher plains and lowland lake basins (Blumenschine 1987).

Carnivore competition in the open habitats of the secondary grassland habitat is usually severe, and carcasses are quickly consumed by their predators and a succession of scavengers following them (Domínguez-Rodrigo 1999). Carcasses are highly dispersed in this habitat, most notably during the wet season when the herds of grazers have dispersed to feed on the grassy plains. Therefore, both carcass completeness/yield once located and carcass availability in a spatial sense is generally low in these open habitats. An exception is the late dry season, when there is a carcass glut near the remaining waterholes due to animals having succumbed to the drought. From a nutritional aspect, these carcasses however are largely useless to hominins because they are severely fat-depleted: this is the lean-meat season of this savanna habitat, and only the internal organs or the marrow of lower leg bones yield some nutritional value (Bunn and Ezzo 1993; Speth 1987; Speth and Spielmann 1983).
The only feasible significant scavenging opportunity in this habitat is therefore during the early dry season in the riparian habitats along drainage lines between the piedmont uplands and lake basins. Migrating herbivores

come to these riparian corridors for access to water, and predators take advantage of this and produce carcasses in the riparian habitat. Being a closed habitat, carcasses are less easily spotted by vultures, who usually attract hyaenas, and hence remnants of predatory kills escape attention by these non-human scavengers (Blumenschine 1987). Once the carcass is abandoned (voluntarily or not) by the predators, a subsequent hominin scavenger moving in would therefore experience little or no competition from hyaenas or other animal scavengers. Unlike those of the late dry season, these carcasses of the early dry season still have enough fat reserves to be nutritious. Carcasses in the riparian habitats of the dry secondary savanna are therefore a viable source of food for hominins during the early dry season.

Studies by Domínguez-Rodrigo of carcass yields in the riparian habitats of the Masaai Mara National Reserve in Tanzania suggest that because predators are relieved of pressure by scavengers in this closed habitat, they tend to prolong their feeding and stay at these carcasses for a long time. As a result, predatory carcass exploitation is thorough and the carcasses are almost completely defleshed when finally abandoned (Domínguez-Rodrigo 1999). The relative absence of bone cracking hyaenas in this habitat however preserves the nutritious marrow as a potential resource for hominin scavengers equipped with hammer stones.
The predators (lions) that produced and consumed the carcasses in the Domínguez-Rodrigo study, tended to divide their feeding at the carcass into multiple interrupted stages, resting near it in between. This is in contrast to lion feeding in an open habitat, which is a singular and quick event (Domínguez-Rodrigo 1999). While the end result of lion feeding in a closed riparian setting is an utterly defleshed carcass leaving only (although very nutritious) marrow for a hominin scavenger, intervention in an early stage of the prolonged, multiple-staged feeding process of these carnivores would potentially yield serious amounts of meat in addition to the marrow content of the carcass. In itself, this would in theory be a serious incentive for adaptation of a confrontational scavenging strategy by hominins, because it potentially would yield serious nutritional profit. Indeed, such has been recently proposed by Domínguez-Rodrigo (2002). By contrast, due to the intense competition and pressure of other scavengers, such a confrontational strategy would likely be much less successful and profitable in an open setting. It would also be more dangerous in such a setting, because it would involve interaction with a larger number of predators and other scavengers (some of which, e.g. hyaena, are formidable) and less opportunity for strategic withdrawal: in a closed riparian setting by contrast interaction would be with a smaller number of opponents, and trees would provide the opportunity of a quick dash to reach safe refuge, as well as a potential source of defense material (branches, sticks).

Forging a link between African early Acheulean sites and scavenging in a secondary grassland environment

During the Early Pleistocene, roughly from 1.7-1.4 Ma onwards and following the emergence of dry secondary savannas in Africa, Acheulean assemblages emerge, and these and 'non-Acheulean' assemblages of Oldowan affinities ('Developed Oldowan') then co-occur in Africa for a considerable time (Isaac 1984; Gowlett 1988; Clark 1994). It has been noted that Acheulean assemblages, characterized by large percentages of bifaces usually made on flakes and sometimes accompanied by low numbers of smaller tools (Leakey 1971, 1975), seem to correlate to a distinctive habitat, most notably inland riverchannel and overbank contexts (Isaac 1975: 516; Leakey 1975: 491-492; Isaac 1984: 58; Gowlett 1988; Gamble 1993: 125; Clark 1994: 466). These are the geomorphic locations that would correspond to the closed riparian environments, particularly riparian corridors between upland plains and lowland basins (Blumenschine 1987; Peters and Blumenschine 1995). Developed Oldowan sites (Leakey 1971, 1975) on the other hand (including variants like the *Karari industry* (Harris and Isaac 1976)), which are characterized by a very low percentage or absence of bifaces, while the few that are present notably distinguish in their technological characteristics (Jones 1994), occur both near upland seasonal streams and at lower basin lake margins, in open and in riparian habitats (Leakey 1975; Harris and Isaac 1976; Isaac 1984; Gowlett 1988; Rogers *et al.* 1994). They clearly are distributed over a much wider array of habitats in the landscape than Acheulean assemblages. Acheulean and Developed Oldowan overlap spatially, for example at Kilombe (Gowlett 1988), but it is the Acheulean element which has the more restricted distribution. At Olduvai, Acheulean does not occur within one kilometre of the shore of the saline lake, where by contrast Developed Oldowan occurrences are present (Isaac 1984: 58; Gowlett 1988: 13). At Koobi Fora (Isaac and Isaac 1997) Acheulean sites only occur in streamchannel contexts situated well inland and not near the palaeolake. At Peninj, Acheulean sites occur within fluvial and proximal alluvial fan depositional environments, while contemporary Oldowan sites occur in more distal alluvial fan and lacustrine floodplain environments (Domínguez-Rodrigo *et al.* 2001). In the Middle Pleistocene deposits in the area around the Bodo hominid site in the Middle Awash Valley of Ethiopia, although quite young (approximately 0.65 Ma) in comparison with the other sites discussed in this chapter, Acheulean appears in the piedmont Wadi fan environments close to seasonal water courses (Clark *et al.* 1994), while Oldowan assemblages (which are surprisingly young here) disappear in favour of Acheulean assemblages in conjunction with a shift from alluvial plain deposits to these overbank and channel deposits, and the excavators explicitly mention that: *"the Middle Awash change from core (chopper-) based Oldowan assemblages to assemblages with large quantities of Acheulean bifaces*

appears to reflect the use of different technologies in different geographic settings" (Clark *et al.* 1994: 1909). Similar changes in industry that appear to reflect a change in local palaeo-environment occur at Olduvai Gorge, while there is a suggestion of a similar pattern at 'Ubeidiya in Israel (see chapter 1.4).

When we compare the restricted distribution of early African Acheulean bifaces (handaxes and cleavers) in the landscape with scavenging opportunities in a dry secondary savanna as outlined above, the presence of Acheulean assemblages seems to match that particular landscape facet which during the early dry season would yield the only feasible, productive scavenging opportunity within these secondary savannas, as outlined earlier. Handaxes have often been functionally interpreted as butchery tools, and indeed serve well for such a purpose in experiments (Jones 1980; see also Isaac (1984) and references therein), while early European Acheulean flint handaxes provide use-wear evidence for use as butchery tools (see chapter 4: I am however not quite certain whether this later evidence from Europe should without any caution be transferred to the early African Acheulean). We might therefore legitimately investigate along the line of a cautious link between the early African Acheulean and early dry season scavenging in the riparian habitats of the emerging dry secondary savanna.

Exploring the *Acheulean-dry season scavenging* link

The hypothesis that the early African Acheulean is tied to scavenging behaviour in the riparian habitats of the African dry savanna during the early dry season has a number of implications. Ultimately, it might provide the explanation for the early Acheulean remains being restricted to Africa (or more exactly: African savanna type habitats, including those of the Early Pleistocene Near East) until well after the first 'Out of Africa' at approximately 1 Ma ago. This point will be discussed in a separate chapter. Below, I will focus on the behavioural implications with regard to the early Acheulean and its wider archaeological context in Africa.

Earlier, it has been pointed out that felid-produced carcasses in the riparian habitat of the African dry secondary savannas are thoroughly defleshed, as indicated by the research of Domínguez-Rodrigo (1999). Therefore the focus of a hominin passive scavenger, which would move in only after the carnivores have permanently left the kill remnants, would be on marrow extraction from already defleshed longbones. A large cutting tool like a handaxe or cleaver would not likely be employed in such a scavenging context. Instead, one would expect to find hammerstones/choppers for bone breaking, and scrapers for periosteal removal (the Developed Oldowan toolkit). The use of large cutting tools like handaxes would however certainly come into view when hominins, instead of being passive scavengers, engaged in active confrontational scavenging and intervened in an early stage of the prolonged multiple-stage feeding behaviour displayed by felids in these riparian habitats (see Domínguez-Rodrigo 1999) such as outlined earlier in this chapter. Indeed, the presence of large cutting tools in these riparian settings, as is well documented archaeologically, implies either that, and in contrast to modern riparian settings, Early Pleistocene predators in this habitat abandoned carcasses which still yielded considerable amounts of meat or that Early Pleistocene Acheulean hominins appropriated felid kills while still largely meat-bearing by active confrontational scavenging (a third option of course would be that these large cutting tools have nothing to do with the exploitation of carcasses. See for example the phytolith evidence of Domínguez-Rodrigo *et al.* (2001), a point to which I will return later). In theory, this should be discernable in the pattern of bone modifications at Acheulean sites. When abandoned carcasses were still meat-bearing but no longer completely fleshed, a pattern of many cutmarks related to the removal of meat scraps should be present. By contrast, when passive scavenging of defleshed bones was practised, emphasis should be on breakage of long bones (for marrow acquisition) with negligible cutmarks. Finally, when active scavenging of still largely meat-bearing kills was practised, one would expect cutmarks at major articulation points only, little bone breakage and skeletal profiles where certain preferred body parts appear to be missing. It is not likely that carcasses and carcass parts would be completely processed at the locality of procurement. Rather, with the predators of the carcass still close by in this scenario, time spent with the carcass would likely be as limited as possible. It is most likely that active confrontational scavenging involved a quick and rough disarticulation, followed by retreat and transport of carcass parts to a safe spot.

Some characteristics of handaxes might corroborate a function in an active confrontational scavenging scenario. Much has been written, from various angles, about the apparent 'overdesign' of handaxes in terms of symmetry, size, and the prolific numbers at many sites. Basically, a handaxe is however a very sturdy cutting tool, very useful for 'quick and dirty' butchering tasks of 'hit and run' style, and many if not all of the mentioned 'overdesigned' and distributional characteristics might find an explanation in this.

In a scenario such as sketched above, whereby hominin scavengers appropriate still meat-bearing prey from felines in the riparian habitats of the savanna, and certainly if active confrontational scavenging was employed, actions had to be of 'hit and run' style given the danger of interaction with these predators. Employed stone tools would have to be ready, reliable and appropriate to the task, minimizing time spent in the danger zone and the chance of unwelcome surprises such as inappropriate tools or tools severely damaging in the act of use. Handaxes, when employed in the sense as outlined above, would fit these characteristics well. They would classify as examples of "reliable" technology *sensu* Bleed (1986).

Bleed points out that a tool design must be "effective" for its purpose. Such effectiveness can be reached in different ways, involving choices in emphasis on particular aspects of the character of tools and toolkits. Social factors (associated with identity, a point which I will leave aside in this discussion) and cost-related measures concerning the minimal level of effectiveness are involved in shaping the character of a tool or toolkit. The last aspect depends amongst others on the context of use. A simple and relevant cost-related measure is availability of the tool, which can be expressed in two modes of design: reliability or maintainability. The first one can be achieved by overdesigning the tool (making it extra sturdy, or with multiple similar working edges – interestingly, handaxes have both these elements involved in their design) or by using it below the maximum carrying capacity. Reliable (*sensu* Bleed) technology usually has a clearly scheduled separation between the times the system is in use and the time of maintenance and repair (Bleed 1986).

Maintainable systems *sensu* Bleed, characterize by offering the possibility of multipurpose use (when a tool is broken or exhausted, e.g. using a bow to spear a rabbit when one has run out of arrows), easy repair and adjustment potential, and by the fact that, unlike reliable systems, there is typically not a clear and scheduled separation between the times these systems are in use and the time of maintenance and repair (Bleed 1986).

It should be pointed out, as Bleed does, that the two are not mutually exclusive. The ideal toolkit has elements of both (and indeed, a careful reader will note that the two modes overlap in some elements, and that handaxes have elements of both). Bleed points out that reliable systems have costs that make them less than optimal in some situations: they are costly in terms of time, raw materials and other resources. They can only be justified in situations where the advantages of increased availability outweigh the added design costs, and where the benefits of increased availability can be judged in advance. Maintainable systems are more appropriate for generalized undertakings that have continuous need but unpredictable schedules. Reliable systems are more appropriate for undertakings that have a short but highly certain schedule of employment. Thus, both aspects are connected to a toolkit which is used to obtain a critical resource for which vital demands exist, but reliability is the optimal solution when the pattern of toolkit employment (with regard to task and timing) is clear and predictable (as it is with handaxes in a scavenging scenario as outlined earlier), while maintainability is the optimal solution when those conditions are not met. A handaxe, when employed in an active confrontational scavenging environment as outlined earlier in this chapter, therefore might have and indeed appears to have clear affinities with "reliable" technology *sensu* Bleed.

It is important to note that African early Acheulean handaxes do *not* appear to be *ad hoc* tools manufactured on the spot. They are almost never found with their production debitage. African Acheulean handaxes were typically made by preparing a face on a boulder core and then knocking a large flake off it. This flake blank, often side struck, was then fashioned into a handaxe by flaking the ventral face and if necessary by some further trimming of the edges. Apparently, the handaxe was then taken away, over a short but meaningful distance (up to a few kilometres), and employed in the riparian environment. The handaxes are never accompanied by boulder cores at African early Acheulean sites and seldom by large amounts of related debitage (Toth 1987; Toth and Schick 1986), and by consequence where boulder cores are present (e.g. at FxJj33, Koobi Fora (Isaac and Isaac 1997)) there are no bifaces. An exception is an ignimbrite workshop and quarry site at Gadeb (Ethiopian highlands) where large flake blanks for handaxe manufacture were directly knocked off the face of an ignimbrite outcrop (Clark and Kurashina 1979: 36-38). This quarry site is clearly a different context however from that of the typical Acheulean site in a riparian environment. With regard to the latter more typical type of Acheulean site, handaxes were clearly brought there in a finished state. It stands to reason that they were also used at the place where they were subsequently discarded.

Domínguez-Rodrigo *et al.* (2001) provide evidence that handaxes from the early Acheulean site of Peninj (Tanzania) have been employed in woodcutting tasks. They found wood phytoliths, probably from *Acacia*, on two handaxes (and a flake), while the absence of similar phytoliths from the sediments which contained the artefacts suggest that these phytoliths are not due to contamination by these sediments. While this makes clear that the hardwood phytoliths on the tools are very likely to be use-related, which would seem to argue against a function of handaxes as butchery tools, it also points out that these tools apparently were not deposited in an environment with *Acacia*, although they were at some point used to cut *Acacia* hardwood. This begs the question why these handaxes were transported after being used to cut hardwood, the more so since they were left in a part of the landscape which as outlined earlier is typical for handaxe occurrences and restricted in comparison to the distribution of other artefact types. In addition, why cut wood with handaxes? These do not seem to be the ideal tool for such activities. Chopping-tools would work as well or even better in branch cutting since only a small part of the cutting edge is used in such activities (see e.g. experimental results by Jones (1994: 295-295)), while the continuous sharp edge of handaxes would necessitate some protection while handling, which would not be necessary for a chopping-tool. Cobble material for chopper production would in many instances be well available in the stream channel context of Acheulean sites.

A possible answer could be, that handaxes served a role in both woodcutting and carcass butchery, with the latter following the first or the first preceding in preparation for the latter. We might think of for example the cutting of thick (and as Guthrie recently pointed out: thorny) *Acacia* branches in prepararation for defensive/offensive actions

against predators during carcass appropriation (in line with a confrontational scavenging scenario). Alternatively, it could have concerned the preparation of digging sticks for embedded exploitation of resources like rootstock at the stream margins (see e.g. Peters and Blumenschine 1995), to dig for water, or in preparation for digging carbohydrate-rich tubers on the dry open plains. The latter necessitate sturdy digging sticks because of their depth of burial (Vincent 1984). It appears difficult to test these different options against each other using the archaeological record.

Apart from scavenging opportunities, riparian woodlands along streams would provide a diversity of fruits during the dry season (Sept 1986; Peters and Blumenschine 1995) which would be another reason why subsistence foraging could have been highly focused on this landscape facet during the dry season.

Developed Oldowan

The occasional handaxe occurs in Developed Oldowan assemblages: typically, they make up to 2 to 9% of a Developed Oldowan assemblage only. Compared to Acheulean handaxes, Developed Oldowan handaxes are usually smaller, thicker and less elongated, show more variation and are predominantly made on cobbles instead of flakes. They have undergone a larger amount of reduction as attested by the degree of secondary retouch (Jones 1994; Leakey 1975). Developed Oldowan handaxes appear to be items that have been carried around for some time, experiencing considerable reduction by resharpening, as suggested by Jones (1994).

Developed Oldowan (the main artefact types of which are small retouched tools, spheroids, core tools, and debitage (Leakey 1971, 1975)) extends over a larger part of the landscape than Acheulean occurrences do (including landscape units in which Acheulean occurs, as well as in those in which the latter is absent). The reduced character of the Developed Oldowan handaxes and spheroids suggests that they could have been embedded in a long chain of use (see Schick and Toth (1994) concerning spheroids). This would indicate that they are highly mobile items that might have served in an exploitation strategy which included a rather large extended foraging round through the landscape. They are frequently found in association with small tools, cores and core-tools and considerable amounts of flake debitage. Given that usually little of the flake debitage can be refitted to cores and core-tools (Leakey 1971; Toth 1987; Binford 1989), these latter presumably signify a similar wide stretched spatio-temporal mobility.

Contrasting Developed Oldowan and Acheulean

When we compare the Developed Oldowan and the Acheulean, a contrast emerges whereby Acheulean handaxes point to a rather restricted employment of tools made in preparation for activities on a rather short timescale in a specific part of the landscape. Handaxes are made at locality A and discarded at a landscape-specific locality B without further reduction. Developed Oldowan handaxes and spheroids attest to activities extended over multiple cycles of use in various parts of the landscape: they are made at locality A and then used, reused and resharpened at presumably several localities before being discarded, the latter without a landscape specific point of discard. In Bleed's (1986) terminology, Developed Oldowan handaxes are therefore more akin to "maintainable" technology which has many modes and moments of employment, whereas Acheulean handaxes have more affinities with "reliable" technology. The Acheulean tools serve in procurement activities (carcass exploitation in the riparian habitats in my model) with a short but predictable schedule which would be rather punctuated in time and space, while the Developed Oldowan tools were employed in a more continuous and probably more varied (and hence less predictable in time and space) schedule of procurement. Developed Oldowan would signify subsistence procurement outside the early dry season focussing on plant foods with some scavenging for marrow and only limited meat eating, as well as perhaps procurement of plant foods in the context of the Acheulean early dry season scavenging activities. During the peak of the dry season, which is the "lean meat season" of Speth (Speth 1987; Speth and Spielmann 1983), the only nutritious (least fat depleted) body parts are marrow from the lower leg bones, and the internal organs. During the short seasonal glut of carcasses near the remnants of the water sources at the peak of the dry season, these would yield potential but limited scavenging opportunities while competition and danger from other predators/scavengers would be relatively low. During the wet season, the only and limited scavenging opportunity would be marrow from defleshed long bones, to which could perhaps be added small amounts of meat from tree-cached leopard kills.

This hypothesis could perhaps be tested by means of microwear research on Developed Oldowan tools and analysis of hominid modified faunal remains at Developed Oldowan sites. Microwear analysis should yield clear indications for exploitation of plant materials. Hominid modified faunal remains should show evidence for a dominance of marrow exploitation and limited but present traces of butchery of partly or completely fleshed carcasses. The latter opportunities would potentially be provided all year round, although in limited quantities, by tree-cached leopard kills, and during the peak of the dry season by abundant but lean-meat carcasses of bovids that died of starvation. In the latter season, fat-rich internal organs of the occasional complete carcass would be resources for which limited amounts of cutting tools like Developed Oldowan handaxes (which perhaps could serve a double role as cores for servicable flakes) were needed.

These tools would also serve for disarticulation of lower leg bones prior to marrow extraction.

Microwear evidence on the use of Developed Oldowan tools is available for a small number of small chert tools from roughly 1.6-1.5 Ma old "Karari industry" sites FxJj 18, 20 and 50 in the Okote Member of Koobi Fora (Keeley and Toth 1981; Isaac and Isaac 1997), where "Karari industry"appears to be a local variant of the Developed Oldowan (Harris and Isaac 1976). Working of a soft wood type, cutting of silica-rich plants (grasses or reeds) and cutting or slicing meat or fresh hide are in evidence. Keeley (in Isaac and Isaac 1997) believes the evidence for meat processing is connected to light butchery related to final processing and consumption of products from initial butchery elsewhere. The full suite of activities evidenced would apply to those expected for a wet season site and/or a 'safe' location, where the products of 'hit and run' style confrontational scavenging of the early dry season would have been further processed and consumed. Indeed, these sites were located in a palaeo-environment that has been reconstructed as consisting of seasonal streams with some gallery forest embedded within an open plain well away (i.e. reconstructed distances of up to 20 kilometres) from the palaeo-lake margins (Isaac and Isaac 1997), and the sites have indeed been regarded as possible wet season sites (Bunn in the comments section in Blumenschine (1987)). If this is largely correct and if by contrast the palaeo-lake margins of roughly contemporaneous Olduvai Gorge Upper Bed II represent mainly peak of dry season exploitation instead, this could perhaps be an explanation for the two notable differences between the Developed Oldowan of Olduvai and the Developed Oldowan ('Karari industry') of the Karari escarpment at Koobi Fora: the apparent relative lack of handaxes from 'Karari' assemblages, and the absence of spheroids. The relative insignificance of handaxes would be explainable since wet season scavenging in the relatively open landscape of the Okoto Member would be limited (and probably be a by-product of foraging for open savanna foods like tubers) and strongly focused on marrow and small meat scraps, hence hammerstones and core-flake dominance. At the palaeo-lake margin of Olduvai, the peak of dry season carcass glut would introduce some possible (but limited) demand for handaxes used for disarticulation of (partly) complete carcasses of animals that died of starvation, and possibly for extraction of internal organs. The dry-wet season contrast proposed for Olduvai Developed Oldowan and Koobi Fora Karari sites would indicate that the enigmatic spheroids, which are present at Olduvai but absent at Koobi Fora, would be artefacts serving in (peak of) dry season activities. If they are indeed highly curated, highly mobile hammerstones for stone flaking (Schick and Toth 1994) then they could have a connection to the highly reduced, highly mobile (see Jones 1994) Developed Oldowan handaxes.

The faunal patterns at Koobi Fora sites like FxJj50 (Bunn et al. 1980; Isaac and Isaac 1997) show a bias towards many limb bones and almost no axial elements. Limb bones display strong shaft fragmentation, with impact scars from hammering present, indicating marrow exploitation. A straightforward prediction and interpretation of cutmark and bone breakage patterns however is difficult to produce, because it can be expected that this landscape unit served both during wet season and (as locales receiving body parts obtained by confrontational scavenging) early dry season exploitation. One would expect a composite palimpsest pattern with meaty bones showing cutmarks indicating disarticulation and perhaps subsequently broken for marrow extraction (early dry season), as well as bones primarily broken for marrow and/or showing signs of removal of meat scraps (wet season).

For Developed Oldowan sites near the lake margin of Upper Bed II Olduvai (as well as the palaeolake margins in Koobi Fora, where sites with modified bone but no stone tools have been found, e.g. GaJi5: see Isaac and Isaac 1997) a similar mixture of exploitation patterns, but this time of peak of dry season and wet season activities, would be expected: peak of dry season activities would produce patterns of bone modification indicating disarticulation of partly complete or complete carcasses with subsequent removal of skin/meat from the lower limb bones (not for consumption but to get at the marrow) and subsequent breakage with the sole purpose of getting at the marrow, while wet season activities would produce broken limb (and mandibular) bones with cutmarks indicating removal of scraps of meat, with subsequent bone breakage for marrow. Indeed, this is not unlike the documented GaJi5 patterns from the Koobi Fora palaeo-lake margin (Isaac and Isaac 1997: 442).

It should be re-emphasized that exploitation of non-animal resources (plant foods, roots, tubers, bulbs, nuts) instead of the products of scavenging probably were the major elements in daily food acquisition outside the early dry season. These would necessitate relatively large daily rounds through the landscape. Availability of such food items would be a complex matter of seasonal variations in availability (see Sept 1986) and seasonal variations in access to water sources (see e.g. Peters and Blumenschine 1995). During the dry season, a lack of water sources would prohibit prolonged exploitation of certain landscape units for both food and lithic raw materials. Yet, some use of the dry open plains would have had an incentive in the form of the presence there of rich patches of tubers, which are a source of carbohydrates necessary as a complementary component of the diet during this season (Speth 1987). During the wet season, landscape foraging rounds would probably have been at their largest (Peters and Blumenschine 1995) and cover most landscape units. The open savanna, as opposed to riparian habitats, potentially could have provided a rich source of carbohydrates in the form of tubers. These would, because of their depth of burial, however necessitate digging tools (see e.g. Vincent 1984). The current evidence for termite digging tools from the South African sites (Backwell and d'Errico 2001) indicates that nothing precludes this possibility.

Interesting with regard to an interpretation of the Koobi Fora Okote Member sites as predominantly wet season sites and the microwear evidence for use of tools in cutting thin soft wooden stakes and stems of siliceous plants like grasses (Keeley in Isaac and Isaac (1997)) is that the reconstructed broader palaeo-ecotone in which the sites FxJj 50, 20 and 18 were found is comparable to the ecotone (the transitional zone between open woodland and short-grass plain in a relatively dry wooded savanna), where modern chimpanzees at Assirik forage for termites during the early wet season. They preferentially forage there because this ecotone yields concentrations of the right kind of shrubs for making termite fishing probes (McGrew 1992: 171). In addition, cutting of soft wooden stakes could be related to harvesting not-yet-ripe fruits in the channel margins and/or alluvial plains. As Sept (1994) remarked, this would be a potential strategy to optimize returns and mitigate competition by other fruit consumers. The cutting evidence could indicate a harvesting strategy whereby fruits were collected and taken on the branch rather than picked from the branch.

Implications with regard to behaviour and cognition

To summarize: elaborating on an earlier (3.5-2 Ma) trend to trade closed woodland environments for the open woodland with edaphic grassland ecotone, the period of 2 to 1.5 Ma appears to document a shift in subsistence behaviour whereby an all round foraging strategy is traded for a seasonally organized strategy in an ecological domain (now including the emergent dry secondary grasslands) which is structured quite differently from previously occupied ecological domains. This shift probably includes a shift to other resources, and/or reorganization of rank of importance of resources.

There might be connections to other phenomena observable during this timespan. The same period documents an increase in brain size which is probably connected to a reorganization of the hominin gut system (Aiello and Wheeler 1995). Brains are energetically costly organs. The energy to sustain larger brains needs to be released by a reorganization of the metabolic system. One way to do this is by reducing the gut system, and anatomical evidence (such as changes in the shape of the postcranial skeleton, e.g. ribcage shape) suggests that this happened around the time of early Homo, most notably Homo ergaster (see Aiello and Wheeler 1995; Aiello 1998). A reduced gut system entails a dietary shift from low quality vegetable food (foliage, fibrous plants and fruits) towards more high-quality, easily digested food. Examples of the latter are meat and nuts and soft fruits, which as explained are seasonal resources on the secondary savanna. There therefore appears to be a matching interconnection between increasing brain size and a shift to seasonal subsistence strategies such as outlined above.

The interesting thing is that there appear to be various and complex interconnections between diet, brain size and behaviour which reinforce each other. Dunbar (1993) and Aiello and Dunbar (1993) have pointed out that there appear to be relations between brain neocortex size, group size, and social behaviour in primates. According to their research, larger neocortex sizes in primates relate in law-like ways to larger group sizes, and in turn a relatively large amount of time needed for social interaction (e.g. grooming) in order to sustain these larger group sizes. The brain expansion documented for Plio-Pleistocene hominins is setting in between 2 and 1 Ma. It would indicate that hominin group sizes likely became larger during this period, and social interaction more intensive. Changing hominin diet related to an emergent shift to subsistence based on the more seasonal secondary grassland savanna resources therefore would have connections with gut size reduction and related brain expansion. The latter also would have interconnections with increasing group sizes and, notably, increasing sociality among early hominins. Increasing sociality and intelligence of hominins in itself could serve to reinforce the changing patterns of subsistence behaviour: increased social cooperation for example would serve well to stimulate cooperation in securing carcasses as part of the Acheulean repertoire of scavenging activities outlined earlier, making these activities more successful. This would stimulate the selection of traits towards incorporation of more meat and other high quality resources, which would stimulate further brain expansion. Thus a process of runaway selection would be started in which dietary shifts, brain expansion and increasing social behaviour would reinforce each other in a progressive way. To summarize, brain expansion and more social cooperation would become possible due to a shift to more high-quality foods (allowing gut-size reduction freeing metabolic space for brain expansion), but would also stimulate the process to continue as more social cooperation and increasing intelligence would open effective ways to exploit these more difficult to obtain resources on the secondary savanna.

Seasonal resource exploitation and variability selection

An adaption to seasonal variability in food resources such as proposed here, a shift to new food sources and a reorganization of the gut system such as proposed by Aiello and Wheeler (Aiello and Wheeler 1995; Aiello 1998), entails a serious divergence in subsistence pattern between the *Australopithecinae* and early *Homo* (*Homo ergaster/erectus*). An important point is the development of a tolerance of serious inter-annual variability in food supplies (as well as clear variation with landscape unit) and the inclusion of new food and variable food sources in the subsistence package. These developments can be seen as signalling a process of "variability selection", a concept recently introduced by Potts (1998). Potts coined the concept of "variability selection" to account for a process whereby evolutionary selection would not select for trend-following habitat-specific adaptation as the result of directional trends such as cooling, deforestation etc., but would select for a tolerance of variability suited to circumstances of complex environmental change (for a more elaborate discussion of this complex concept of "variability selection", see Potts 1998). A tolerance of seasonal food resource fluctuations of increasing magnitude and a reorganization of subsistence behaviour involving different strategies for different seasons and landscape units, is one step towards such a process, on the smallest time-scale involved. The emergence of clearly complementing stone tool technologies with different landscape distributions, perhaps connected to seasonal subsistence strategies (e.g. my model for Developed Oldowan and Acheulean), instead of one basic broad spectrum stone tool technology (Oldowan) can be seen as an archaeological signal to that point. A radiation into previously unoccupied subenvironments, such as the high plain savanna of the Gadeb and Dmanisi (see earlier in this chapter), is a biogeographic sign of this process. It is ultimately expanded when it leads to the first dispersal into Eurasia, into environments substantially different from the African savanna and high altitue savanna. It leads to a difference in strategies of stone tool employment between different geographic regions: the 'Movius line' phenomena. The latter events would seem to be clear, archaeologically visible products of this process of 'variability selection'.

Occupation of temperate Eurasia, with its environments highly variable in geographic space as well as variable on very short (inter-annual) *and* long term (glacial cycle) timescales, in all reality became possible only because of the development of a tolerance of complex variability in early hominins, an environmentally tolerant hominin more specifically signified by *Homo erectus*.

Note added: just as the manuscript of this work was finished, a paper by Manuel Domínguez-Rodrigo appeared in the *Journal of World Prehistory* (Domínguez-Rodrigo 2002). In it, he questions the whole concept of Plio-Pleistocene (Oldowan) hominins as passive scavengers based on a new approach towards cutmark and toothmark frequencies on bones from the Oldowan sites FxJj50 and FLK 22 'Zinj'. He makes a strong argument that hominins were the primary agents of carcass exploitation at these sites (which date to 1.8-1.5 Ma). They obtained carcasses in a very early stage, either by confrontational scavenging or hunting. Domínguez-Rodrigo's work is not uncontroversial, but it should be well noted and if true has implications for what I set out in the current chapter. Where FxJj50 could perhaps be accomodated in the model as representing a locality whereto the products of confrontational scavenging in a riparian environment were brought and further prepared, this is less easy for FLK 22 'Zinj'. If these Oldowan sites represent confrontational scavenging decoupled from my model of confrontational scavenging in riparian woodlands along drainage lines, this would seem to generate a problem for the role I ascribe to the emergence of the Acheulean as a product of confrontational scavenging and acquiring carcasses in an early stage. On the other hand, it could then be argued that the kind of behaviour which I suggest here as a background to the African early Acheulean, found its origin in an emergent confrontational scavenging during the later Oldowan. The emergence of Acheulean tools and behaviours then could be seen as the result of adaptation of these behaviours to the changes in ecological structure, and the new opportunities and intensification of seasonal confrontational scavenging emerging, introduced by the emerging of the secondary savanna with riparian corridors.

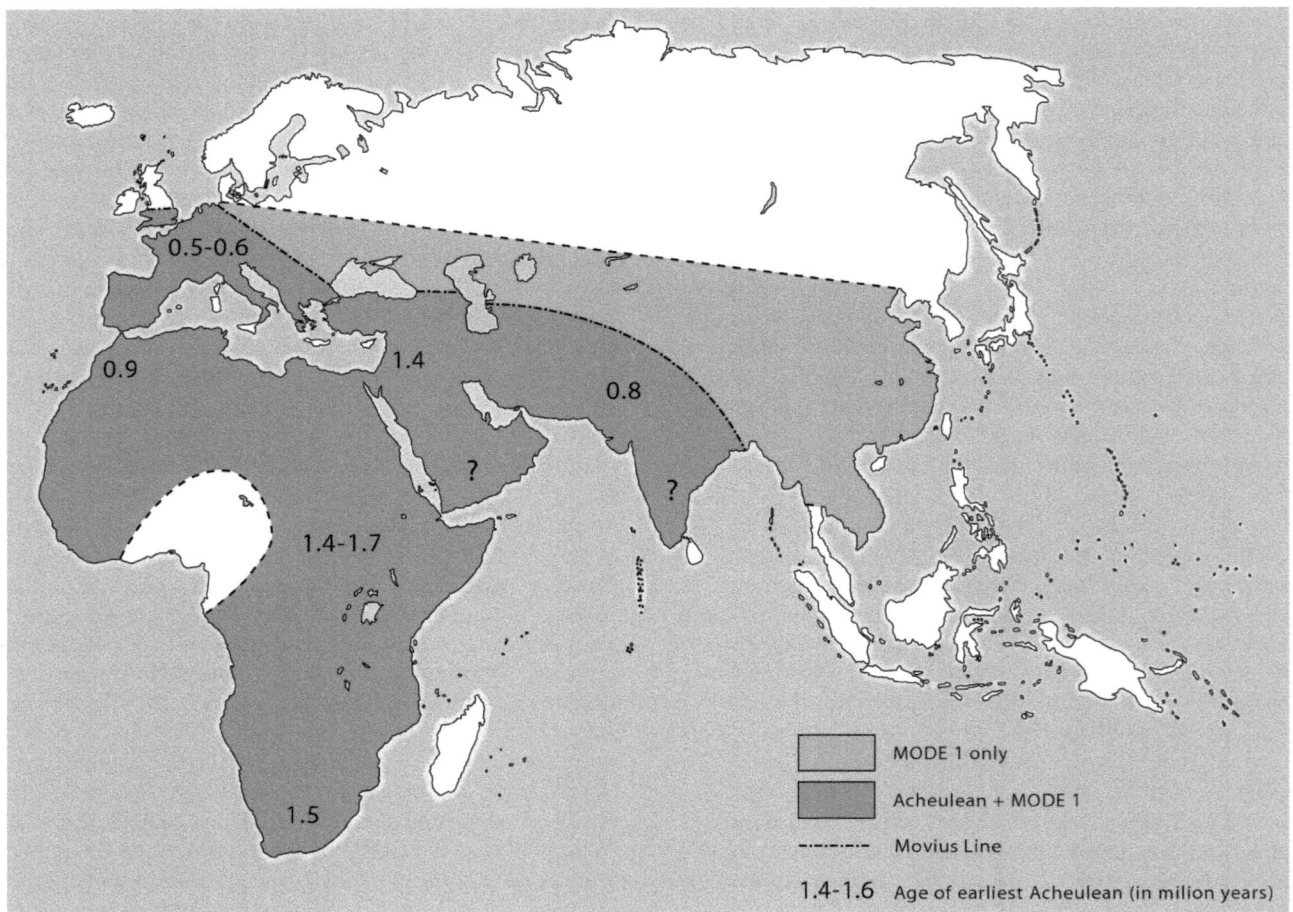

Figure 8: map of the 'Movius line', showing the geographic dichotomy between exclusively 'mode 1' industries in eastern Eurasia, and the presence of 'mode 2' Acheulean alongside 'mode 1' industries in Africa and western Eurasia (separated by the 'Movius line'). The age of earliest occurrences of Acheulean for the latter areas is indicated, in million years. For a discussion of the patterning and possible causes of the dichotomy, see the text (drawing made by Medy Oberendorff).

Chapter 3.2   Out of Africa 1 and the Movius Line enigma

As outlined in the previous chapter, hominins changed subsistence strategies and developed a tolerance of more seasonal environments following the emergence of the dry and more seasonal secondary grasslands in Africa after 1.7 Ma ago. Inside the African/West Asian savanna realm, this led to the development of the Acheulean-Developed Oldowan complex. Geographically, as a prelude to 'Out of Africa 1', the first local steps into previously unoccupied areas with environments more temperate but closely allied to the African savanna were made around 1.5 Ma ago. This concerns the African higher plains (e.g. Gadeb) inside Africa itself and the West Asian fringe of the savanna realm (Dmanisi).

This initiation of occupation of more temperate high-altitude grassland is followed by a move into definite non-tropical environments around 1.3 Ma ago as outlined in chapters 2.2 and 2.3. East Asia up to 40 degrees latitude North, and perhaps parts of the southern Mediterranean fringe of Europe up to a similar latitude were occupied first.

Again, it should be emphasized that this dispersal into the more temperate, seasonal environments of Eurasia was not in any way influenced by the emergence of the Acheulean technocomplex in Africa and neighbouring West Asia. Rather, both phenomena (the emergence of the Acheulean inside the African savanna realm and the nearly contemporaneous first dispersal from Africa into Eurasia) are *symptoms* resulting from a deeper lying cause. It was not the Acheulean which made the dispersal possible: Acheulean did not spread beyond the borders of the initially occupied parts of Africa and West Asia at this stage in prehistory. It was the emergence, forced by eco-climatic changes in Plio-Pleistocene Africa, of a tolerance of more seasonal environments and the development of a certain flexibility in subsistence structuring to cope with seasonal resources which led to both the Acheulean and 'Out of Africa 1'. This increased flexibility in structuring subsistence strategies led to related variations in lithic technology, in which the character of lithic technology became closely adapted to the particularities of the local environment. Different types of environmental structuring led to different types of technological structuring, both on a regional and a continental scale. Hence the emergence of contemporaneous and varied lithic technologies inside Africa (the Acheulean - Developed Oldowan technocomplex) and on a larger scale the emergence of contrasts in the character of the organization of lithic technology between the African savanna realm and the temperate environments of Eurasia. As a result, with this first Early Pleistocene 'Out of Africa' a phenomenon

known as 'the Movius line' (see introductory chapter) emerges in the archaeological record. East Asian (and possibly South European) artefact assemblages from this period appear to be exclusively mode 1 assemblages. This contrasts with the abundant distribution of mode 2 (Acheulean) assemblages in contemporaneous Africa. The dividing line between the geographic areas with and without biface occurrences is known as the 'Movius line'.

It is worth exploring this regional as well as geographic bimodality between mode 1 and mode 2 in lithic technology in more detail. In the previous chapter (3.1), it has been outlined how the Acheulean of Early Pleistocene Africa appears to be a technocomplex which is strictly tied to subsistence strategies unique to the ecological structure of the dry secondary savanna. With this hypothesis in mind, the Movius dichotomy between the lithic industries of Africa/West Asia on the one hand and East Asia on the other immediately is put into perspective. There was no African type dry secondary savanna in those areas of Eurasia where early Pleistocene lithic technology is of an exclusive mode 1 character. This is exactly the reason why it is of an exclusively mode 1 character. The absence of Acheulean east of the Movius line during the Early Pleistocene has therefore nothing to do (contra Swisher *et al.* 1994; Larick and Ciochon 1996; Walker and Sieveking 1962) with a supposed early (Plio-Pleistocene) hominine expansion out of Africa before the 'invention' of the handaxe, nor with cognitive retardation of East Asian hominines (contra Movius 1948), a forest filter barrier (contra Watanabe 1985), nor a (too) quickly advancing expansion combined with hypothetical limited linguistic capacities causing a loss of tradition as in the absence of practice lithic traditions could not be handed over to offspring by oral traditions (contra Toth and Schick 1993). In addition it has in all likelihood no primary cause in availability of alternative raw materials in the form of bamboo in Asia (contra Pope 1985; Watanabe 1985).

The character of the technological dichotomy between 'Asia' and 'Africa' during the Early Pleistocene is consistent with what would be expected from the character of assemblage differentation inside Early Pleistocene 'Africa'. In chapter 3.1, the occurrence within Africa of mode 1 technology (Oldowan and Developed Oldowan) alongside mode 2 (Acheulean) was linked to seasons and landscape parts with necessarily large size daily foraging rounds, high carnivore competition and limited, dispersed resource availability. To a certain extent similar characteristics of resource distribution and foraging character are to be expected from Pleistocene temperate Eurasia. In temperate grasslands, resources are more dispersed and patchy, less predictable and many are highly seasonal, with a notable winter dearth in availability of many of these resources. Plants with 'underground storage organs' (USO's), an important carbohydrate source, seasonally have a poor above-ground visibility (Marean 1997). Many of the plant foods in temperate environments come in small packages only and require intensive collection strategies (Marean 1997). As a result, it is to be expected that hominine subsistence strategies in these environments will be highly variable, and that they will include large daily foraging rounds and extended time budgets. Resource encounters and gathering events will generally be of an *ad hoc* character, often unpredictable in time and space and character. Toolkits employed can be expected to show characteristics adapted to versatility in use and ease of production linked to lack of predictability of action. A flake-core technology is an example of such a simple and versatile technology and therefore one of the archaeological signatures expected for the earliest occupation of Eurasia. Hominines would be expected to carry cores and raw materials rather than tools, and to produce simple but efficient tools from these *ad hoc* as the situation demanded when encountering resources in the landscape. Hominines would need to possess flexibility to cope with these kinds of situations. This flexibility already had to be in existence before any successful attempt could be made to enter temperate latitudes. As was argued in a previous chapter, this flexibility was born of the increasing seasonality and emergence of the dry secondary savanna in Africa.

For the earliest occupation prior to 0.5 Ma the chrono-geographic pattern outlined in chapter 2.3 amounts to an apparent northern limit of dispersal at 40° Northern latitude throughout Eurasia. Limits to hominine dispersal would be set by resource densities and time budgets. The winter would be the most critical barrier at temperate latitudes. During wintertime, resources are at a low and daylight time is at a minimum, putting critical constraints on foraging time budgets. This while demands for energy intake would be at a high, because daily foraging area sizes would be stretched to their limits. The 40° Northern latitude limit to Early Pleistocene dispersal in Eurasia corresponds (*cf.* Dennell and Roebroeks 1996) to a minimum daylight duration of 10 hours, indicating an approximate minimum daily foraging time threshold of that extent. This would imply that foraging time budgets were stretched to their very limits during the earliest occupation of temperate Asia and especially southern Europe.

It appears that changes in mobility and foraging strategy in connection with versatility of mind rather than technology were the keys to 'Out of Africa'. The character of toolkits would be determined by employed, and available choice of, foraging strategies and time budgets. Hence, it appears totally inappropriate to consider perceived technological advances (e.g. the handaxe) as the mechanism that made dispersal possible. It also points out that comparative studies into technological complexity of (stone) artefacts do not necessarily yield results related to the relative level of cognition of the hominines who made them, although such a relationship is often assumed in such studies. A very 'simple' stone tool technology can be embedded in a very complex (in a cognitive sense) subsistence strategy allowing survival under harsh conditions. Australian Aborigines are ethnographic examples which witness to that. It is the cognition behind the strategy of stone tool employment which carries significance.

Part IV

Breaching the "Movius line' and re-establishing it, and the structure of the earliest Acheulean of Europe

Part III concluded with an hypothesis for the early Pleistocene 'Movius line' phenomenon. In the period of 0.9-0.5 Ma, this Early Pleistocene 'Movius line' is breached as Acheulean sites start to appear in areas where they were previously absent. In the case of Europe, this appears to coincide with the earliest occupation of Europe north of the Pyrenees. Part IV starts with a brief chronological outline of when and where the 'Movius line' is breached. It then ponders the structure of the earliest Northwest European Acheulean, by means of an in-depth study of handaxe production and discard at the 0.5 Ma British Acheulean site of Boxgrove, prying for clues with relation to planning depths and degrees of 'displacement'. Differences are noted with regard to the African Early Pleistocene Acheulean.

Chapter 4.1   Geographical developments in the spreading of Acheulean technology, 0.9-0.5 Ma ago

In chapter 3.1, it is discussed how Acheulean technology appears in Africa around 1.4 to 1.7 Ma ago. The FAD ('First Appearance Date') of the Acheulean is still floating somewhat. The oldest securely dated Acheulean site is that of Konso-Gardula in Ethiopia, where Acheulean tools have been recovered from underneath a tuff layer which has associated ^{40}Ar/^{39}Ar ages of 1.34 ± 0.4 and 1.38 ± 0.7 Ma (Asfaw *et al*. 1992). Some of the earliest Acheulean occurrences in Olduvai Gorge might date as far back as 1.6-1.7 Ma (Clark 1994). During this early period of Acheulan occurrence, the presence of the Acheulean is geographically restricted to the African tropical savanna environments. At that time, these occur in East and Southeast Africa, as well as in parts of West Asia (e.g. the Levant), as outlined in chapter 2. An explanation for this 'Movius line' phenomena has been summarized in chapter 3.2.

A new 'Movius line'

Starting around 0.8-0.9 Ma, after an apparent stasis of at least 0.5 and possibly 0.8 Ma during which the Acheulean does not appear outside the mentioned African savanna realm, the geographical area over which the Acheulean is present expands. This expansion culminates in the intrusion of both the Acheulean and the first hominines into Northwest Europe around 0.5 to 0.6 Ma, after which this proliferation of the Acheulean appears to come to a halt. There is no solid evidence for the occurrence of bifacial tool technologies in Asia until after 0.2 Ma (Schick 1994; see also chapter 2.1). As has been discussed in chapter 2.1, recently presented evidence for a purported early Acheulean occurrence in East Asia as early as 0.8 Ma (the Baise sites from southern China) is weak.

This phenomenon is strongly reminiscent of the earlier Early Pleistocene 'Movius line'. It is less easy to explain, for at the time of this second Acheulean 'explosion' the old correlation with a typical African savanna habitat is abandoned. The strong correlation of Acheulean sites with a drainage line context also disappears. The role of Acheulean technology therefore seems to change, perhaps because it is included in changing subsistence behaviour. This would explain why the Acheulean undergoes an expansion in the period 0.8-0.5 Ma as documented below. The reappearance of a second 'Movius line' with an altered geographical location remains something of an enigma, though perhaps it has to do with east-west trends in continentality across Eurasia and the ways this is influencing ecological structure.

0.9-0.8 Ma: the appearance of Acheulean in Marocco

As related in chapter 1.5, the first evidence for hominine occupation in the Casablanca sequence of Atlantic Morocco dates to just before the Brunhes-Matuyama geomagnetic reversal, i.e. about 0.8-0.9 Ma ago. The oldest dated site is the Thomas-1 Quarry site, dated to about 0.9 Ma by means of the reversed palaeomagnetic polarity of the sediments and biostratigraphy (Raynal *et al*. 1995b, 2001). Thomas-1 Quarry concerns an Acheulean site. Hence it clearly concerns both the initial occupation of this area and the extension of the geographical area over which the Acheulean occurs.

0.8-0.6 Ma: the appearance of Acheulean in Pakistan

Around the same time, the first Acheulean sites appear in Pakistan. At Dina and Jalalpur, artefacts including Acheulean handaxes have been recovered from an *in situ* stratigraphic context (Rendell and Dennell 1985; Dennell 1998). Their sedimentary context consists of folded Upper Siwalik sediments. A combination of fission track datings and palaeomagnetic investigations of the Eastern Potwar anticline suggests that the folding took place between 0.4 and 0.6 Ma; the Acheulean tools embedded *within* these folded sediments hence date to *before* 0.4 to 0.6 Ma. At Dina, palaeomagnetic investigations suggest that the Brunhes-Matuyama boundary occurs just below the find horizon (Rendell and Dennell 1985; Dennell 1998) indicating an age close to 0.8 Ma.

Occurrence of the Acheulean of a similar age in the peninsula of India is much less well established. Many rich Acheulean assemblages on the Indian peninsula remain undated but are at least of Middle Pleistocene (>0.35 Ma) age (Misra 1987; Mishra 1992; Clark 1994). One find locality has been suggested to date to the earliest Middle Pleistocene. At Bori (Maharasthra, in the western part of peninsular India), 152 artefacts including 6 rather crude bifaces of 'Abbevillian' type have been recovered from fluviatile deposits that are both under- and overlain by a volcanic ash that has been ^{39}Ar/^{40}Ar dated to 0.67 ± 0.03 Ma (Mishra *et al*. 1995). If the ash that forms a thin tephra band in the fluviatile clay deposits above the find horizon is not reworked sediment from the thick basal tephra deposit lower in the sequence, in which the fluviatile gravel deposit containing the artefacts is incised, this would date the earliest Acheulean of peninsular India to the same timespan as that of Pakistan, slightly older than the earliest Acheulean sites in Europe and slightly younger than those in the Casablanca area of Northwest Africa. Yet, there remain some questions about the age of this site, that warrants caution. The radiometric dates are disputed and it has been suggested, based on similarities in mineralogy, that the tephra is actually tephra from the 0.075 Ma Toba eruption (Mishra 1999). Note that Mishra's argument for validity of the older age (Mishra 1999: 84) is not a strong argument It is solely based on a typological argument in which the roughness of the handaxes leads to an assignment to the 'Early Acheulean'.

0.6-0.5 Ma: the appearance of Acheulean in Europe

In southern Europe, Acheulean sites appear around 0.5 Ma. One of the oldest dated Acheulean sites in this part of Europe is Fontana Ranuccio, where handaxes and other artefacts were recovered from a tephra layer dated by K/Ar to 458 ± 6 ka, while the fauna indicates an age equivalent to OIS 11 and a temperate, open environment (Segre and Ascenzi 1984; Mussi 2001). In addition to stone handaxes, this site yielded some interesting examples of bifaces fashioned from elephant bone.

The oldest Acheulean sites in Northwest Europe are of similar age and at the same time represent the oldest occupation of this part of Eurasia. Boxgrove in Sussex, Great Britain (see chapter 4.2), is one of those earliest sites, if not the earliest site, with an age of about 0.42-0.52 Ma on combined stratigraphic and biostratigraphic grounds, correlating to OIS 13 (Roberts and Parfitt 1999). The oldest Acheulean Somme Valley sites at Cagny have ages of about 0.5 to perhaps 0.6 Ma (Tuffreau and Antoine 1995; Tuffreau et al. 1997a), spanning OIS 10-15.

0.8 Ma: new Acheulean dispersals through the Israeli Rift Valley?

The discussed evidence suggests an 0.9-0.5 Ma Acheulean proliferation into the western parts of Eurasia. It may concern multiple proliferation phases, one of which takes place around the Brunhes-Matuyama reversal at 0.8 Ma, another around 0.6-0.5 Ma. It concerns a proliferation in areas some of which were previously occupied but lacked the Acheulean, and some of which were not occupied at all until these hominines with Acheulean technology appeared. It also concerns environments, certainly in the case of Northwestern Europe, which are unlike the African savanna in ecological structure (see chapter 2.3).

Additional and intriguing evidence for a possible new flux of the Acheulean from Africa to Eurasia at 0.8 Ma comes from the Near East. At this age, it lines up well with the evidence from Eurasia itself for a new Acheulean proliferation. At Gesher Benot Ya'aqov in the Israeli rift valley, an occurrence of an Acheulean of a rather unusual kind for this area has been excavated (Goren-Inbar et al. 2002, 2000, 1992, 1991; Saragusti and Goren-Inbar 2001; Werker and Goren-Inbar 2001; Goren-

Inbar and Saragusti 1996; Belfer-Cohen and Goren-Inbar 1994; Belitzky et al. 1991). Gesher Benot Ya'aqov is a spectacular site where numerous handaxes and cleavers along with other tools (flake tools, choppers) have been preserved, as well as abundant organic material. The assemblage bears characteristics which are unlike those of other Acheulean assemblages from the Early/Middle Pleistocene Near East (both earlier sites such as 'Ubeidiya, Evron and Latamne, and later sites) and later Acheulean sites in Eurasia, but does have parallels in Africa (Goren-Inbar and Saragusti 1996; Goren-Inbar et al. 2000; Saragusti and Goren-Inbar 2001). There is a strong emphasis on basalt as raw material for both handaxes and cleavers. Blanks for handaxes were struck from prepared boulder cores, a common technique for making bifaces in the African Early Acheulean. This is the first occurrence outside Africa of a biface assemblage where bifaces are systematically fashioned on large flakes (Goren-Inbar et al. 2000: 946).The cleavers make up 40% of the bifacial tools at Gesher Benot Ya'agov, which is a very high percentage, and again something only encountered in the African Early Acheulean. One of the techniques employed to fashion the cleavers is the Kombewa technique: at an age of 0.8 Ma, this is the oldest occurrence of the Kombewa technique outside east Africa (Goren-Inbar et al. 2000: 946) and the only Eurasian one on this scale. The reduction sequences at the site are complex and vary with regard to tool type. Different raw materials were chosen for different tool categories. The chaines operatoires are much more complex than at 'Ubeidiya (Belfer-Cohen and Goren-Inbar 1994).

The site consists of multiple archaeological levels. Palaeomagnetic investigations show that these straddle a polarity transition from reversed to normal, a transition which is interpreted to represent the Brunhes-Matuyama transition at 0.8 Ma. The archaeological levels yield a Biharian fauna, pointing to the end of the Early Pleistocene or the start of the Middle Pleistocene. This fauna primarily derives from the upper half of the sequence, and contains African as well as Asian taxa. The full sequence of archaeological layers at Gesher Benot Ya'agov probably represents some 0.10 to 0.15 Ma, which would largely place Gesher Benot Ya'agov in OIS 19 (Goren-Inbar et al. 2000). Apart from the stone tools and rich faunal assemblage, the site contains evidence for the consumption of nuts, evidence which consists of pitted hammers and anvils as well as botanical remains of several edible nut species (Goren-Inbar et al. 2002). In addition, an intriguing wooden artefact has been recovered: a polished plank of Salix wood, carefully cut diagonally to the plane of a large branch or treetrunk (Belitzky et al. 1991).

The palaeoenvironment of the site complex represents a lake shore, the shore of palaeo-lake Hula. The presence of a rich Acheulean in such a context differs markedly with what is known for the Early Acheulean in Africa, where the Acheulean occurs in a drainage line context only (see chapter 3.1). It foreshadows, however, the patterns later found in the Acheulean of Europe. This could indicate that the expansion of the Acheulean around 0.8 Ma represents a shift in hominine behaviour, and it could indicate a changing role for Acheulean technology. Signs of this changing role might be present in other aspects of the lithic assemblage too. For example, both handaxes and boulder cores occur together at Gesher Benot Ya'agov (Belfer-Cohen and Goren-Inbar 1994; Goren-Inbar and Saragusti 1996), which is unlike the African Early Acheulean (it should be added that it is not clear whether the handaxes found at Gesher Benot Ya'agov and the boulder cores form one local sequence from core working to endproduct discard. Why this is of interest, will become clear in chapter 4.2 on the handaxe reduction sequence at Boxgrove).

The possible shift in behaviour could have induced the renewed colonization event(s) in the period 0.8-0.5 Ma, of which the primary occupation of Europe north of the Alps is part. It is tempting to consider a shift from confrontational scavenging towards full-scale hunting, such as evidenced for the early occupation of northwest Europe (e.g. Schöningen), as an important aspect of this behavioural shift and accompanying colonization process.

Re-enter the 'Movius line'

One of the enigmatic aspects of the 0.8-0.5 Ma proliferation of the Acheulean into Eurasia is that it does not reach east Asia. From well-represented in western Europe, the Near East and the Indian peninsula, it grades into less well abundant in the eastern part of Europe and the western part of central Asia, to nonexistent in east and southeast Asia. This re-appearance of a (geographically altered) Movius line is difficult to explain. An attempt to sum up some possible related issues will be made in chapter 4.

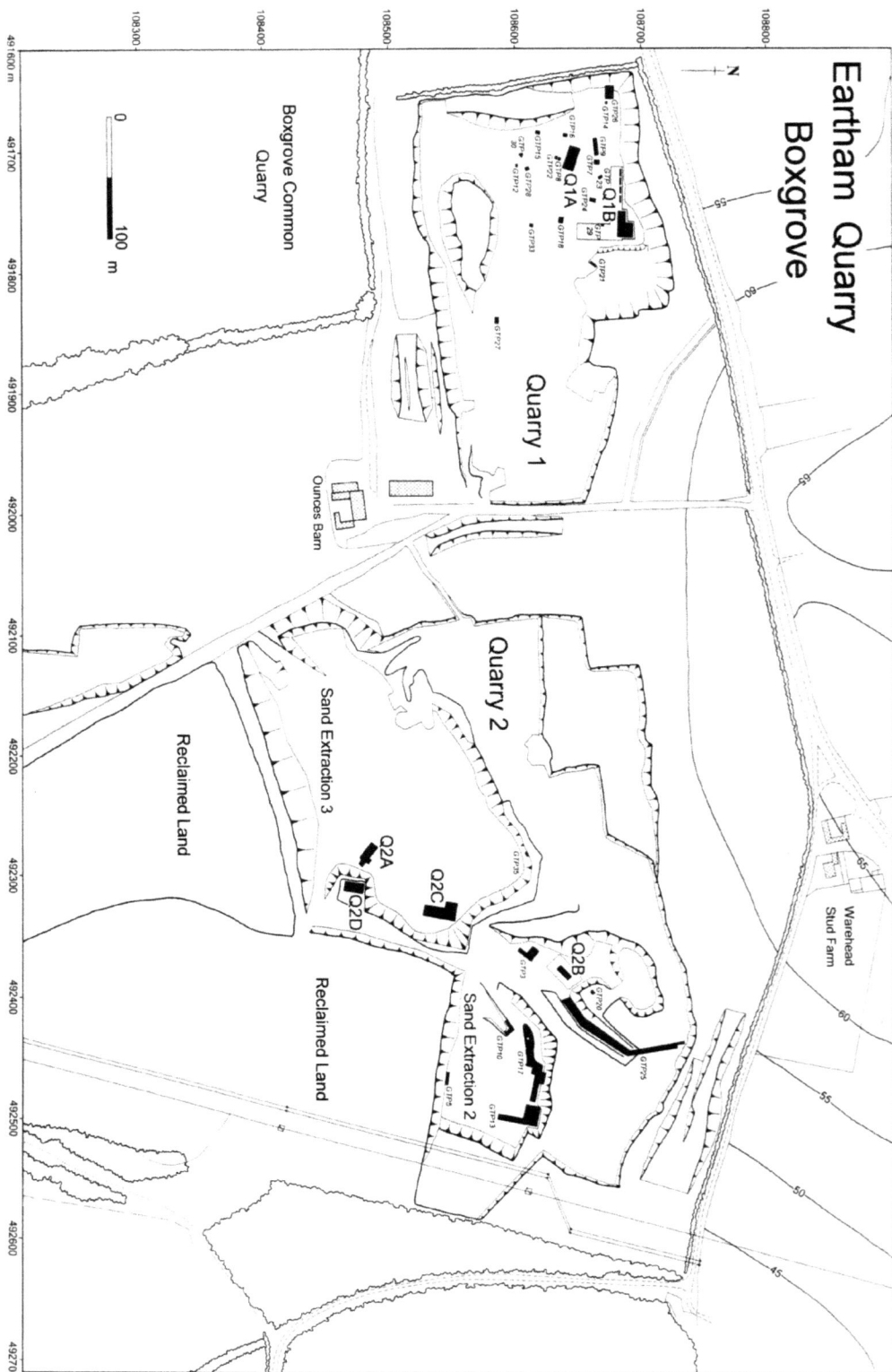

Figure 9: map of Boxgrove quarry, Sussex, Great Britain (from Roberts and Parfitt 1999)

Chapter 4.2   A Veil of Handaxes: a 'scatters and patches' approach to the Acheulean landscape at Boxgrove, Sussex, and beyond [1]

1.   This chapter is dedicated to the memory of the late Cees Klaassen (1926-2000), one of the colourful members of the 1996 Dutch team at Boxgrove.

Introduction: palimpsests, statics and dynamics

Behavioural reconstructions for the Palaeolithic are traditionally heavily biased towards intra-site analysis of high density sites from a presumably undisturbed context with a high temporal integrity. This has yielded problems for the Middle and Lower Palaeolithic where, unlike the Upper Palaeolithic, unambiguously structured intra-site spatial patterning appears to be elusive. This in turn has promoted views where indeed archaic hominine behaviour is thought to have been less structured, most notably with regard to structuring principles such as planning and curation, or a structured use of space. The lack of these in turn is usually taken to indicate a lack of social/organizational structure.

Problems with discerning 'structure' in patterning and, if present, giving meaning to those perceived structures in the archaeological record, are abundant. These problems range from issues like the reality and meaning of 'living floors' which provide the basal referring unit (discussed a.o. by Binford (1987)) to the related but more general problems of time depth and spatio-temporal resolution of archeo-geological deposits (e.g. Binford 1987; Stern 1993, 1994). This all boils down to problems with the palimpsest character of the archaeological record in which the dynamics of multiple temporally unrelated activities are transformed into one static (and often fragmentary) record (e.g. Binford 1982; Stern 1993), or multiple of such and difficult to link static records. These problems will have to be addressed before other problems can be tackled such as infering organisational structure from inter- or intra-site structure. While structure in spatial patterning on intra-site level remains elusive for the major part of the Lower and Middle Palaeolithic (cf. Kolen 1999), structure on an inter-site level, or landscape scale, must exist. Both a niche geography (associated with a primate pattern of land use) and a cultural geography (associated with modern human ethnographic examples of land use) cf. Binford (1987), lead to structured patterning on a landscape scale because in both systems specific locales in the landscape will see different activities or combinations of activities. If we are to optimize our understanding of the broader organizational structure of palaeolithic societies, we must therefore not only look at structure on an intra-site level (in the sense of:

structure on a scale of a few square metres), but most notably for structural variation on a landscape scale. Of course, this does not mean that patterning on intra-site level is irrelevant. But it can be questioned whether it can be meaningfully resolved, with structures distinguished and interpreted, without the context of inter-site patterning on a landscape scale. Archaeology is concerned with both long-term stability and change of systems (see Binford 1992). Intra-site activity as a suite of anecdotal events with an unknown time depth therefore is only interesting when put into a context of wide-scale organizational systems, and changes therein. It is not interesting to get engrossed in what series of difficult to relate events happened on site B and who sat where while knapping scatter 'z', for the purpose of a holistic site re-enactment approach only. It is more important to know how and why all these behavioural elements eventually came to be performed at site B as part of the overall behavioural strategies of its performers. We learn from placing activities at site-level or intra-site level in a wider behavioural system. Taking that step is a problem because the structure of the archaeological record hampers attempts at putting observable singular chains of behavioural events into a wider behavioural context with each other (by singular chains of behavioural elements are meant reconstructable events like a knapping episode as reconstructed from refitting: this is both a chain of events as well as a singular event because the temporal dimension with regard to other discernable singular events at the site cannot be established). The problem is therefore not just, and not primarily, that unrelated temporally disparate activities 'diffuse' into each other at intra-site scale because of a palimpsest problem. The problem is that this also obscures the possibility of discerning the links between the elements that make up the dynamic system of behaviour behind it, in which people move through the landscape and live according to the way their life and therefore behaviour in the landscape was structured. The problem is not that we cannot discern what belongs together; the problem is that we cannot discern what does not belong together while still being part of one behavioural system. This has been discussed in depth by Binford (1982). A major problem is that we have difficulty in discerning the repositioning of behavioural systems in the landscape (Binford 1982) because we can only discern either singular chains of behavioural events, or their static palimpsest outcome. This is important to understand, because this repositioning of behavioural systems is the essence of system dynamics. There is a suite of reasons why the translation from the visible patterning of the archaeological record on a landscape scale to operational system dynamics of past hominine societies is not straightforward. This static archaeological pattern is due to the precipitational effect of a multitude of dynamic actions performed as part of one or more dynamic systems of behaviour (cf. Binford 1982). The preserved picture not only has a palimpsest character, even when a very short formational timescale can be ascertained, but it is, to quote Binford (1982: 17), also due to an "*interaction between the cultural system and the processes which are conditioning burial of cultural debris*". We should add that this includes long-term taphonomic history.

Defining 'landscape' in an archaeological sense certainly is a problem. Extensively preserved stretches of palaeo-landscapes, or major parts of palaeo-landscapes are very rare. Moreover, with only few exceptions a 'living' landscape is a dynamic, constantly changing entity; only a static outcome of this can be preserved however. Added to the problems of time depth and timescale resolution (cf. Stern 1993) of depositional units, this makes the concept of 'palaeo-landscape' a problematic one (Stern 1994). 'Palaeo-landscapes' are not preserved, only palimpsest landscapes are. For the sake of convenience, I will retain the term 'palaeo-landscape' in this chapter, while noting that it does refer to an idealized and therefore immobilized 'static' snapshot of a past dynamic system.

One of the seemingly most problematic archaeological aspects of both inter- and intra-site data, as Binford (1982: 17) has pointed out in his seminal work *The Archaeology of Place*, is that "*demonstrably associated things may never have occurred together as an organized body of material during any given occupation*". This is a serious point to consider, because this element is important in the analysis of the archaeological record of Boxgrove now following. One and the same locale (or 'site') may have served several different activities at different moments in time, even if these activities were performed as part of one single system of behaviour, because these systems were continuously repositioned in the landscape due to mobility and seasonal or even daily variations in activity.

Moreover, even spatio-temporally closely associated, different activities yielding different artefacts may not be directly related in terms of a functionally integrated performance – there may be a long-term relation however, if some of these are preparatory (whether consciously or not) to activities at another landscape locality. Such preparatory actions may be very divers in character. They are linked however to activities elsewhere in the landscape.

One thing that is certain is that inter- and intra-site patterns are clearly related and mutually dependent, because both have an origin in the same dynamic system(s). A solution should be sought which is based on this realization. Even if singular events of a palimpsest on intra-site scale are impossible to link, and even if it would be possible to ascertain that they are *not* linked in the sense of one continuous temporal-behavioural action, it might be possible that they can be successfully 'hyperlinked' if they can be assigned their proper place in the larger dynamic system (or systems) on a landscape scale. This is in the first place highly dependent on the temporal resolution of the sedimental envelope in which they are contained (cf. Stern 1993), and even if that time depth can be ascertained to be relatively concise, there still is a blurring factor because multiple behavioural systems can be in use at the 'same' time, and even single systems can be expected to show a clear variational 'bandwidth' in forms of behaviour, in which for example the mood of the individual or the make-up and/or size of a group influences whether a Levallois flake or a handaxe is used.

All this has a bearing on investigating archaeological inter-site patterning. Such patterning represents a "*long repetitive pattern in the 'positioning' of adaptive systems in geographic space*" (Binford 1982: 6) and therefore also a palimpsest outcome of the continuous repositioning of exploitational systems in the landscape in all their forms of random variation allowed by the behavioural 'bandwidth' of the system. It is a sum of the activity affordance of the landscape units mixed with constraints by the behavioural 'bandwidth'. Likewise, intra-site patterns are such a sum for a given locality (see Binford 1982 for a view from an ethno-archaeological perspective; and Roebroeks *et al.* 1995 for an archaeological case study). An obvious trap that emerges from this realization with regard to intra-site interpretations, is that preparatory actions to activity 'x' and the spatio-temporal distinct final act of 'x' itself, because of the interplay between the continuous repositioning of adaptive systems in the landscape and the palimpsest character of the archaeological record, can become associated at one locale and be mistaken for one singular *ad hoc* on the spot action with little planning depth involved. In intra-site interpretations, it probably has been mistaken as such many times. For example, I will argue that this has happened with regard to the topic of handaxe fabrication and use at Boxgrove. We should look for Middle Range Theory which is able to discern between real *ad hoc* artefact fabrication with little planning depth, and the situation whereby different stages in a reduction sequence performed in a spatially distinct way become spatially associated solely through the interplay between palimpsest formation and behavioural system repositioning through time (at various shorter and longer timescales). There lies a challenge. What is needed is to bring back the dynamics behind the formation of the static record.

A significant first step is taken if for example items that appear to be consistently associated as an organized body of materials from one organizational system at site localities - e.g. handaxes and handaxe manufacturing debris - can be shown to be not, in the sense of not representing a behavioural continuum. How to take this step?

In this chapter, the focus will be on the life trajectory of handaxes from the early stages of the European Lower Palaeolithic, with Boxgrove in the UK providing a case study. This exercise will provide us with a partial glimpse of the dynamics of organization in the European Acheulean. Although partial, it will be informative with regard to strategic aspects employed by the Acheulean hominines in question, providing a touch of insight into degrees of planning depth and (parts of) subsistence strategies.

Methodology: Isaac's "scatters and patches"

When viewed on a landscape scale, archaeological materials occur as spatially restricted dense patches (traditional 'sites') which are often embedded in a low density scatter of isolated or small sets of artefact occurrences (Isaac 1981; Isaac et al. 1981; Stern 1993; Roebroeks et al. 1995). This concept of "patches" in a low density "scatter" has been well articulated by Isaac (e.g. 1981) and archaeologically probed by a.o. Blumenschine and Masao (1991) for Lower Palaeolithic Olduvai, Stern (1993) for Lower Palaeolithic Koobi Fora, and Roebroeks et al. (1995) in the Saalian (Middle Palaeolithic) levels of the Dutch Maastricht Belvédère quarry.

One of the research questions of these studies was whether or not the "patches" differ in character from the low density background "scatter" in which they are embedded beyond just differences in artefact density. Whether or not they are, is case dependent. For example, they clearly are in the Saalian levels of the Dutch Maastricht Belvédère quarry (Roebroeks et al. 1995). They appear to be not so in the Lower Okote Member of Koobi Fora (Stern 1993), where the "patches" appear to be places where the palimpsest of the "scatter" simply is thicker (for a similar observation concerning the 'living floors' at several African Early Palaeolithic localities, see Binford (1987)). A "scatter and patches" approach thus gives clues to the spatially continuous or discontinuous character of different activities in the landscape during formation of the archaeological record in question. It tracks different modes of formation of the archaeological palimpsest. The archaeological precipitation patterns of some activities are spatially continuous, some are not and spatially restricted. The interplay between these two might provide a route towards a better understanding with regard to organizational aspects of hominine behaviour. It should be stressed, however, that the pattern might be different for different landscape units and therefore should not necessarily be equated with the full extent of organizational structure of archaic hominine behaviour: this would produce the danger of creating contrasts which are only due to sample problems by virtue of differential behaviour in various landscape units and not due to real 'grand' organizational aspects of past hominine behaviour. In this sense for example, the apparent contrast between the Koobi Fora LOM (Stern 1993) and the Belvédère quarry Saalian levels (Roebroeks et al. 1995) should not be overstressed. Ideally, one should seek to sample multiple landscape units but it is here that problems of temporal-spatial correlation become paramount.

A proper "scatter and patches" approach looks at both density and assemblage content variations over the landscape, and not just at one of these only. It takes note of technology, typology, raw materials distribution, and takes into account refit information as well as geological and taphonomical information. It seeks to link various stages of lithic reduction or faunal processing, as far as discernable, and their distributional aspects. Individual items (artefacts) should not be regarded as typological items only, but it should be acknowledged that there is a history behind all of them before they became embedded in the static archaeological record which is the end product of these cumulative histories. Somewhere in this static record, traces of the historical dynamic trajectory should be present, because these (and not just the end results) can also fossilize. In a few occasions, they are indeed discernable. Information is to be gained from them when the links can be re-established, bringing back some dynamism to the static palimpsest. Such is the endeavour undertaken below.

Boxgrove (OIS 13, Sussex, UK): a case study

The Boxgrove (Eartham Quarry) site in Sussex, in the southern part of Great Britain, represents one of the oldest, if not the oldest, archaeological site of Northwest Europe. It also is a very spectacular site, with well-preserved archaeology on a large stretch of a preserved palaeo-landscape representing a fossil beach. The following short outline of the basic geology of the site is based on the site monography (Roberts and Parfitt 1999).

The site context represents a raised beach that once stretched in front of a large chalk cliff (which has been estimated to have been at least 60 metres high). The fossil beach deposits stretch for several tens of kilometres (at least 30), and are exposed in several quarries. They are now located some 12 km north of the current shoreline, and have been raised to +43 m OD. The marine and lagoonal deposits in question are known as the 'Slindon Sands and Silts', while the fossil beach is designated as the

85

Goodwood-Slindon raised beach. The relevant part of the sedimentary sequence which contains the rich Acheulean archaeology are lagoonal silts (the Slindon Silts), designated as unit 4. They overlie the marine Slindon Sands (unit 3). Unit 4 is capped by a paleosol (unit 4c), which itself is overlain by a brickearth (unit 5), representing a phase of deteriorating climate. At points, there is chalk rubble from a cliff collapse which caps unit 4. Unit 4 sediments show signs of loading, attesting to a wet soft substrate. Within unit 4, an extensive scatter of *in situ* archaeology has been preserved, most notably in unit 4c/d, including a few hundred finely made handaxes, some informal cores and a few flake tools, and large amounts of debitage. The latter can for a large part be related to the knapping of handaxes. Primary knapping scatters are recognizable, up to the point of suggestions as to the actual position of the flintknapper in respect to the preserved scatter. Hence horizontal disturbance is minimal in at least some parts of the site. The archaeological horizon can be traced almost continuously over several hundreds of metres at Boxgrove Quarry. It has been sampled with several archaeological trenches and geological test pits, spread over two sub-quarries: Quarry 1 (Q1) in the west and Quarry 2 (Q2) in the east. A very rich concentration of handaxes was encountered in a part of Quarry 1 (Quarry 1B), in deposits which suggest the presence of a freshwater spring. In the same part of the quarry, a hominine tibia and tooth remains have been found.

The unit 4c/d sediments represent a comparatively short timespan, to be measured in hundreds of years rather than thousands or ten thousands of years. The extremely well-preserved, relatively undisturbed archaeological horizon and the large extent over which it has been sampled, along with the probably short timespan it represents, make Boxgrove a unique case of a well-sampled set of activities on a palaeo-landscape, with high temporal integrity. As such, Boxgrove provides a unique opportunity for an in-depth analysis of behavioural patterning in the early European Acheulean.

Discernable lithic stages

From flake attribute and refitting studies, three separate stages of handaxe production are evidenced within the archaeological assemblages which sample the Boxgrove unit 4c/d palaeo-landscape artefact distribution. These distinct elements are represented by:

1.	*decortication debitage and debitage from primary working (thinning) of nodules (up to creation of a handaxe 'roughout');*
1a.	*isolated roughouts;*

2.	*debitage from a further thinning and finishing phase;*
3a.	*isolated finished handaxes (sometimes with refitting tranchets);*
3b.	*isolated resharpening flakes (tranchets).*

These listed elements are distinct. Refitting evidence is available for all three main phases, with sequences of refitting decortication and initial nodule reduction debitage, and sequences of refitting thinning and finishing flakes. But hardly any direct refitting evidence links one phase to another. There are no examples of thinning and finishing debitage sequences fitting to any of the recovered handaxes. All that fits to the handaxes are occasional tranchet flakes, presumably representing resharpening. Likewise, it seems that no sequence through to thinning and finishing, which includes the phase of decortication, is present. So basically, the three separate behavioural elements that make up the record are:

1.	*decortication and roughing out;*
2.	*thinning and finishing;*
3.	*employment of finished handaxes.*

And these appear to be spatio-temporal *separate* behavioural elements.

Non-handaxe context

Apart from various debitage phases of handaxe manufacture and finished handaxes, the Boxgrove assemblage contains a limited but clear number of cores and core reduction sequences with a rather expedient/unstandardized character (see e.g. Bergman and Roberts 1988; Roberts and Parfitt 1999). Apparent hammerstones, bone percussors and antler percussors are present. Antler percussors are well worn, attesting to a long lifespan; the bone percussors look more 'expedient' and suggest the use of fresh bones (Pitts and Roberts 1997). Retouched flakes and flake tools are few but present, as are a number of 'used flakes'. Interestingly, it appears that some flakes produced as part of the handaxe thinning/finishing sequences were set apart and used.

Some refitting examples

The three separate behavioural elements discussed for the Boxgrove handaxe production and use sequence can all be demonstrated by refit examples from the site:

Figure 10: refitted nodule from Boxgrove (GTP 17, Quarry 2) with a central cavity representing an handaxe roughout. This refitted nodule represents the primary decortication and roughing-out stage in handaxe manufacture (phase 1 in this study). The missing roughout has been characteristically transported for further finishing elsewhere (from Pitts and Roberts 1997; photograph courtesy of Mark Roberts, the Boxgrove project).

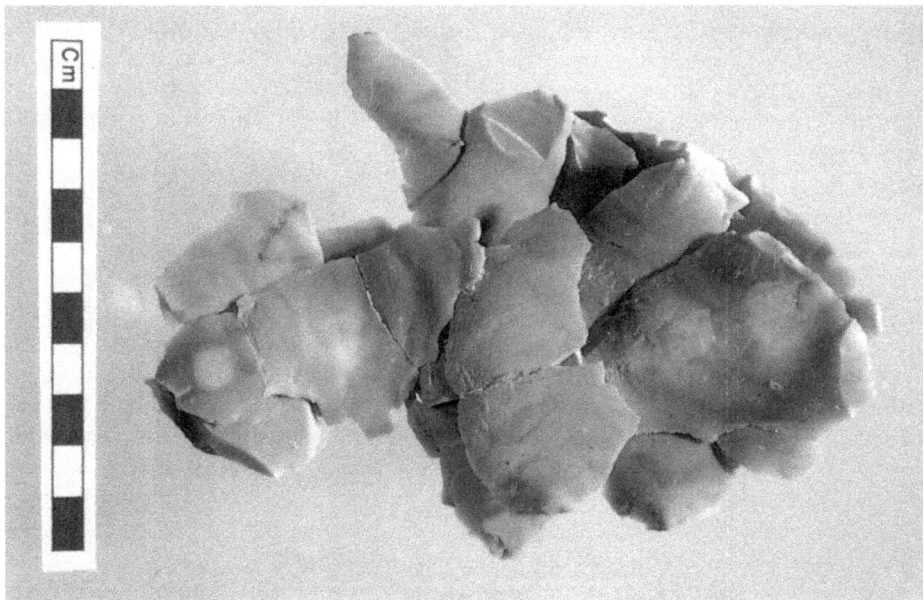

Figure 11: refitted handaxe thinning and finishing flakes, representing phase 2 in this study (from Pitts and Roberts 1997; photograph courtesy of Mark Roberts, the Boxgrove project)

87

Figure 12: finished Boxgrove handaxe, representing phase 3a in this study. Without exception, no debitage from the thinning and finishing stages fit to handaxes at Boxgrove. Only tranchet flakes (resharpening flakes, phase 3b) do. Photograph by author.

phase 1 - one of the most 'complete' examples of a refitting sequence comes from GTP17 (the "Horse Butchery Site") in Quarry 2 and it is a very instructive one. Here, a nodule initially containing at least 70% cortex was reduced to a handaxe roughout: there the sequence stops and the resulting roughout is missing (Roberts and Parfitt 1999: 373. A fine photograph of this refitted nodule can be found in Pitts and Roberts 1997, figure 27).

Q2A contains an example of 35 refitting large cortical flakes. Together, they form the outer cortical surface of a nodule (Roberts and Parfitt 1999: 360). Likewise, Q2D contains a comparatively large number of primary cortical flakes, indicating primary reduction of nodules. None of this seems to go beyond the roughout stage (or alternatively, flake core production).

phase 2 - Q1B contains several groups of refitting finishing/late thinning stage flakes. These groups consist of 6 to 13 flakes each (Roberts and Parfitt 1999: 350). Small series of refitting handaxe finishing debitage have been recovered from Q1A unit 4c; here, the largest refitting group numbers only four of these flakes (Roberts and Parfitt 1999: 320). All however attest to a thinning/finishing phase following initial roughing out and thinning elsewhere, and none fit to a finished handaxe, indicating export of the final product.

The most spectacular example of this phase however comes from Q1A unit 4b, which is a slightly earlier level

(in the sense of: perhaps a few centuries) than the other archaeology discussed here. In Q1A unit 4b, an extremely well-preserved knapping scatter has been found in the form of a dense concentration of both large and very small waste, covering an area of about a quarter of a square metre. Of 198 larger flakes and flake fragments from this scatter, 132 could be refitted into two groups (Roberts and Parfitt 1999: 335). Both represent the final thinning and finishing of a (non-present) handaxe, starting from a roughout with a break surface from end-shock. This roughout must have been produced elsewhere.

Interestingly, it appears that a number of larger flakes of this thinning episode was selected and set aside of the main scatter (Roberts and Parfitt 1999: 335), anticipating future use as flake tool? At least two large flakes of these refitted series are missing.

phase 3a - finished handaxes are numerous (some 450 have been recovered). They scatter as a low-density veil over the whole quarrying area, but the vast majority comes from Q1B which represents a denser concentration over a limited surface, coinciding with a concentration of large mammal bones, and Roberts and Parfitt (1999: 380) explicitly mention that: "*It is worth considering that amongst the finished handaxes recovered from Boxgrove there are very few which can be considered failures (<2%)*". Notably too is that refits to the handaxes are very rare. The most 'complete' refits so far concern 3 tranchet flakes which fit to the tip of a handaxe from Q2A (Roberts and Parfitt 1999: 360); and 3 flakes refitting to a rather rough handaxe (a roughout essentially) from Q1B. In the latter case, which is instructive, this flaking episode apparently exposed a flaw that spoiled the production of a proper working edge (and thus finishing into a handaxe), after which the piece was discarded (Roberts and Parfitt 1999: 344).

phase 3b - like handaxes, tranchet flakes are present all over the excavated surface. In rare cases, these are the only items refitting to finished handaxes. Apparently, they mainly represent a resharpening phase, both for continued use of handaxes on the spot and anticipating future use in a location elsewhere; sometimes handaxes were abandoned on the spot after this resharpening phase, but it also seems as if frequently handaxes were subsequently carried away.

Sometimes tranchets may perhaps have been produced with the intention of producing a flake tool. As an instructive case of handaxe resharpening/finishing by means of a tranchet blow followed by subsequent export of the handaxe in question, Q2D contains no handaxes but 11 tranchet flakes. Q2C contains as much as 30 of these, with only 5 tranchet-sharpened handaxes recovered (Roberts *et al*. 1997: 341-344).

"Scatters" and "patches"

A look at the character of the distribution of the archaeology over the palaeo-landscape as revealed by the excavation trenches and test pits indicates some subtle patterning, already hinted at in the above descriptions. Some items are to be found in every trench and pit, as a low-density level 'veil' or 'scatter' of archaeological residue (Isaac's "scatter between the patches"). Others appear more clustered and spatially limited, some in the form of distinct "patches" and some not.

The "scatter" - Finished handaxes are the most visible items in the continuous low density 'veil' of artefacts distributed over the Boxgrove unit 4c/d palaeo-landscape. They are joined by tranchet flakes –some refitting to handaxes, most not – and limited amounts of handaxe final shaping/finishing debitage, none of which fit to the handaxes or debitage from earlier manufacturing stages. Some elements of this thinning debitage appear to be used as flake tools. Every now and then the odd flake core is present, along with both hard and soft percussion tools. The character of this low density "veil of handaxes" is best represented by the assemblage from Q1A, but it is present as a 'background' in all trenches, both in Quarry 1 and in Quarry 2.

Type I patches - The presence of primary handaxe manufacture and nodule decortication debitage is distinctly concentrating in the east quarry (Quarry 2). It takes the form of small relatively dense 'patches' with a high refitting percentage. It is distinctly different from the content of the low-density 'veil of handaxes' scattering over the palaeo-landscape. The "Horse Butchery Site" (GTP17) is a good example of such a type I 'patch'. This site contains some interesting aspects, perhaps giving a clue to how these distinct patches relate to the activities which formed the low-density veil, from which these type I patches differ sharply, but to which they nevertheless seem to be linked.

Type II patches - A concentration of most notably finished handaxes, coinciding with a concentration in the bone density, occurs over a limited area in the west quarry (Quarry 1), and represented by some trenches of Q1B. The archaeology of this second type of 'patch' has the same basic characteristics as the archaeology in the 'veil of handaxes' over the palaeo-landscape, but it is much denser in artefact numbers, most notably finished handaxes.

Interpreting activities in the landscape: life trajectory and employment of a Boxgrove handaxe

Transport of tools and tool roughouts in various stages of reduction is well recognizable in the above outline of the Boxgrove archaeology. One thing that becomes evident from the outline above (cf. also Austin (1994) for an earlier articulation of many aspects of the discussed patterning) and the 'scatter and patches' approach is that the Boxgrove handaxes (as bifaces elsewhere, e.g. Roebroeks *et al.* 1988) were *not* made on the spot in one continuous episode as a direct reaction to an emergent need, after transport of a freshly quarried nodule over a small distance to the place of action (*contra* Gamble 1999), not even at the "Horse Butchery Site", I suggest (*contra* White 2000: 45). Handaxes were highly mobile items with a considerable history behind them when discarded. They were probably made some kilometres away from the place where they were discarded, on the same long shoreline of the Goodwood-Slindon Beach along which the cliff with it's seams of flint stretched for tens of kilometres. A detailed argument for this will be presented below.

Not only handaxes were transported, roughouts were as well, *and this is highly instructive*. It appears that the transformation from initial raw flint nodule to finished handaxe involved movement along a chain (or 'path', as Gamble calls it (1998, 1999)) of *at least three,* and sometimes more, distinct localities, with activities at each locality apparently anticipating activities at the next *and even beyond the next*. It is the latter point which suggests that the discernable pattern is the result of intentions.

A handaxe would have started its conception at a location where nodules were quarried and initial decortication and roughing out took place. Then the roughout would become mobile. It was taken, perhaps over a considerable distance, to a second spot. *Here they double served as a blank to be transformed into a finished handaxe, and a portable core.* The question is whether the roughouts were flaked with the *intention* of *both* producing a finished handaxe and producing servicable flakes. It is my feeling that the answer is probably "yes". Handaxes apparently were not just cores which by chance ended up in handaxe shape (contra Davidson and Noble 1993). In their final handaxe form, they clearly had a *structural* function as a tool, not an occasional function, and in combination with their typical multiphased way of production there are reasons to think that this was anticipated.

Flakes from the final handaxe thinning and finishing episode appear to have been set aside and used. The end product, a finished handaxe, then entered another mobile phase, being taken to yet another location *and to be used there*. In some cases this was not the end of its life: the many tranchet flakes without handaxes at Boxgrove indicate that handaxe mobility could be prolonged after this stage, (sometimes) following resharpening. The separation of the stages of roughout production at type I patch localities and their finishing into handaxes elsewhere as part of the activities creating the 'veil', suggest to me that the roughouts in the minds of their producers *did consciously double up* as cores *and* blanks for finishing into handaxes. The refitting evidence suggests that the handaxe resulting from the thinning and finishing was systematically *not* discarded at the finishing locality, but was carried away to another spot and was thus made in preparation for future use. This three-stage production behaviour in space and time only makes sense if the roughouts doubled up as cores. The separation of roughout production and the use as a core halfway its life cycle in its transported roughout stage, leading to a finished handaxe, as well as the transformation into and use as a butchery tool in its finished handaxe stage elsewhere, and most notably the consistent combination of these stages, indicate planning and an aim not only for a core, but for a finished handaxe in a later stage as well. Yet, I agree that it remains difficult to provide strong unambiguous arguments warranting the step from the observed patterning to ascribing intentions behind them. This is the everlasting problem faced by archaeologist: how to proceed from observing actions to ascertaining intentions? I will try to make as strong an argument as I can, in the current discussion of the Boxgrove evidence.

A palimpsest of activities

The discussed later events in the life of a handaxe occurred all over the vast foreshore plain, and they created the continuous 'veil of handaxes' over the palaeo-landscape. As pointed out, this 'veil' does not only consist of finished handaxes but also of final finishing and thinning waste, some of which was utilized as tools. Use-wear studies on handaxes from Hoxne and Boxgrove suggest a primary employment as butchery tools (Keeley 1993; Pitts and Roberts 1997; Roberts *et al.* 1997), a suggestion corroborated by experiments which show how highly useful these tools are for such purposes (Jones 1980; Pitts and Roberts 1997). It has been argued above that handaxe roughouts doubled up as portable cores, producing the scatter of thinning/finishing waste and used flakes. The presence of finished handaxes, utilized flakes (and rare flake tools), and bones, some of which bear cutmarks, in the low density 'veil' which forms a carpet of finds over the palaeo-landscape suggests that the 'veil' primarily represents a palimpsest created by the archaeological precipitation of countless small episodes of 'direct subsistence procurement activities' (*sensu* Roebroeks *et al.* 1995 for the Belvédère quarry), including the acquisition and utilization of animal carcasses, obtained either by hunting or scavenging (or both). The type II 'patch' in Q1B underlines this. Here a relative enhancement in handaxe density co-occurs with a relative enhancement in bone density. Apart from matters of artefact density, the content of the patch however is similar to that of the wider

low-density 'veil'. If not due entirely to site formation processes, this 'patch' might be connected with the freshwater spring and small lake/pond that must have been in this area judging from its sedimentology (cf. Roberts and Parfitt 1999). This freshwater source may have acted as a focal point in the foreshore plain for both animals and hominines. As a result, it was visited more frequently and the palimpsest of the 'veil' is 'thicker' here, both for artefacts and bones.

Some connection between the handaxes, used flakes and (some of the) bones in an indirect sense is provided by the use-wear evidence on the handaxes, and the cutmarks on the bones. While conjecture, it is perhaps not too much conjecture to interpret the used flakes, originating from handaxe thinning episodes (the use of roughouts as both cores and blanks for bifaces) as directly connected to the events in which handaxes were employed for carcass butchery. These flakes might very well be tools employed in further processing the carcass yield after initial butchery. There is evidence from cutmarks on the hominine teeth found at Boxgrove which suggest that the hominines cut things with flint tools while holding the material between their teeth (Roberts and Parfitt 1999). In any case, these used flakes from handaxe thinning episodes clearly are part of the same general repertoire of 'direct subsistence procurement' events creating the 'veil' as the handaxes. These used flakes are also coupled to these handaxes in the sense that they are part of the handaxe reduction chain. They are therefore, in a broad sense, behaviourally linked on a rather short timespan compared to the time depth of the unit 4c/d sediments.

Contrary to the 'veil', primary decortication and thinning episodes of nodules notably concentrate in Quarry 2 (east quarry), relative to Quarry 1 (west quarry). Here they are present in the form of the distinctive type I 'patches' of debitage. In contrast to the 'veil' and the type II 'patch' of Q1B, these type I patches seem to represent distinct episodes of 'technology maintenance' (*sensu* Roebroeks *et al.* 1995 for the Belvédère quarry). The suggestion is that the area of Quarry 2 was a focal point for such activities, indicating the possible presence of a flint extraction point nearby (e.g. a large cliff collapse, providing easy access to large numbers of good quality nodules). The nearby presence of such a raw materials source could have been an additional reason why handaxes were so easily discarded at the spring locality 'focal point' of Q1B.

A persistent element: comparison with the Acheulean sites of Cagny (France)

The way, described above, in which activities in the landscape were structured at the late Cromerian Goodwood-Slindon raised beach of Boxgrove seems to be not unique to this locality. Elements of this organizational pattern can be recognized in other roughly contemporary Northwest European Acheulean sites, and they closely resemble those in non-Acheulean (and distinctly non-contemporary!) Middle Palaeolithicsites such as those of the Dutch OIS 7 Maastricht Belvédère quarry Unit IV (see also the remark in Austin 1994).

From the late 1970s to the early 1990s, a series of Acheulean sites spanning OIS 9-12 have been excavated by Tuffreau *et al.* in the surroundings of Cagny, just south of Amiens, in the French Somme terraces (see Tuffreau *et al.* 1997a for an overview). The largest surface excavated is that at the early OIS 10 Ferme de l'Epinette site. This site, situated on what was a terrace edge and close to both a small drainage channel and a flint-bearing chalk tallus, contains debitage, a clear percentage of cores including Levallois cores, in addition to flake tools (mainly denticulates), bifaces and some chopping tools. Like Boxgrove, none of the debitage fit to the handaxes except for one single flake, indicating that the bifaces were imported items (this is underlined by the fact that one of these is in an 'exotic' flint type). Biface finishing flakes and biface roughouts are present (Tuffreau *et al.* 1997a, b). A considerable percentage of refits has been established among the debitage, and they appear to form refitting groups falling into distinct refitting categories, which include a distinct biface finishing phase, without the resulting biface, as well as a distinct nodule roughing out phase, with the resulting roughout missing (Tuffreau *et al.* 1997b). Thus the three elements of Boxgrove (roughing out (decortication) - handaxe finishing - transported individual handaxes) are also recognizable at Ferme de l'Epinette. Like Boxgrove, the clear presence of a nodule roughing out (decortication) phase seems to be connected to a nearby raw material source; raw materials employed are from the flint-bearing chalk tallus some 100 metres from the main debitage concentration. Again, the relative concentration of artefacts seems to be connected to an identifiable focal element in the site location; a raw material extraction point, added to a strategic position offering a wide vista over the valley below, as well as access to a nearby water source.

The topographic setting of Ferme de l'Epinette is distinctly different from that of Boxgrove, as is its climatological setting (start of a glacial, while Boxgrove is full interglacial). Still, the basic patterning in the Acheulean component of the site is similar. Yet there may be subtle but important and perhaps instructive differences. Unlike Boxgrove, we do not have the details of the extent of the handaxe 'veil', but the handaxe finds from Ferme de l'Epinette appear more akin to the type II patch of Boxgrove Q1B than to the 'veil'. Is the veil absent on the plateaus? For plateaus and terraces, the archaeological fall-out might perhaps be more focused – the veil being much thinner or perhaps even absent, the patches thereby even

more clear and localized. A 'scatters and patches' approach to the archaeology of the terraces and plateaus is desperately needed to investigate possible contrasts to the patterning of the archaeology from the spatially restricted low-lying (and wet) alluvial and foreshore plains.

Tracks through time and space

As distinct as the type I patches of initial decortication and thinning waste at Boxgrove are within the context of the 'veil of artefacts' they are part of, these episodes of 'technology maintenance' nevertheless are linked to the 'direct subsistence procurement' episodes that created the continuous low-density 'veil' of handaxes and finishing/thinning waste. They are connected because the one is the necessary precursor to the other. That is also the case for the episodes of roughout flaking (handaxe shaping/finishing) in relation to the episodes of finished handaxe discard.

The chain of singular but linked events that starts with knapping a roughout, transporting it, and then turning the carried roughout into a finished handaxe which in turn is itself transported, provides a behavioural link between al three stages, though as individual acts they are spatio-temporally distinct (and as singular acts at any given locality are temporally distinct, though sometimes spatially associated with the temporal dimension lost because they have become embedded in a palimpsest). As mentioned earlier, the same applies to the employment of the used flakes that result from handaxe thinning episodes. The important aspect is that handaxes do not start immediately as handaxes but have a 'previous life' as a 'core'. And whenever 'roughout-cores' change into handaxes, these handaxes are always transported. In the case of Boxgrove, there is no evidence (in the form of fitting debitage sequences) that finished handaxes further on in the trajectory were re-employed as core yielding servicable flakes, except perhaps for the tranchet removals. Although information on the flake-core facies of Boxgrove has not been extensively published, from the information available it seems that cores found there are very informal *ad hoc* products (because flaking sequences can be almost fully refitted, e.g. Bergman and Roberts 1988) made from small cortical nodules and clearly different from handaxe roughout cores and handaxes (cf. Bergmann and Roberts 1988). Occasionally they are very clearly larger cores which likewise cannot be products of handaxe recycling. Finished handaxes were therefore consistently transported in order to be employed as handaxes (i.e., possibly employed in butchery tasks), not as cores. There is no evidence at all of a common 'afterlife' of handaxes as cores (at best, these kinds of episodes are anecdotal. For example, among the materials from GTP 27 excavated in

1996, there is a very small, thin, bifacial 'disc'-like implement resembling a highly reduced biface. This could be the product of an occasion where only a handaxe was available while a core was needed). Beyond Boxgrove, the evidence also seems to remain anecdotal (as opposed to structural), for example at Cagny La Garenne where a few bifaces were employed in a Levallois-core fashion, by striking one large flake from along the biface axis after preparing a striking platform (Tuffreau *et al.* 1997a; see also DeBono and Goren-Inbar 2001). It is interesting to ponder the dual way in which the roughout core-handaxe sequence and the handaxe-Levallois core sequence (joined later in the Middle Pleistocene by a Levallois core-handaxe sequence when Levallois flakes were frequently shaped into handaxes) become connected. To go deeper into this issue would go too far in the context of this chapter, however). Perhaps it could be instructive to compare flint-rich environments to flint-poor environments. Re-utilization of handaxes as cores could perhaps increase as the availability of raw materials in the landscape becomes poorer, or more dispersed (or raw material collection more difficult to embed in daily subsistence activities through time constraints). This could be one reason why the importance of handaxes apparently diminishes in east-central Europe.

At Boxgrove there is, in other words, the suggestion of a sequence that implies that handaxe roughouts were seen as both cores for servicable flakes and blanks for handaxes, while the resulting handaxes were seen as handaxes only, with only a few anecdotal exceptions. Once reduced into a finished handaxe, either there was apparently consistently no need for a core anymore (indicating planning in the form of a planned sequence of tasks in the landscape), or these hominines (whether as individuals or as groups) always carried a second resource in the form of a handaxe roughout 'core' together with a finished handaxe.

The first option implies that they knew that they would only need a handaxe at the next locality, or alternatively they knew that raw materials for flake production at the next locality were plentiful enough, leaving only the need for a handaxe to be carried.

The latter option implies that they knew that they were going to have to use both handaxes and 'cores' at a next locality, and not just either of them. In the situation where they did not know whether they would need a core or a handaxe, this dependent on the occasion, carrying a handaxe and recycling it into a core would be an option. This seems to have been one not employed by the Boxgrove hominines, which leaves the earlier suggestion, a deliberate strategic choice as opposed to *ad hoc* behaviour. Indeed the importance of this realization is that it again underlines that decision-making in tool manufacture and planning of tasks was not *ad hoc* and triggered by immediate needs 'on the spot', though it is often pictured as such.

In addition, it again underlines that for these hominines, finished handaxes were finished handaxes and not 'fluid' multi-purpose products. Any further reduction and shape modification were probably solely related to resharpening attempts. The concept of handaxes as the "Swiss army knifes" of the palaeolithic therefore is not tenable for Boxgrove, though of course multiple tasks could be performed with them. The same suggestion applies to Davidson and Noble's (1993) concept of handaxes as a form of bifacial core. While their ideas apply to the handaxe roughout stage, it does not apply to finished handaxes, at least not at Boxgrove. If these Boxgrove handaxes were merely a byproduct of a bifacial core reduction strategy, they should be expected to get recycled as cores. They are not at Boxgrove. Handaxes were resharpened however, indicating that they were tools and as shown in the above outline distinctly regarded as such by the Boxgrove hominines. The "finished artifact fallacy" (cf. Davidson and Noble 1993) with regard to an interpretation of handaxes as distinct tools therefore does not completely apply at Boxgrove.

Contrary to views of an *ad hoc* five minute culture with little strategic planning depth such as frequently ascribed to archaic hominines by e.g. Gamble (Gamble 1993, 1999), there seems to be an element of 'purposeful' strategies, including decisions on both the 'now' and 'then' involved, once the underlying structure of the Acheulean at Boxgrove as described above is realized. It clearly is not just "taking with you what you already have and use it as the need emerges". There is more complex decision-making involved which appears to take into account the character of future activities at other localities.

It becomes clear that the 'veil of handaxes' as well as the type I and II patches are part of a chain or 'path' through the landscape interconnecting each of them. It is this aspect, in which handaxe production from initial nodule quarrying to use and discard of the finished handaxe is *multi-staged in both space and time*, which might point to an extraordinary degree of planning and anticipation, and purpose. The Boxgrove hominines seem to have planned well beyond the next task at the next location. They apparently anticipated that they were going to need a flake core at another location, and a handaxe at the following one. They purposely combined both into one strategy by carrying and then finishing the roughouts, and then carrying the resulting handaxe yet further away. There would appear to be a clear element of 'displacement' in this, and at least a basic element of a 'release from proximity' as these hominines were apparently able to imagine situations beyond activities at the next location, a step further than a simple one-stepped pattern of 'now and then'. Again we turn back to the haunting question whether the observed patterns *must* be intentional or not. If they indeed are, the implications are as profound as suggested above.

Routed Foragers?

One of the important aspects arising from this scatter and patches approach is that while the distributional pattern for subsistence activities related archaeology is spatially continuous, though with density variation, it is the technology maintenance related archaeology only which is discernable spatially restricted. The spatial restriction of the latter has been interpreted above to be tied to a raw materials extraction point acting as a focal point. Density variations in the 'veil' likewise seem connected to identifiable focal points (the spring in Q1B).

Patches such as the type I patch in Q1B and the type II patches in Q2 appear to represent what Binford (1984) has called "magnet locations" in the landscape. It is solely this aspect of these locations which generates their character as 'rich' patches within the low density scatter. The low-density 'veil' of handaxes seems to originate from continuous isolated subsistence activities while moving between these Binfordian "magnet locations". This is the pattern of Binford's (1984: 259-264) "routed feeding" or "routed foraging" mobility model. This model seems the best match for the distributional patterning observed in Boxgrove. Yet, there is some suggestion that these Boxgrove "routed foraging" mobility strategies were well planned.

A comparison to the African Early Acheulean and Developed Oldowan

In chapter 3.1, a model was presented for the African Early Pleistocene Acheulean. When its aspects are compared to the analysis of fabrication, transport and use of Acheulean bifaces at Boxgrove and the Somme Valley (which, it should be emphazised, both are a half to one million years younger than the African sites), clear differences are apparent. Apart from a clear difference in ecological setting, the most notable aspect to emphasize is that the European Early Acheulean compared to the African Early Acheulean complex *sensu lato* is much more akin to the *Developed Oldowan* than to the African Early Acheulean *sensu stricto*. The similarities lie in the prolonged trajectories of fabrication, use and discard of handaxes in space and time, and links with use in the context of a flake-core component. In chapter 3.2, the Developed Oldowan has been tied to (seasonal) subsistence strategies involving long (in space and time) gathering rounds through the landscape as compared to the African Early Acheulean *sensu stricto*. The similarity that has become apparent between the use and life history of handaxes in the African Developed Oldowan and the European Acheulean might provide an argument in favour of a similar situation for Pleistocene Europe: subsistence strategies involving long rounds of mobility through the landscape. This is not surprising, of course, as the need for such strategies when occupying Eurasia were already pointed out in chapter 4.1. It does emphasize that the African Early Acheulean and the European Acheulean should not be lumped together. Although both contain handaxes, the underlying strategies of production and schedules of use are different. This in turn indicates that the Acheulean of 1.5-0.2 Ma ago does not represent a long period of stasis, though it is often portrayed as such, but one of dynamic change concealed in a seeming typological stasis. Although there are conceptual links (deriving probably from evolutionary links), the post 0.5 Ma Acheulean of Europe is dynamically different from the pre 1.0 Ma Acheulean of Africa. It would be interesting to investigate whether a similar dynamic change between 0.5 and 1.0 Ma occurs within Africa.

94

Part V

Synthesis and concluding remarks

Various topics discussed in parts I to IV are brought together into a synthesis, open questions signalled, phenomenon regarding the earliest occupation of Eurasia considered, and some possible avenues to follow suggested.

Chapter 5   concluding synthesis and summary

In Chapter 3, a model was presented in which the early African Acheulean technocomplex is related to seasonal (and probably confrontational) scavenging in a typical African savanna environment. The close tie with the resource structure of the African savanna explains why the Acheulean does not proliferate beyond the African savanna realm when 'Out of Africa 1', a first occupation of Eurasia, takes place around 1.3 Ma. Instead, it appears that early Eurasian industries are exclusively core-flake (mode 1) technologies and Acheulean artefact occurrence remains restricted to the African savanna. This Early Pleistocene 'Movius line' phenomenon now no longer seems enigmatic. It is a consequence of the strong tie between Acheulean technology and behaviour driven by the resource structure peculiar to the African savanna as outlined in chapter 3.

Factors behind 'Out of Africa 1'

As has been explored in chapter 4.1, the expansion of hominin presence to regions outside the tropical grassland realm around 1.3 Ma ago has little to do with the 'invention' of Acheulean technology. Instead, both the appearance of the Acheulean inside the tropical grassland realm, and the first hominin presence outside this region are *symptoms* (not cause and result) of a development in hominine behaviour. As a result of climatic fluctuations, and the emergence of an increasing degree of seasonality with regard to resource availibility on the tropical savanna of Africa and accompanying changes in biotope structure, a process of variability selection was started. This led to the development of an increasing level of tolerance in early *Homo* of fluctuations in resource availibility. On the behavioural side, this was accompanied by a change in diet and procurement strategies. Hominins started to include fluctuating food resources of higher quality into their diet. This process got well underway some 2.5 Ma ago, and an archaeological signature might be the emergence of stone tool technology. An adaptation to the food resources of the emerging dry secondary savanna around 1.7 Ma involved the incorporation of a seasonal focus on foods such as (scavenged) meat, bulbs and tubers. Around 1.7 Ma, meat eating probably had become a seasonal activity, as opposed to an occasional activity, connected to the early dry season and Acheulean tool technology (and its underlying behavioural strategies). Increasing reliance on these seasonal but high quality dietary elements allowed for gut size reduction, freeing metabolic space for an increase in brain size. An increasing brain size allowed for larger group sizes, a higher level of sociality, and a flexibility enhancing opportunities for change in

subsistence strategies. This promoted continuation and elaboration of the changes in subsistence taking place at that time. In the end, the changes in subsistence strategies and increasing levels of flexibility and tolerance to seasonal resource fluctuations led to an increasing tolerance for demanding environments, which eventually led to 'Out of Africa 1', an occupation of temperate and subtropical Eurasia up to 40° Northern latitude beginning around 1.3 Ma ago. As a prelude to this 'Out of Africa 1', hominins appear on the previously unexploited higher altitude savanna in Africa and on the African/west Asian fringe at about 1.5 Ma. Gadeb in Ethiopia and Dmanisi in Georgia are examples of this prelude to 'Out of Africa 1' (see chapter 2.4).

Hence 'Out of Africa 1' is a by-product of developments inside Africa. There are no clear pulling factors involved emerging from Eurasia itself (in the sense of climate and/or environmental affordances turning more favourable, or geographical obstacles disappearing), nor clear pushing factors (in the sense of overpopulation; necessary range extensions of a hominin turning predator (see Walker and Shipman 1996); seeking refuge from a worsening climate; or clear hominin purpose) from Africa. Neither is it the result of a technological innovation (the Acheulean, as tradition demands). It was the unintended by-product of opportunity, an act of contingency and serendipity. The process which led to it was driven by developments in Africa itself, which in essence were and remained completely internal African affairs. When internal events inside Africa had shaped a strain of hominins fit to do it, Eurasia south of 40° Northern latitude was occupied simply because it was available. The first occupation of Eurasia hence was a phenomenon similar to chickens crossing a road: chickens cross a road simply because the other side is available, and they happen to have the means to cross roads without these having been specially developed to cross roads.

'Out of Africa 2'

With regard to occupation patterns, stone tool technology and presumably behaviour, something changes around 0.8 to 0.5 Ma. Geographically, the area with Acheulean occurrences expands, first into northwest Africa and the eastern part of west Asia at 0.8-0.9 Ma (see chapter 4.1). This is suggested by Acheulean sites appearing in areas where hominine occupation and/or the Acheulean previously was absent. It concerns sites such as those from the Casablanca sequence in Morocco, and southwest Asian sites like Dina and Jalapur in Pakistan, while Gesher Benot Ya'agov in Israel provides a tantalizing suggestion of a renewed flux of hominins with Acheulean technology through the Near East corridor between Africa and Eurasia around this time. This is followed by a proliferation of hominin occupation as well as Acheulean technology into Western Europe at 0.6-0.5 Ma, as evidenced by sites such as Boxgrove in Great Britain, the Somme Valley sites in northwest France and Fontana Ranuccio in Italy.

The late proliferation of Acheulean technology into Eurasia, and especially the late introduction into Europe at about 0.5 Ma, seems to points to a different role for this technology in the European realm compared to the earlier Acheulean occurrences in Africa. In the case of northwest Europe, it is clearly coupled to the colonization of new, previously uninhabited environments, with an ecological structure unlike that of the African savanna. Apart from its earlier tie to African savanna biotopes, the Acheulean also loses its earlier strong tie to a drainage line contex around this time. Rich Acheulean sites start to appear in lake-shore contexts (e.g. Gesher Benot Ya'agov – see chapter 4.1) and sea-shore contexts (e.g. at Boxgrove – see chapter 4.2). All this indicates that from 0.8 Ma onwards, the Acheulean probably played a role in subsistence which was different from the role it played in the earliest African Early Acheulean. The Acheulean as a technology seems to become more versatile, as is the way in which it is embedded in a changing and more complex environment of behaviour. This is a point to note, as 'The' Acheulean is usually treated as a unity, a constant over almost one million years. It is not.

The increasing versatility signalled by the changing structure of the Acheulean is again accompanied by a colonization event, signalling a significant increase in behavioural versatility in general. The search should now be for other correlatives of this increasing versatility in behaviour. The kind of capacities for 'displacement' and planning as hinted at by the analysis of the Acheulean assemblage of Boxgrove (chapter 4.2), could be one archaeological signature. This is however difficult to ascertain as long as similar detailed assessments of the African Early Acheulean (including the Developed Oldowan, as certain aspects of Developed Oldowan handaxes appear to foreshadow the reduction cycles in the European Acheulean) are lacking. Chapter 4.2 moreover serves as a grim example that even when working with an extremely well-preserved set of archaeological data, with a (comparatively) high degree of temporal and conservational (and presumably also behavioural) integrity, allowing an extremely detailed look, it is difficult to take a solid step from discerning a pattern of actions towards assigning intentions to them. This is the ever-continuing despair of palaeolithic archaeology, especially when it concerns that period of the Palaeolithic for which each suspicion of intention has to be defended tooth and nail against (rightful) criticism and doubts. In Chapter 4.2 I have tried, and in the minds of many (even that of my own, perhaps) may have failed.

What made 'Out of Africa 2' happen?

Prior to the 0.5 Ma expansion of hominin presence into northwest Europe, the 40° Northern latitude limit of hominin dispersal throughout Eurasia and the informal character of toolkits suggest that foraging rounds through the landscape and foraging time budgets were stretched to their limits (cf. chapter 3.2). The northern latitude limit suggests a minimum daylight threshold of at least 10 hours a day in order to fulfil subsistence needs (cf. also the suggestion by Dennell and Roebroeks 1996), within which subsistence had to be turned to such opportune levels and occasions in order to survive that the toolkits employed developed a highly *ad hoc* character, ready made for unforeseen opportunities because these were the mainstay of subsistence rather than opportunities of a short and precise, well-anticipated character. This again (and seemingly paradoxical compared with the previous treatment of Acheulean technology) is an expression of versatility, but versatility fit to a completely different mode (in a strategic sense) of subsistence. Tactical depth under these conditions demands a highly versatile use of resources. The pitfall is that this results in a stone tool technology which superficially seems highly primitive, thus putting the unwarry archaeologist on the wrong foot.

The 0.5 Ma dispersal north of the 40° latitude boundary in western Eurasia points to a change in this situation, which signifies one of the following options:

a) *A change in environmental structure in that area resulting in minimum foraging round sizes and allowing more opportunities within foraging time budgets;*

b) *A change in hominin behaviour involving new behaviours allowing more effective foraging within existing foraging time budgets and environmental structures;*

c) *A combination of the previous two options.*

Turner's hypothesis: carnivore guilds and scavenging opportunities

Turner (1992) has put forward arguments for a type (a) solution. He points out that around 0.5 Ma, the structure of the carnivore guild in Europe changes. With the demise of some large predators and scavengers, the ratio of carcass scavengers to carcass producers in Europe changes into a situation where fewer scavengers in relation to the number of predators are present. Turner's interpretation is that conditions for a hominin scavenger became more favourable because of less competition from other scavengers (e.g. the large hyaena *Pachycrocuta brevirostris* becomes extinct at the end of the early Pleistocene). This assumes that the number of scavengeable carcasses remained the same and the extinctions were not due to diminishing resources, which begs the question why the several (large) scavengers went extinct. In my opinion, the decrease in relative numbers of scavengers could likely be explained as due to a decrease in scavenging opportunities, leading some scavengers into extinction. This is exactly the opposite of Turner's proposed development of scavenging opportunities for a hominin scavenger. Indeed, the number of carnivore species also goes down at 0.5 Ma, just as the number of scavenger species does (Turner 1992, figure 1). The change in the carnivore guild entails the extinction of the Machairodont cats in Europe, which quite likely were formidable producers of fleshy scavengeable carcasses. In fact, Turner's argument solely relies on the similarity of the carnivore guild after 0.5 Ma to that of current eastern Africa, coupled with Blumenschine's (1987) observations on scavenging opportunities on the secondary savanna of current eastern Africa (cf. Turner 1992: 121). This completely ignores the point that these scavenging opportunities are not primarily the result of the carnivore guild structure, but the result of the very specific ecological and climatological structures of the African secondary savanna, which are unlike those of Pleistocene Europe (see chapter 3). My assessment of scavenging opportunities for a hominin scavenger would be that they decrease after 0.5 Ma.

Viewed in this light, the expansion of hominin presence in Europe just around this time is the more remarkable.

Hunting as a key behaviour

There are two novelties in the Eurasian archaeological record around this time which could indicate that option (b), new hominine behaviour, is a factor behind the dispersal north of 40° latitude. One is the already mentioned expansion of the Acheulean, which previously seemed to be strictly tied to the ecological structure (and subsistence structures) of the African savanna environments. The other novelty is that we have the first indications of full-scale hunting of large mammals, and the first unambiguous hunting equipment, dating roughly to this period. Wooden javelins have been recovered from 0.4 Ma old deposits in the Schöningen quarry, Germany (Thieme 1996, 1997, 1999), along with a bone assemblage with human modifications and a small set of lithic tools. The javelins are true throwing weapons, finely balanced with their centre of gravity at about one third of their length, and the tips made of the most dense parts of the treetrunks from which they were carved (Thieme 1997, 1999). These are not just sharpened branches, they have been carefully constructed. Ongoing analysis of the monospecific bone assemblage (Voormolen *priv. com.*; Roebroeks 2001) reveals anthropogenic modification patterns that point to a highly

standardized utilization of and butchery of the large horses in question (although again it is hard to ascertain whether these are the result of *intentions*). The tip of a (thrusting?) spear of similar age as the Schöningen spears has been recovered from Hoxnian deposits at Clacton, Britain (Oakley et al. 1977). Neither of these sites (Schöningen or Clacton) is an Acheulean site. But a horse scapula with a large circular puncture that has been suggested as being due to the impact of a spear was found at the 0.5 Ma British Acheulean site of Boxgrove (Roberts and Parfitt 1999: 378). Seen as two as yet independent but broadly contemporaneous observations, the structure of the Acheulean as well as the evidence for spear-aided hunting of large mammals in the early Palaeolithic of Europe, allowing for the assumption that these first observations indeed represent the first occurrence, both point to major behavioural change, even more so when put in its context of primary occupation of Northwest Eurasia. I cannot prove it, but it seems not unrealistic to invoke a role for hunting behaviour as one of the major behavioural elements behind the events occurring in Northwest Europe about 0.5 Ma ago. As an element in itself, the evidence for hunting is there. For early palaeolithic European hominins hunting behaviour as such now seems undeniable, though some still do, with archaeological proof as hard as the carefully shaped wooden spears of Schöningen and the clear-cut butchered bones of the Pleistocene horses from this site. The challenge now is to find more clear-cut connections with the primary occupation of Northwest Europe as a process, and the broadly contemporaneous changes in archaeological complexity which appear to be visible, though in many aspects debatable perhaps, when carefully looking at such sites as Boxgrove or the Somme Valley sites. The impression I have is that all these observations try to tell us something, but as yet have not crystallized enough to get a firm grip on them. Important elements still slip like sand through our fingers. Maybe we will have to wait until the evidence strengthens, as parts of it already have with the discovery of amongst others Schöningen. The hypothesis and models set out in this work, so far can be helpful in providing guides to direct research attention and working hypothesis to compare new evidence to.

Let us return to the topic of hunting as a major (and around 0.5 Ma ago new) behavioural mode of survival. Later on in the Pleistocene, hunting was a key subsistence strategy of the Neanderthal descendants of these earliest Europeans. This is born out by recent Neanderthal bone isotope studies which suggest that Neanderthals were top-level carnivores (Fizet *et al.* 1995; Bocherens *et al.* 1999; Richards *et al.* 2000), and new analysis of Neanderthal generated faunal assemblages which point to repeated highly monospecific targeting of prime aged individuals (examples are for example Salzgitter-Lebenstedt, Coudoulous, Mauran, La Borde and Ilskaya: see Gaudzinski and Roebroeks (2000) and Gaudzinski (1996,

1999)), though for the latter it is again difficult to ascertain that these observed patterns represent intentions. Strong reliance on hunting as a key subsistence strategy may have been embedded in high day-to-day hominin mobility (Langbroek 2001).

The hypothesis that the development of hunting as an important subsistence strategy made the occupation of Northwest Europe possible would require that earlier subsistence strategies still primarily focused on scavenging and gathering. This yields testable predictions. It predicts, for example, that there should be differences between the hominin modified faunal assemblages of the earliest occupation of southern Europe such as Atapuerca on the one hand, and the earliest Northwest European sites such as Boxgrove and Schöningen on the other hand. The earlier sites should not show the kind of targeting of large mammals, and their bone modification patterns should be more in line with scavenging. A further prediction is that there should be (perhaps subtle) differences between faunal assemblages from Early Pleistocene Acheulean sites in Africa and Western Asia on the one hand, and Middle Pleistocene Acheulean sites in Europe on the other hand. This because the first would be the result of (confrontational) scavenging, while the second would be due to full-scale hunting.

The earlier prediction probably is easier to recognize. With regard to the second prediction, the difference in exploitation patterns between carcasses obtained through confrontational scavenging and hunting may not be profound (see also Domínguez-Rodrigo 2002). This is an important point to note, because the earlier Acheulean in my model (chapter 3.1) may represent confrontational scavenging whereby carcasses were appropriated from carnivores at a very early stage. Faunal assemblages from Middle Pleistocene Europe compared to earlier Acheulean sites from Africa and Western Asia (e.g. Gesher Benot Ya'aqov in Israel) therefore can be expected to be difficult to distinguish even if the latter are due to (confrontational) scavenging instead of hunting. In the archaeological search for the origins of organized hunting (Roebroeks 2001), this is a point which should be well taken to avoid misinterpretations. This point of equifinality and the difficulty in differentiating appropriation at an early stage of carnivore kills by confrontational scavenging from hunting, has recently also been discussed by Domínguez-Rodrigo (2002).

The least ambiguous picture should be arrived at by comparing early temperate Eurasian hominin modified faunal assemblages from sites with mode 1 lithic industries, like those of Atapuerca or better still the Chinese Nihewan sites, with sites like Schöningen. If scavenging opportunities and competition from other scavengers in the open landscapes of Early Pleistocene temperate Eurasia were similar to those on the *open* parts of the African savanna (see chapter 3.1 and 3.2), as can be expected, and if the Early Pleistocene assemblages were the result of scavenging, then the difference in handling/exploitation of carcasses should be notable. Carcass exploitation in a scavenging mode for these early sites 'in the open' should show a strong focus on marrow extraction, a limited removal of small scraps of meat and in general little exploitation of meaty carcass parts. This contrasts with the evidence for hunting and consumption of fully fleshed carcasses such as is now forthcoming from Schöningen in northwest Europe.

A new 'Movius line'?

When thinking along the line of the transition from scavenging partial carcasses to obtaining fleshed carcasses by full-fledged hunting, the transition from fully mode 1 industries to inclusion of Acheulean elements (bifaces) in Europe becomes less enigmatic. The enigma remains in the fact that the proliferation of bifacial technology seems to have been restricted to the western part of Eurasia.

Why did the 0.5 Ma proliferation of the Acheulean remain restricted to the western part of Eurasia? Why are there (rejecting the Baise evidence from southern China – see chapter 2.1) no clear Acheulean sites in East Asia from 0.5 Ma onwards? This Middle Pleistocene re-establishment of the old 'Movius line', though a geographically altered 'Movius line', remains something of an enigma. A point to contemplate is whether the absence of Acheulean technology has the implication that the new behaviours, connected to the proliferation of the Acheulean into Europe, did not reach East Asia. With the European Acheulean arguably connected to full-scale hunting behaviour, does this mean that full-scale hunting behaviour did only later reach China and southeast Asia, or did not even reach China at all during the Middle Pleistocene?

This should be testable, for it would predict that while Europe would see archaeological signatures of obtaining fleshed carcasses through hunting (e.g. as at Schöningen), East Asian hominin-modified faunal assemblages would continue to show a scavenging signature only. If it is not just a matter of concepts not reaching East Asia, but also the relevant level of cognition not being reached in Asia, the kind of complex chaines operatoires and levels of displacement and planning depth such as deduced from the Boxgrove evidence in chapter 4.2 would fail to show up in the archaeological record of East Asia as well. Carrying out this test would however require Asian sites with similarly good preservation conditions as the few but highly informative sites in Europe which do yield this kind of information.

For the moment, I do not feel confident with such a hypothesis of 'retardation' for Middle Pleistocene Asia. One clear warning that makes one warry of such rash conclusions is that the primary site upon which the evidence for hunting in Middle Pleistocene Northwest Europe rests (Schöningen), is a site with, from the preliminary results published, a mode 1 technology.

There are other options which need to be explored first before the above propositions regarding a hypothetical Middle Pleistocene developmental isolation for Asia can be considered (what could plead in favour of isolation however is the apparent occurrence of endemism among the (southeast) Asian hominin population. For example, the very young ages of 30-100 ka obtained for the latest Indonesian *erectus*, at Ngandong on Java (Bartstra *et al.* 1988: Swisher *et al.* 1996). There is no *Homo erectus* in Africa or the western part of Eurasia after about 0.5-0.4 Ma. An argument for isolation however begs the question how this isolation was created: what prevented advanced hominins of the Middle Pleistocene to reach east Asia? There are no obvious answers to this question except for one: advanced hominins could have failed to settle east Asia, because this already was settled by a well-established population of *Homo erectus*).

Arid-mesic gradients over Eurasia?

One alternative hypothesis to be explored is one in which east-west gradients in environmental structure across Eurasia would introduce differentiation with regard to time budgets available for subsistence procurement and minimum foraging round sizes. As pointed out earlier, where time budgets and minimum daily foraging round sizes would be stretched to their limits, hominins would perhaps be forced to resort to mode 1 technology again, in a similar vein as the differentiation due to seasonal differences in subsistence opportunities between the Acheulean and Developed Oldowan in the early Acheulean of Africa. In essence, the ecological contrast to be explored could be between the oceanic part of Europe and the more continental parts of Eurasia. There is little data for the earlier part of the Middle Pleistocene, but from the middle part of the Middle Pleistocene onwards, there does seem to be an east-west (or southeast-northwest) gradient in ecology, most notably with regard to openness of the landscape and presumably biomass density. Evidence for such is discussed by Von Koenigswald (1992), Gamble (1995) and Guthrie (2001). According to Von Koenigswald (1992) the oceanic influence in western Eurasia had a smoothing effect on climate fluctuations, creating a more stable faunal and floral environment than in continental Europe and Asia. For example, according to him a pronounced difference in continentality should have existed between west and east Europe on one side and central Europe on the other, with the western part of Europe being much more temperate. In addition, central Europe was much more influenced over time by climate shifts, a difference felt especially during cold periods (Von Koenigswald 1992). According to Gamble (1995), key factors that may have distinguished the continental from the oceanic parts of Eurasia would have been prey density, its mobility and reliability:

"this ameliorating [oceanic] effect could, combined with the zonal distribution of upland and mountain in Europe, have pronounced the dual mosaic pattern that had the effect of concentrating animal resources in the western arm of the Eurasian landmass" (Gamble 1995: 283).

Guthrie (2001) has recently explored possible geographical contrasts in the arid-mesic character of the Eurasian palaeoenvironment during glacial periods and briefly touches upon a possible 'north-south' (but more 'southwest-northeast' if we look at his map) contrast in western Eurasia (Guthrie 2001: 565). If there is a link between the Middle Pleistocene Eurasian 'Movius line 2' and this gradient in continentality, it may have to do with the effects of available time budgets again, just as in the (seasonal) contrast between Developed Oldowan and early Acheulean in Africa during the Early Pleistocene. This would have the implication that in general time budget constraints were less demanding for the oceanic environment of western Europe than for the continental rest of Eurasia.

A related archaeological signature in this regard could be the evidence that transport distances for raw materials appear to be longer in eastern Europe than in western Europe during the Middle Palaeolithic (Roebroeks *et al.* 1988). This could point to an increased level of mobility, which indeed influences time budgets and time budget strategies.

One question remaining is whether these results and ideas regarding arid-mesic gradients over Eurasia, as they are actually shown only for a specific period (and climatic situation) of the Pleistocene, can be generalized as a pattern *grosso modo* valid throughout the Middle Pleistocene. Of course, the proposed contrast could have (and probably has) waxed and waned over time during the Pleistocene. If the second 'Movius line' phenomenon is related, this has the implication that the exact position of this 'line' changed repeatedly during the Pleistocene, which is interesting in the context of for example the suggestions by White (2000) for "the Clactonian question" (It would go too far to further explore this digressive avenue in this chapter).

The context of the earliest occupation of Europe

There clearly is much to explore here, which however falls outside the scope and limits of this work. I hope that the subjects discussed in this work emphasize that, if we are to properly understand the process of the earliest occupation of Europe and the apparent technological differences between Europe and the rest of Eurasia during the Middle Pleistocene, we should look beyond the borders of Europe itself. We should look at what happens in Africa and Western Asia both prior to and contemporary with the period in question, and at what happens in East and Southeast Asia. Likewise, we should do so with regard to the primary occupation of Asia, as well as the apparent technological differences between Africa and the occupied part of Eurasia around 1 Ma. Only with such a diachrone and inter-continental scope can we provide a proper and helpful context for the earliest occupation of Eurasia. A focus on Eurasia, and certainly Europe, alone only provides archaeologists with (by nature imperfect) glimpses of symptoms, but not of processes behind the evolutionary events which led to the dispersal of hominins out of the African realm. The causes of Out of Africa 1 around 1.0-1.3 Ma have to be studied while balancing the evidence from both the source area (Africa) and the receiving area (Eurasia). The same is true for Out of Africa 2 around 0.5 Ma. A look at this wide a scale demands high levels of abstraction. At the same time, a look at details and variation at the level of a site or small region can be instructive (if the archaeological record and research history of a given area or timespan allows such a detailed look at all), to gain extra and relevant insight into some of the elements upon which the grand model is built. And of course, ultimately the test of models at a high abstraction level (and the fuel for generating and maintaining them), models at continental or inter-continental scales and highly diachrone, results from detailed looks at site-level. Refining and amending high abstraction level models will have to be done by employing research at lower abstraction levels. In this work I have tried to look at multiple levels of abstraction, in different chapters, as both avenues of research are relevant for building these kinds of models and structures. I do hope that my attempt shows the value of such an approach, by providing both plausible explanatory scenarios (with avenues for testing) as to processes behind phenomena visible in the archaeological record, and stringent models against which to test new archaeological data.

Concluding summary

In this work, I have presented as well as employed a stringent model against which to test archaeological evidence for early occupations. From this, I have proceeded to construct a critical chronology of Old World hominin dispersals from about 2.5 Ma to about 0.3 Ma. These two can serve as a guideline for further research as well as for the assessment of both old and new archaeological data pertinent to the question of 'earliest occupations'. Building on this, and adding known data on changes in climate and environment, as well as on the changing archaeological record of Africa and Eurasia between 2.5 and 1.0 Ma, I have built a model of behavioural constraints and change, trying to make sense of the chronological picture of early hominin dispersal,

as well as the peculiar characteristics of the archaeological record of the time. I have connected these elements in trying to discern developments in hominin behavioural and cognitive evolution in the Plio-Pleistocene hominin source area (Africa and part of western Asia), developments which eventually enabled the first occupation of Eurasia around 1.3 Ma. In constructing this model, I have also put forward an explanation for the limited distribution of the early Acheulean around the time of this first occupation. In my assessment, the early Acheulean is a phenomenon strictly tied to a particular type of environment, the African secondary savanna, as the result of a mode of behaviour (early dry season active scavenging making use of carcasses in the riparian areas of the African secondary savanna) which can only be employed in this geographically restricted type of environment. This mode of behaviour is one, regional, expression of an increased capability in early Pleistocene hominins to deal with increasing variability in resource availibility. The same increased capability allowed for the first dispersal into Eurasia below 40° Northern latitude, as well as an opportunistic infill of previously void sub-environments in Africa, and at its fringes, a process which seems to slightly precede Out of Africa 1 proper.

Less grip can be asserted on a second dispersal event. A prelude to this may have occurred around 0.8 Ma and involved a further spread of Acheulean technology. This phenomenon breaks through around 0.5 Ma, coinciding with the first occupation of Northwest Europe. There are tantalizing hints in the archaeological record of increasing tactical and planning depths, and changing behaviours. Occupying previously uninhabited parts of Eurasia is a clear sign of change, but the conditions allowing this phenomenon remain shrouded in darkness. Small glimmers and avenues for further research are perhaps that Acheulean technology seems to attain a different tactical role in subsistence behaviour (but even a detailed look at one of the best preserved Acheulean sites of Europe does not provide a proper grip on it, only suggestions), and the first clear archaeologically visible signs of full-scale hunting (with hunting equipment) appear. The possible influence of variations in Middle Pleistocene Eurasian environmental structures on regional, temporal as well as continent-wide scales with regard to the variation and some remarkable contrasts (e.g. absence of Acheulean technology in the eastern part of Eurasia) in the archaeological record remain points which should be high on the agenda. But even the basics of this possible spatio-temporal variation in environmental structure are still poorly documented, and at present this topic is still too much shrouded in darkness to be properly explored. From a positive viewpoint, let us welcome this, for it means that there still is work to be done.

Part VI

Appendix and bibliography

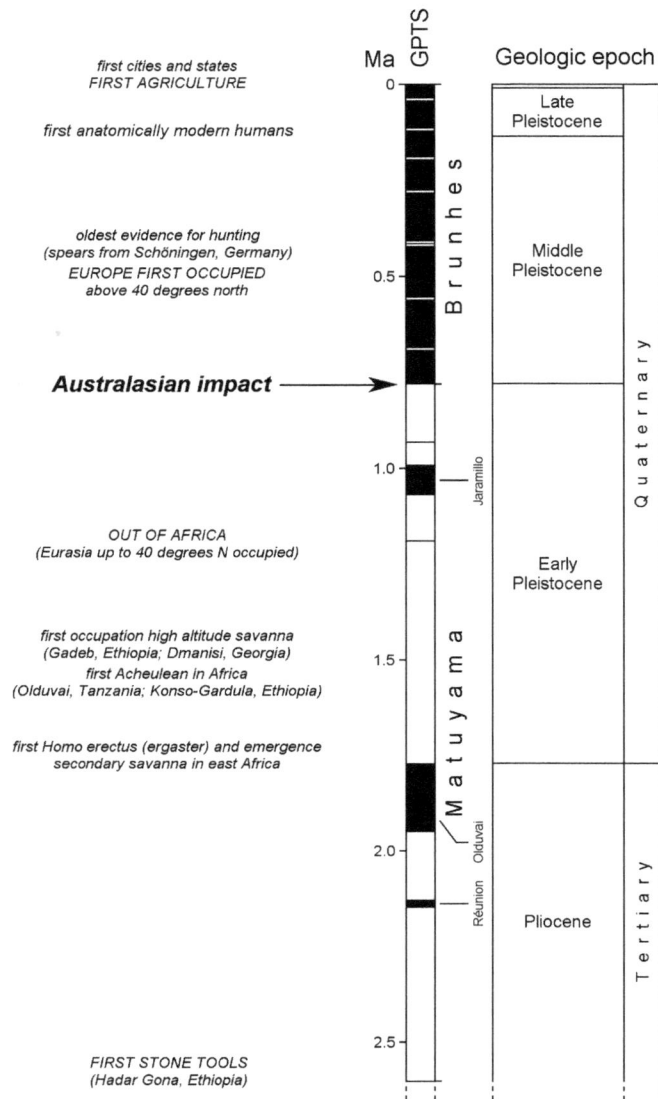

Figure 13:   Timeline showing the Australasian impact put chronologically in context with key events in Human evolution.

Appendix 1

Narrowing down the significance of a large cosmic impact catastrophy in southeast Asia for early Asian *Homo erectus*

Impacts and evolution

As a result of the research following the famous Alvarez *et al.* (1980) paper on the cause of the Dinosaur extinction at the K/T boundary, cosmic impact is now recognized as a potentially serious factor in the evolution of life. The evidence of past extinctions due to giant cosmic impacts has resulted in concern about the possible threat that such impacts pose to humanity (Chapman and Morrison 1994). Yet, little attention is given to the fact that humanity (defined as all species of the genus *Homo*) already experienced – and survived – a large impact at least once in its 2.4 million year history, as was pointed out by Langbroek and Roebroeks (2000) and Paine (2001). This appendix tries to make the active link between impact science and the science of Palaeoanthropology by exploring some of the significance of the mentioned impact on early hominin presence and evolution in southeast Asia.

A significant asteroid/comet impact at 0.8 Ma

Around the time of the Brunhes-Matuyama geomagnetic polarity reversal, a cosmic body of roughly one kilometre in size is known to have impacted in Indochina in what must have been one of the largest impacts of the past few million years. Around the time of impact, early hominins (*Homo erectus*) were either present or at the point of arriving in southeast Asia (see chapter 1.1 and chapter 2.2), and they were certainly present in China at the time of the impact (see chapter 2.1). The impact event can be ranked as crossing the lower limit of the 'global effects threshold' of Chapman and Morrison (1994). This means that it would have had potential (but mild) effects on a global scale with regard to short-term perturbation of climate and environmental productivity. For southeast Asia the results must have been considerable, for the impact must have caused serious ecological havoc over a significant part of the Sunda shelf. If hominins were present in southeast Asia around the time of impact, they would have suffered severely, and it seems likely that local hominin extinction on the mid-Sunda shelf would have occurred in the aftermath of the impact.

The formation of the Australasian strewnfield

Planetary geologists are well aware of the large impact that occurred 0.8 Ma ago in Indochina. Although the impact crater remains yet to be located (Blum *et al.* 1992; Glass 1993; Schmidt and Wasson 1993; Hartung and Koeberl 1994; Schnetzler and McHone 1996; Lee and Wei 2000), evidence of this impact, believed by some to be one of the largest impacts on Earth in several million years (e.g. Schnetzler and McHone 1996), is present in the form of a large strewnfield of abundant tektites and microtektites (glassy impact ejecta) covering an area of 5×10^7 km^2, or about 10% of the Earth's surface. This is the Australasian strewnfield which stretches from southern China to the south of the Australian continent, including a large part of the Indian Ocean (up to Madagascar) and parts of the Pacific Ocean (see map in Glass *et al.* 1997). By various methods including K-Ar and fission track dating, the formation of the tektites has been dated at around 0.7-0.8 Ma, roughly contemporary in age to the Brunhes-Matuyama geomagnetic polarity reversal that marks the transition between the Lower and Middle Pleistocene (Izett and Obradovich 1992; Fudali 1993). A much more precise age in relation to the Brunhes-Matuyama polarity reversal has been determined from the stratigraphic position of micro-tektites in deep sea sediment cores. From a detailed analysis of two cores (ODP sites 767 and 769 taken near the Philippines), Schneider *et al.* (1992) conclude that the impact and strewnfield formation must have occurred during the later part of Oxygen Isotope Stage 20, an estimated 12 ka before the Brunhes-Matuyama polarity change, with an uncertainty of only a few thousand years. A similar conclusion has been reached by Lee and Wei (2000) from analysis of two cores, MD972142 in the South China Sea and MD972143 in the West Philippine Sea. They provide an age estimate of 0.793 Ma for the impact.

Strength and direct effects of the 0.8 Ma Australasian impact on southeast Asia

From the structure of the strewnfield, Schmidt and Wasson (1993) estimate this strewnfield to be caused by

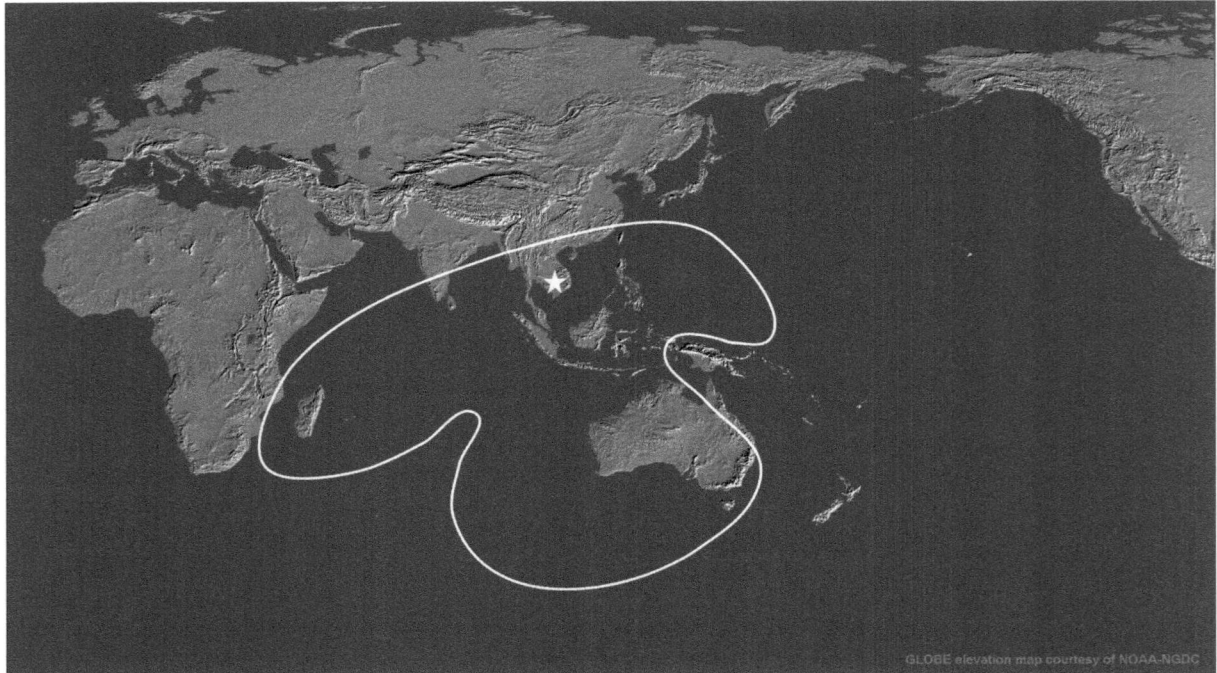

Figure 14: map of the 0.8 Ma Australasian tektite strewn field, originating from an asteroid impact in Indochina (strewnfield outline after Glass *et al.*, 1997). The star marks the probable impact location

an impact with an energy release in the order of 5×10^4 to 1×10^5 MT. In the impact hazard assessment model of Chapman and Morrison (1994), this would be an impact at the lower limit of the "global effects threshold". In the Chapman and Morrison model, a global catastrophy is defined as one that would disrupt modern agriculture on a global scale due to acid rains and (most notably) impact winter effects caused by dust ejected into the stratosphere. The stratospheric dust blocks sunlight and thereby decreases average temperatures by several degrees for some time. That the Australasian impact reaches this lower limit of the 'global effects threshold' shows that it indeed must be considered a very significant impact.

Airblast and wildfire damage

Apart from possible short-term effects due to stratospheric dust release, ozone depletion and acid rains, simple scaling relationships from the Chapman and Morrison paper also show that an area of about 150 000 to 200 000 square kilometres, or an area 500 kilometre in diameter, would be directly affected by severe air blast phenomena. Such an area is significant in size: it amounts to as much as about one third of the longitudinal diameter

of the Southeast Asian peninsula/Sunda shelf at this location. In a larger area of Indochina with a size of roughly 1000 km, impact ejecta in the form of large Muong-Nong type tektites occur. Muong-Nong tektites are large, have a layered structure, are believed to be ballistic ejecta from the impact crater (Fiske 1996), and lack the solidified aerodynamic shapes of smaller tektites. These Muong-Nong tektites are believed to have been still plastic and "hot" upon landing (Fiske 1996), introducing the possibility that they started wildfires in their area of occurrence, an area which covers a significant part of the Indochinean peninsula. When all these effects are taken together, the result suggests considerable ecological havoc on a sub-continental scale.

Presence of hominins at the time of impact

When this large impact occurred, early hominins were already venturing outside Africa. Whether hominins had already reached the area of impact is less certain. But they were certainly close by. Hominin presence in China is established from at least 1.2 Ma onwards (see chapter 2.1), well before the impact event occurred. For southeast Asia, the dates are still controversial (see chapters 1.1 and 2.2).

Hominin presence cannot be secured for the actual impact area (believed to be in the area of Laos-Cambodia-Vietnam: see Lee and Wei 2000) before roughly 0.5 Ma, but the paucity of faunal assemblages dating to before the later Middle Pleistocene for this area suggests this to be perhaps due to sampling bias (see chapter 2.2). A few purported 'archaeological' sites believed to date to the Lower-Middle Pleistocene transition (and thus to the time of the impact) on the mainland of southeast Asia are highly problematic. This includes the Baise sites from southern China, believed to date to the time of impact and to preserve evidence of impact-generated forest fires (Hou *et al.* 2000 – see chapter 2.1). Java (Indonesia) might have been settled as early as the Jaramillo geomagnetic subchron, but the chronology is very poor and there is a remote possibility that this part of the Sunda shelf was in reality not colonized before early Brunhes times (see chapter 1.1). Evidence for a 0.8 Ma occupation of Walacea, from the island of Flores, is doubtful (chapter 2.2). In summary, early hominins (*Homo erectus*) had colonized east Asia (China) well before the impact occurred. Southeast Asia may have been occupied already during the time of the impact, depending on whether one accepts a 1.1 Ma occupation date for Java (chapter 1.1).

This makes the Asian population of *Homo erectus* a contemporary or near-contemporary of the impact event that created the Australasian tektite strewnfield. If Java was occupied around the time of the impact, then chances are high that the actual impact area was as well, for hominins first had to cross this area before reaching Java. Does this mean that the first human victims of a significantly large impact catastrophy occurred 0.8 Ma ago? This would bring death through impact out of the hypothetical realm and into the realm of reality, as far as humans is concerned. In the current debates on the significance of a threat of cosmic impact, this is an important conclusion. It shows that the danger of humanity experiencing a large impact is real. The evidence is there to show that it has happened before.

Significant effects?

While very significant on a sub-continental scale and perhaps (and inevitably if they indeed were present in the actual impact affected area) leading to the extinction of a local subgroup of *Homo erectus*, there is no evidence that the impact and its aftermath led to long-term climatic/environmental disturbance, or seriously affected human evolution. A detailed study of Deep Ocean Drilling Core data by Schneider *et al.* (1992) revealed no evidence for significant climatic perturbations on a timescale of 1 ka or longer: compared with the strong effects of glacial cycles, this impact was hardly a ripple in the ocean. Likewise, even if local *Homo erectus*

inhabitants of the impact area were wiped out (as seems likely) on a sub-continental scale, this seems to have had little evolutionary effect. Once the dust settled, the population was simply restocked with *Homo erectus* from outside the impact-affected area. Such abandonment and repopulation of areas were probably common in the Pleistocene, certainly in this area, and connected to events that had nothing to do with impacts but were of similar scale or even scales surpassing the effects of the impact: an example being the strong effects of cyclical flooding and re-emergence of the Sunda shelf just south of the impact area, which were due to the cycles of sea-level change connected to the glacial cycles. Outside southeast Asia, the effects of the glacial cycles were even more profound in shaping human evolution and human biogeography, as is shown by the history of Upper Pleistocene human occupation of Europe.

Impacts shaping human evolution?

It appears that only the largest of impacts would have had the potential to seriously shape human evolution: and with this is meant the very rare impacts of K/T size, which are not likely to have happened during the past 5 to 8 million years of hominin evolution (such an impact would have yielded clearly discernable signs in the geological and palaeontological record, in the form of mass extinctions of a considerable part of the global fauna and flora, as well as a widespread (=global) presence of impact ejecta). Any smaller impacts will simply have had effects which were insignificant compared to the powerful driving force of the glacial cycles of the last few million years. Cosmic impact effects would have been very local and temporary when seen in that context, being hardly more than ripples in the ocean, whereby an area was temporarily depopulated and subsequently repopulated again. Where climatic effects (and by inference ecological effects) remain short term and do not wipe out significant parts of the global or continental biomass (and there is no evidence for such non-short term, non-local effects due to impact in palaeoclimatological and biochronological proxy data of the past million years, while these effects should be discernable if they did occur), evolutionary effects will probably remain very minor and will probably not lead to either profound extinctions or profound speciation events. Only under very specific conditions could a theoretical role in shaping evolution come about from smaller impacts. This would for example happen when effects of an impact would open up a route to an unoccupied (sub-)continent. With regard to the Australasian impact, if we accept a 1.1 Ma occupation of Java, the impact would have occurred too late to assign it a possible role in opening up a route to Java by breaching a hypothetical ecological barrier on the southeast Asian mainland. Significant as it was, the truth is that the impact apparently has had little effect on Asian hominin evolution and biogeography. Evidence points out that *Homo erectus* was in Asia before the impact, and *Homo erectus* was in Asia after the impact.

Bibliography

Agusti J., Oms O. and Pares J.M., 1999: Calibration of the Early-Middle Pleistocene transition in the continental beds of the Guadix-Baza Basin (SE Spain). *Quat. Sci. Review* 18, 1409-1417.

Aiello L.C., 1998: The 'expensive tissue hypothesis' and the evolution of the human adaptive niche: a study in comparative anatomy. In: Bailey J. (ed.), *Science in Archaeology. An agenda for the future*, p. 25-36. English Heritage, London.

Aiello L.C. and Dunbar R.I.M., 1993: Neocortex Size, Group Size, and the Evolution of Language. *Current Anthropology* 34, 184-193.

Aiello L.C. and Wheeler P., 1995: The Expensive Tissue Hypothesis: the brain and the digestive system in human and primate evolution. *Current Anthropology* 36, 199-221.

Aitken M.J., 1990: *Science-based Dating in Archaeology*. Longman, London.

Aitken M.J., 1995: Chronometric techniques for the Middle Pleistocene. In: Roebroeks W. and Van Kolfschoten T. (eds.), *The earliest occupation of Europe, Proceedings of the ESF workshop at Tautavel (France), 1993*, p. 269-277. Leiden University Press, Leiden.

Albrecht G. and Moser J., 1996: Geröllgeräte aus Schottern des Mekong? In: Campen I., Hahn J, and Uerpmann M. (eds.), *Spuren der Jagd – Die Jagd nach Spuren (Tübinger Monographien zur Urgeschichte* 11), p. 133-146.

Alvarez L.W., Alvarez W., Asaro F. and Michel H.V., 1980: Extraterrestrial cause for the Cretacious-Tertiary extinction. *Science* 208, 1095-1108.

An Z. and Ho C.K., 1989: New Magnetostratigraphic Dates of Lantian *Homo erectus. Quaternary Research* 32, 213-221.

Arambourg C., 1949: Sur la présence dans le Villafranchien d'Algérie de vestiges éventuels d'industrie humaine. *C. R. Acad. Sci. Paris* 299, 66-67.

Ascenzi A., Bidditu I., Cassoli P.F., Segre A.G. and Segre-Naldini E., 1996: A calvarium of late *Homo erectus* from Ceprano, Italy. *Journal of Human Evolution* 31, 409-423.

Asfaw B., Beyene Y., Suwa G., Walter R.C., White T.D., WoldeGabriel G. and Yemane T., 1992: The earliest Acheulean from Konso-Gardula. *Nature* 360, 732-735.

Atapuerca Excavation Team, 1992: *Excursion a los Yacimentos Mesopleistocenicos de la Sierra de Atapuerca (Ibeas de Juarros / Atapuerca, Burgos), 1 julio 1992.*

Austin L., 1994: The life and death of a Boxgrove biface. In Ashton N. and David A. (eds.), *Stories in Stone*, p. 119-126. Lithic Studies Society Occasional paper no. 4.

Aziz F., Shibasaki T. and Suminto, 1985: Pucung site. In: Watanabe N. and Kadar D. (eds.), *Quaternary geology of the hominid fossil bearing Formations in Java. Report of the Indonesia-Japan Joint Research Project CTA-41, 1976-1979*, p. 87-90. Geological Research and Development Centre special publication no. 4, Bandung.

Backwell L.R. and d'Errico F., 2001: Evidence of termite foraging by Swartkrans early hominids. *Proc. Nat. Acad. Sci. USA* 98, 1358-1363.

Baksi A.K., Hsu V., McWilliams M.O. and Farrar E., 1992: ^{40}Ar/^{39}Ar Dating of the Brunhes-Matuyama Geomagnetic Field Reversal. *Science* 256, 356-357.

Balter M. and Gibbons A., 2000: A Glimpse of Humans' First Journey Out of Africa. *Science* 288, 948-950.

Balter M. and Gibbons A., 2002: Were 'Little People' the First to Venture Out of Africa? *Science* 297, 26-27.

Bandet Y., Sémah F., Sartono S. and Djubiantono T., 1989: Premier peuplement par les mammifères d'une région de Java Est à la fin du Pliocène, âge de la fauna du Gunung Betak, près de Kedungbrubus (Indonésie). *C.R. Acad. Sci. Paris* 308-II, 867-870.

Bartstra G., 1982: *Homo erectus erectus*, the search for his artifacts. *Current Anthropology* 23, 318-320.

Bartstra G., 1983: Some remarks upon: fossil man from Java, his age, and his tools. *Bijdragen tot de Taal-, Land- en Volkenkunde* 139, 421-434.

Bartstra G., 1985: Sangiran: the stone implements of Ngebung and the Palaeolithic of Java. *Mod. Quat. Res. SE Asia* 9, 99-113.

Bartstra G. and Basoeki, 1989: Recent work on the Pleistocene and the Palaeolithic of Java. *Current Anthropology* 30, 241-244.

Bartstra G., Soegondho S. and Van der Wijk A., 1988: Ngandong man, age and artifacts. *Journal of Human Evolution* 17, 325-337.

Bartstra G., Keates S.G., Basoeki and Kalupa B., 1991: On the dispersion of *Homo sapiens* in Eastern Indonesia: the palaeolithic of South Sulawesi. *Current Anthropology* 32, 317-321.

Bar-Yosef O., 1994: The Lower Paleolithic of the Near East. *Journal of World Prehistory* 8, 211-265.

Bar-Yosef O., 1995: The Lower and Middle Palaeolithic in the Mediterranean Levant: Chronology and Cultural entities. In: Ullrich H. (ed.), *Man and Environment in the Palaeolithic (Études et Recherches Archéologiques de l'Université de Liège* 62), p. 247-263. Liege.

Bar-Yosef O., 1999: Lower Paleolithic sites in south-western Asia – evidence for "Out of Africa" movements. *Anthropologie* 37, 51-69.

Bar-Yosef O. and Goren-Inbar N., 1993: *The lithic assemblage of 'Ubeidiya, a Lower Palaeolithic site in the Jordan valley*. Qedem (Monographs of the Institute of Archaeology) 34, Jerusalem.

Bar-Yosef O. and Shea J., 1999: Lithic Assemblages from New (1988-1994) Excavations at 'Ubeidiya: A Preliminary Report. *Journal of the Israel Prehistoric Society* 28, 5-20.

Belfer-Cohen A. and Goren-Inbar N., 1994: Cognition and communication in the Levantine Lower Palaeolithic. *World Archaeology* 26, 144-157.

Belitzky S., Goren-Inbar N. and Werker E., 1991: A Middle Pleistocene wooden plank with man-made polish. *Journal of Human Evolution* 20, 349-353.

Bellon H., Maury C.S., Soeria-Atmadja R., Polvé M., Pringgoprawiro H. and Priadi B., 1989: Chronologie 40K-40Ar du volcansime Tertiaire de Java Central (Indonésie): mise en évidence de deux épisodes distincts de magmatisme d'arc. *C. R. Acad. Sci. Paris* 309-II, 1971-1977.

Bellwood P., 1987: The Prehistory of Island Southeast Asia: a multidisciplinary review of recent research. *Journal of World Prehistory* 1, 171-224.

Bergman C.A. and Roberts M.B., 1988: Flaking technology at the Acheulean site of Boxgrove, West Sussex (England). *Revue archéologique de Picardie* 1-2, 105-113.

Bermúdez de castro J.M., Arsuaga J.L., Carbonell E., Rosas A., Martínez I. and Mosquera M., 1997: A hominid from the Lower Pleistocene of Atapuerca, Spain, possible ancestor to Neanderthals and modern humans. *Science* 276, 1392-1395.

Binford L.R., 1981: *Bones: Ancient men and modern myths*. Academic Press, New York.

Binford L.R., 1982: The Archaeology of Place. *Journal of Anthropological Archaeology* 1, 5-31.

Binford L.R., 1983: *In Pursuit of the Past. Decoding the Archaeological Record*. Thames and Hudson, London.

Binford L.R., 1984: *Faunal Remains from Klaasies River Mouth*. Academic Press, New York.

Binford L.R., 1987: Searching for Camps and Missing the Evidence? Another look at the Lower Palaeolithic. In: Soffer O. (ed.), *The Pleistocene Old World, regional perspectives*, p. 17-31. Plenum Press, New York.

Binford L.R., 1989: Technology of Early Man: An Organizational Approach to the Oldowan. In: Binford L.R. (ed.), *Debating Archaeology*, p. 437-463. Academic Press, New York.

Binford L.R., 1992: Seeing the Present and Interpreting the Past – and Keeping Things Straight. In: Rossignol J. and Wandsnider L. (eds.), *Space, Time and Archaeological Landscapes*, p. 43-59. Plenum Press, New York.

Biswas D.K., Hyodo M., Taniguchi Y., Kaneko M., Katoh S., Sato H., Kinugasa Y. and Mizuno K., 1999: Magnetostratigraphy of Plio-Pleistocene sediments in a 1700-m core from Osaka Bay, southwestern Japan and short geomagnetic events in the middle Matuyama and early Brunhes chrons. *Palaeogeography, Palaeoclimatology, Palaeoecology* 148, 233-248.

Bleed P., 1986: The optimal design of hunting weapons: maintainability or reliability. *American Antiquity* 51, 737-747.

Blum J.D., Papanastassiou D.A., Koeberl C. and Wasserburg G.J., 1992: Neodymium and Strontium isotopic study of Australasian tektites: new constraints on the provenance and age of target materials. *Geochimica et Cosmochimica Acta* 56, 483-492.

Blumenschine R.J., 1987: Characteristics of an Early Hominid Scavenging Niche. *Current Anthropology* 28, 383-407.

Blumenschine R.J. and Masao F.T., 1991: Living sites at Olduvai Gorge, Tanzania? Preliminary landscape archaeology results in the basal Bed II lake margin zone. *Journal of Human Evolution* 21, 451-462.

Blumenschine R.J. and Cavallo J.A., 1992: Scavenging and Human Evolution. *Scientific American* 267, 70-76.

Bocherens H., Billiou D., Marioti A., Patou-Mathias M., Otte M., Bonjean D. and Toussaint M., 1999: Palaeoenvironmental and palaeodietary implications of isotopic biochemistry of last interglacial Neanderthal and mammal bones in Scladina cave (Belgium). *Journal of Archaeological Science* 26, 599-607.

Bonifay E. and Vandermeersch B. (eds.), 1991: *Les premiers Européens*. Editions CTHS, Paris.

Braüer G. and Schultz M., 1996: The morphological affinities of the Plio-Pleistocene mandible from Dmanisi, Georgia. *Journal of Human Evolution* 30, 445-481.

Bromage T.G. and Schrenk F., 1995: Biogeographic and climatic basis for a narrative of early hominid evolution. *Journal of Human Evolution* 28, 109-114.

Bromage T.G., Schrenk F. and Juwayeyi Y.M., 1995: Paleobiogeography of the Malawi rift: age and vertebrate palaeontology of the Chiwondo beds, Northern Malawi. *Journal of Human Evolution* 28, 37-57.

Brunnacker K., Boenigk W., Bruder G., Hahn G.G., Ronen A. and Tillmanns W., 1989: Artefakte im Altquartär von Obergaliläa (Nordisrael). *Eiszeitalter und Gegenwart* 39, 109-120.

Bunn and Ezzo J.A., 1993: Hunting and Scavenging by Plio-Pleistocene Hominids: Nutritional Constraints, Archaeological Patterns, and Behavioural Implications. *Journal of Archaeological Science* 20, 365-398.

Bunn H., Harris J.W.K., Isaac G., Kaufulu Z., Kroll E., Schick K.D., Toth N. and Behrensmeyer A.K., 1980: FxJj50: an Early Pleistocene site in northern Kenya. *World Archaeology* 12, 109-136.

111

Carbonell E., Bermudez de Castro J.M., Arsuaga J.L., Diez J.C., Rosas A., Cuenca-Bescos G., Sala R., Mosquera M. and Rodriguez X.P., 1995: Lower Pleistocene Hominids and Artifacts from Atapuerca-TD6 (Spain). *Science* 269, 826-830.

Chapman C.R. and Morrison D., 1994: Impacts on the Earth by astroids and comets: assessing the hazard. *Nature* 367, 33-39.

Ciochon R.L. and Olsen J.W., 1986: Palaeoanthropological and Archaeological Research in the Socialist Republic of Vietnam. *Journal of Human Evolution* 15, 623-633.

Ciochon R., Vu T., Larick R., González L., Grün R., De Vos J., Yonge C., Taylor L., Yoshida H. and Reagan M., 1996: Dated co-occurrence of *Homo erectus* and *Gigantopithecus* from Tham Khuyen Cave, Vietnam. *Proc. Natl. Acad. Sci. USA* 93, 3016-3020.

Clark J.D., 1958: The Natural Fracture of Pebbles from the Batoka Gorge, Northern Rhodesia, and its bearing on the Kafuan Industreis of Africa. *Proc. Prehist. Soc.* 24, 64-77.

Clark G., 1977: *World Prehistory in new perspective.* Cambridge University Press, Cambridge.

Clark J.D., 1992: The Earlier Stone Age/Lower Palaeolithic in North Africa and the Sahara. *Africa Praehistorica* 5, 17-37.

Clark J.D., 1994: The Acheulian Industrial Complex in Africa and Elsewhere. In: Corruccini R.S. and Ciochon R.L. (eds.), *Integrative Paths to the Past, Palaeoanthropological Advances in Honor of F. Clark Howell*, p. 451-469. Prentice Hall, New Jersey.

Clark J.D. and Kurashina H., 1979: Hominid occupation of the East-Central Highlands of Ethiopia in the Plio-Pleistocene. *Nature* 282, 33-39.

Clark J.D. and Schick K.D., 1988: Context and content: impressions of Palaeolithic sites and assemblages in the People's Republic of China. *Journal of Human Evolution* 17, 439-448.

Clark J.D., De Heinzelin J., Schick K.D., Hart W.K., White T.D., WoldeGabriel G., Walter R.C., Suwa G., Asfaw B., Vrba E. and Haile-Selassie Y., 1994: African *Homo erectus*: old radiometric ages and young Oldowan assemblages in the Middle Awash valley, Ethiopia. *Science* 264, 1907-1910.

Cook J., Stringer C.B., Currant A.P., Schwarcz H.P. and Wintle A.G., 1982: A Review of the Chronology of the European Middle Pleistocene Hominid Record. *Yearbook of Physical Anthropology* 25, 19-65.

Curtiss G., Swisher C. and Lewin R., 2000: *Java man, How Two Geologists Changed the History of Human Evolution.* Little, Brown and Company, London.

Dennell R.W., 1989: Reply to Hemingway and Stapert (1989). *Current Anthropology* 30, 318-322.

Davidson W. and Noble I., 1993: Tools and language in human evolution. In: Gibson R. and Ingold T. (eds.), *Tools, Language and Cognition in Human Evolution*, p. 363-388. Cambridge University Press, Cambridge.

Dean D. and Delson E., 1995: *Homo* at the gates of Europe. *Science* 373, 472-473.

DeBono H. and Goren-Inbar N., 2001: Note on a Link between Acheulian Handaxes and the Levallois Method. *Journal of the Israel Prehistoric Society* 31, 9-23.

DeMenocal P.B., 1995: Plio-Pleistocene African Climate. *Science* 270, 53-59.

Dennell R.W., 1998: Grasslands, tool making and the hominid colonization of southern Asia: a reconsideration. In: Petraglia M.D. and Korisettar R. (eds.), *Early Human Behaviour in Global Context. The Rise and Diversity of the Lower Palaeolithic Record*, p. 280-303. Routledge, London.

Dennell R.W. and Roebroeks W., 1996: The earliest colonization of Europe, the short chronology revisited. *Antiquity* 70, 535-542.

Dennell R.W., Rendell H.M. and Hailwood E.A., 1988a: Early tool-making in Asia, two-million-year-old artefacts in Pakistan. *Antiquity* 62, 98-106.

Dennell R.W., Rendell H.M., and Hailwood E., 1988b: Late Pliocene Artefacts from Northern Pakistan. *Current Anthropology* 29, 495-498.

Dennell R.W., Hurcombe L.M., Coard R., Beech M., Anwar M. and Ul Haq S., 1993: The 1990 field season of the British Archaeological Mission to Pakistan in the Baroth area of the Pabbi Hills, Northern Pakistan. In: Adalbert G.J. and Mevissen G.J.R. (eds.), *South Asian Archaeology 1991*. Franz Steiner Verlag, Stuttgart.

Dennell R.W., Rendell H.M., Hurcombe L. and Hailwood E.A., 1994: Archaeological Evidence for Hominids in Northern Pakistan Before One Million Years Ago. *Courier Forschungs-Institut Senckenberg* 171, 151-155.

De Terra H., 1943: Pleistocene Geology and Early Man in Java. *Transactions of the American Philosophical Society* 32, 437-464.

De Vos J., 1985 : Faunal Stratigraphy and Correlation of the Indonesian Hominid Sites. In: Delson E. (ed.), *Ancestors: The Hard Evidence*, p. 215-220. Alan R. Liss Inc., New York.

De Vos J. and Sondaar P.Y., 1994: Dating Hominid Sites in Indonesia. *Science* 266, 1726.

De Vos J., Sondaar P.Y., Van den Bergh G.D. and Aziz F., 1994: The *Homo* Bearing Deposits of Java and its Ecological Context. *Courier Forschungs-Institut Senckenberg* 171, 129-140.

Dincauze D.F., 1984: An Archeo-logical Evaluation of the Case for Pre-Clovis Occupations. *Advances in World Archaeology* 3, 275-323.

Ding Z.L. and Yang S.L., 2000: C_3/C_4 vegetation evolution over the last 7.0 Myr in the Chinese Loess Plateau: evidence from pedogenic carbonate $\delta^{13}C$. *Palaeogeography, Palaeoclimatology, Palaeoecology* 160, 291-299.

Domínguez-Rodrigo M., 1999: Flesh availability and bone modification in carcasses consumed by lions. *Palaeogeography, Palaeoclimatology and Palaeoecology* 149, 373-388.

Domínguez-Rodrigo M., 2001: A study of carnivore competition in riparian and open habitats of modern savannas and its implications for hominid behavioral modelling. *Journal of Human Evolution* 40, 77-98.

Domínguez-Rodrigo M., 2002: Hunting and Scavenging by Early Humans: The State of the debate. *Journal of World Prehistory* 16, 1-54.

Domínguez-Rodrigo M., Serrallonga J., Juan-Tresserras J., Alcala L. and Luque L., 2001: Woodworking activities by early humans: a plant residue analysis on Acheulian stone tools from Peninj (Tanzania). *Journal of Human Evolution* 40, 289-299.

Dubois E., 1894: *Pithecanthropus erectus, eine Menschenaehnliche uebergangsform aus Java*. Landesdruckerei, Batavia.

Dunbar R.I.M., 1992: Neocortex size as constraint on group size in primates. *Journal of Human Evolution* 22, 469-493.

Dzaparidze V., Bosinksi G., Bugianasvili T., Gbaunia L., Justus A., Klupotovskaja N., Kvavadze E., Lordkipanidze D., Majsuradze G., Mgeladze N., Nioradze M., Pavlenisvili E., Schminke H., Sologasvili D., Tusabramisvili D., Tvalcmelidze M. and Vekua A., 1989: Der Altpaläolitische fundplatz Dmanisi in Georgien (Kaukasus). *Jahrbuch des Römisch-Germanischen Zentralmuseums Mainz* 36, 67-116.

Etler D.A. and Zhou G., 1998: Asian fossils and African origins. *Abstracts for the Palaeoanthropology Society Meetings, Seattle, 24-25 March 1998 (Journal of Human Evolution 34, A6)*.

Falguères C., Bahain J.J., Yokoyama Y., Arsuaga J.L., Bermudez de Castro J.M., Carbonell E., Bischoff J.L. and Dolo J.M., 1999: Earliest humans in Europe: the age of TD6 Gran Dolina, Atapuerca, Spain. *Journal of Human Evolution* 37, 343-352.

Fiske P.S., 1996: Constraints on the formation of layered tektites from the excavation and analysis of layered tektites from northeast Thailand. *Meteoritics and Planetary Science* 31, 42-45.

Fiske P.S., Putthapiban P. and Wasson J.T., 1996: Excavation and analysis of layered tektites from Northeast Thailand: results of 1994 field expedition. *Meteoritics and Planetary Science* 31, 36-41.

Fiske P.S., Schnetzler C.C., McHone J., Chanthavaichith K.K., Homsombath I., Phouthakayalat T., Khenthavong B. and Xuan P.T., 1999: Layered tektites of Southeast Asia: Field studies in Central Laos and Vietnam. *Meteoritics and Planetary Science* 34, 757-762.

Fizet M., Mariotti A., Bocherens H., Lange-Badré B., Vandermeersch B., Borel J. and Bellon G., 1995: Effect of diet, physiology and climate on carbon and nitrogen stable isotopes of collagen in a Late Pleistocene anthropic palaeoecosystem: Marrillac, Charente, France. *Journal of Archaeological Science* 22, 67-79.

Freeman K.H. and Colarusso L.A., 2001: Molecular and isotopic records of C_4 grassland expansion in the late Miocene. *Geochimica et Cosmochimica Acta* 65, 1439-1454.

Fudali R., 1993: The stratigraphic age of Australites revisited. *Meteoritics* 28, 114-119.

Fullagar R.L.K., Price D.M. and Head L.M., 1996: Early human occupation of Northern Australia: archaeology and thermoluminiscence dating of Jinmium rock-shelter, Northern Territory. *Antiquity* 70, 751-773.

Gabunia L. and Vekua A., 1995: A Plio-Pleistocene hominid from Dmanisi, East Georgia, Caucasus. *Nature* 373, 509-512.

Gabunia L.K., Jöris O. Justus A., Lordkipanidze D., Muschelisvili A., Nioradze M., Swisher C.C., Vekua A.K., Bosinski G., Ferring R.C., Majsuradze G.M. and Tvalcmelidze M., 1999: Neue hominidenfunde des Altpaläolitischen Fundplatz Dmanisi (Georgien, Kaukasus) im kontext aktueller grabungsergebnisse. *Archäologisches Korrespondenzblatt* 29, 451-488.

Gabunia L., Vekua A. and Lordkipanidze D., 2000a: The environmental contexts of early human occupation of Georgia (Transcaucasia). *Journal of Human Evolution* 38, 785-802.

Gabunia L., Vekua A., Lordkipanidze D., Swisher C.C., Ferring R., Justus A., Nioradze M., Tvalchrelidze M., Antón S.C., Bosinski G., Jöris O., De Lumley M-A., Majsuradze G. and Mouskhelishvili A., 2000b: Earliest Pleistocene Hominid Cranial Remains from Dmansis, Republic of Georgia: taxonomy, Geological Setting, and Age. *Science* 288, 1019-1025.

Gaignepain J., Hedley I., Bahain J.J. and Wagner J.J., 1992: Etude magnétostratigraphique du site de Ca'Belvedere di Monte Poggiolo (Forlì, Italie) et de son contexte stratigraphique. Premiers résultats. In: Peretto C. (ed.), *I primi abitanti della Valle Padana: Monte Poggiolo. Nel quadro delle conoscenze Europee*, p. 319-336. Jaca Books spa, Milano.

Gamble C., 1993: *Timewalkers. The prehistory of global colonization.* Penguin books, London.

Gamble C., 1994: Time for Boxgrove Man. *Nature* 369, 275-276.

Gamble C., 1995: The earliest occupation Of Europe: the environmental background. In: Roebroeks W. and Van Kolfschoten T. (eds.), *The earliest occupation of Europe, Proceedings of the ESF workshop at Tautavel (France), 1993*, p. 279-295. Leiden University Press, Leiden.

Gamble C., 1998: Palaeolithic society and the realease from Proximity: a network approach to intimate relations. *World Archaeology* 29, 426-449.

Gamble C., 1999: *The Palaeolithic Societies of Europe.* Cambridge University Press, Cambridge.

Gaudzinsky S., 1996: On bovid assemblages and their consequences for the knowledge of subsistence patterns in the Middle Palaeolithic. *Proc. Prehist. Soc.* 62, 19-39.

Gaudzinsky S., 1999: The faunal record of the Lower and Middle Palaeolithic of Europe. remarks on human interference. In: Roebroeks W. and Gamble C. (eds.), *The Middle Palaeolithic occupation of Europe*, p. 215-233. Leiden University, Leiden.

Gaudzinsky S. and Roebroeks W., 2000: Adults only. Reindeer hunting at the Middle Palaeolithic site Salzgitter-Lebenstedt, northern Germany. *Journal of Human Evolution* 38, 497-521.

Gibbons A., 2001: American Association of Physical Anthropologists meeting: Studying Humans-and Their Cousins and Parasites. *Science* 292, 627-629.

Gibert J., Arribas A., Martinez B., Albadalejo S., Gaete R., Gibert L., Oms O., Peñas C. and Torrico R., 1994: Biostraigraphie et magnétostratigraphie des gisements à présence humaine et action anthropique de Pléistocène Inférieur de la région d'Orce (Granada, Espagne). *C. R. Acad. Sci. Paris* 318-II, 1277-1282.

Gibert J., Campillo D., Arqués J.M., Gracia-Olivares E., Borja C. and Lowenstein J., 1988a: Hominid status of the Orce cranial fragment reasserted. *Journal of Human Evolution* 34, 203-217.

Gibert J. Gibert Ll., Iglesias A. and Maestro E., 1988b: Two "oldowan" assemblages in the Plio-Pleistocene deposits of the Orce region, southeast Spain. *Antiquity* 72, 17-25.

Ginsberg L., Ingavat R. and Sen S., 1982: Découverte dún faune d'age Pléistocéne moyen terminal (Loangien) dans le nord de la Thaïlande. *C. R. Acad. Sci. Paris* 294-II, 295-297.

Glass B.P., 1993: Geographic variations in abundance of Australasian microtektites, implications concerning the location and size of the source crater. *Meteoritics* 28, 354.

Glass B.P., Muenow D.W., Bohor B.F. and meeker G.P., 1997: Fragmentation and hydration of tektites and microtektites. *Meteoritics and Planetary Science* 32, 333-341.

Goren-Inbar N. and Saragusti I., 1996: An Acheulian Bifacial Assemblage from Gesher Benot Ya'aqov: indications of African affinities. *Journal of Field Archaeology* 23, 15-30.

Goren-Inbar N., Zohar I. and Ben-Ami D., 1991: A New Look at Old Cleavers – Gesher Benot Ya'aqov. *Journal of The Israel Prehistoric Society* 24, 7-33.

Goren-Inbar N., Belitzky S., Verosub K., Werker E., Kislev M., Heimann A., Carmii I. and Rosenfeld A., 1992: New Discoveries at the Middle Pleistocene Acheulian Site of Gesher Benot Ya'agov, Israel. *Quaternary Research* 38, 1176-128.

Goren-Inbar N., Feibel C.S., Verosub K.L., melamed Y., Kilsev M.E., Tchernov E. and Saragusti I., 2000: Pleistocene Milestones on the Out-of-Africa Corridor at Gesher Benot Ya'aqov, Israel. *Science* 289, 944-945.

Goren-Inbar N., Sharon G., Melamed Y. and Kislev M., 2002: Nuts, nut cracking, and pitted stones at Gesher Benot Ya'aqov, Israel. *Proc. Nat. Acad. Sci. USA* 99, 2455-2460.

Gowlett J.A.J., 1988: A case of Developed Oldowan in the Acheulean? *World Archaeology* 20, 13-26.

Grün R., Huang P., Wu X., Stringer C.B., Thorne A.G. and McCulloch M., 1997; ESR analysis of teeth from the palaeoanthropological site of Zhoukoudian, China. *Journal of Human Evolution* 32, 83-91.

Grün R., Spooner N.A., Thorne A., Mortimer G., Simpson J.J., McCulloch M.T., Taylor L. and Curnoe D., 2000: Age of the Lake Mungo 3 skeleton, reply to Bowler and Magee and to Gillespie and Roberts. *Journal of Human Evolution* 38, 733-741.

Guenca-Bescós G., Laplana C. and Canudo J.I., 1999: Biochronological implications of the *Arvicolidae* (Rodentia, Mammalia) from the Lower Pleistocene hominid-bearing level of Trinchera Dolina 6 (TD6, Atapuerca, Spain). *Journal of Human Evolution* 37, 353-373.

Guérin C., Bar-Yosef O., Debard F., Faure M., Shea J. and Tchernov E., 1996: Mission Archéologique et Paléontologique dans le Pléistocene ancien d'Oubéidiyeh (Israël), resultats 1992-1994. *C. R. Acad. Sci. Paris* 322-II, 709-712.

Guo S., Hao X. and Chen B., 1996: Fission track dating of Paleolithic site at Bose in Guangxi, south China. *Acta Anthropologica Sinica* 15, 347-350.

Guo S., Huang W., Hao X, and Chen B., 1997: Fission track dating of ancient man site in Baise, China, and its significances in space research, paleomagnetism and stratigraphy. *Radiation Measurement* 28, 565-570.

Guthrie R.D., 2001: Origin and causes of the Mammoth steppe. A story of cloud cover, wooly mammoth tooth pits, buckles, and inside-out Beringia. *Quaternary Science Reviews* 20, 549-574.

Harris J.W.K. and Isaac G. Ll., 1976: The Karari Industry: Early Pleistocene archaeological evidence from the terrain east of Lake Turkana, Kenya. *Nature* 262, 102-106.

Harrison T., 1975: Tampan, Malaysia's Palaeolithic reconsidered. *Mod. Quat. Res. SE Asia* 1, 53-70.

Hartung J. and Koeberl C., 1994: In search of the Australasian tektite source crater: the Tonle Sap hypothesis. *Meteoritics* 29, 411-416.

Hemingway M.F. and Stapert D., 1989: Early Artefacts from Pakistan? Some Questions for the Excavators. *Current Anthropology* 30, 317-318.

Herzog M, 1952 (?): *De Annapurna Expeditie. De eerste top van 8000 m in de Himalaja bedwongen.* Scheltens & Giltay, Amsterdam.

Hoorn C., Ohja T. and Quade J., 2000: Palynological evidence for vegetation development and climatic change in the Sub-Himalayan Zone (Neogene, Central Nepal). *Palaeogeography, Palaeoclimatology, Palaeoecology* 163, 133-161.

Hou Y., Xu Z. and Huang W., 1999: Some new stone artifacts discovered in 1997 at Longgupo, southern China. *Longgupo Prehistoric Culture* 1, 69-80.

Hou Y., Potts R., Yuan B., Guo Z., Deina A., Wang W., Clark J., Xie G. and Huang W., 2000: Mid-Pleistocene Acheulean-like Stone Technology of the Bose Basin, South China. *Science* 287, 1622-1626.

Huang W., Leng J., Yan X and Xie G., 1990: Advanced opinions on the stratigraphy and chronology of Baise stone industry. *Acta Anthropologica Sinica* 9, 105-112.

Huang W., Ciochon R., Yumin G., Larick R., Fang Q., Schwarcz H., Yonge C., De Vos J. and Rink W, 1995: Early Homo and associated artefacts from Asia. *Nature* 378, 275-278.

Hublin J.J., 1985: Human fossils from the North African Middle Pleistocene and the origin of *Homo sapiens*. In: Delson E. (ed.), *Ancestors: The Hard Evidence*, p. 283-288. Alan R. Liss Inc., New York.

Huffman O.F., 2001: Geologic context and age of the Perning/Mojokerto *Homo erectus*, East Java. *Journal of Human Evolution* 40, 353-362.

Hurcombe L. and Dennell R.W., 1989: A pre-Acheulean, Lower Pleistocene Industry in the Pabbi Hills, Northern Pakistan? *South Asian Archaeology 1989*, 133-136

Hussain S.T., Van den Bergh G.D., Steensma K.J., De Visser J.A., De Vos J., Arif M., Van Dam J., Sondaar P.Y. and Malik S.B., 1992: Biostratigraphy of the Plio-Pleistocene continental sediments (Upper Siwaliks) of the mangla-Samwal Anticline, Azad Kashmir, Pakistan. *Proc. Kon. Ned. Akad. Wet.* 95, 65-80.

Hutterer K.L., 1985: The Pleistocene Archaeology of Southeast Asia in Regional Context. *Mod. Quat. Res. SE Asia* 9, 1-23.

Hyodo M., Sunata W. and Susanto E.E., 1992: A Long-Term geomagnetic Excursion from Plio-Pleistocene Sediments in Java. *Journal of Geophysical Research* 97B, 9323-9335.

Hyodo M, Watanabe N., Sunata W., Susanto E.E. and Wahyono H., 1993: Magnetostratigraphy of Hominid Fossil Bearing Formations in Sangiran and Mojokerto, Java. *Anthropol. Sci.* 101, 157-186.

Hyodo M., Nakaya H., Urabe A. Saegusa H., Xue S., Yin J. and Ji X., 2002: Paleomagnetic dates of hominid remains from Yuanmou, China, and other Asian sites. *Journal of Human Evolution* 43, 27-41.

Isaac G.Ll., 1975: Stratigraphy and Cultural patterns in East Africa During the Middle ranges of Pleistocene Time. In: Butzer K.W. and Isaac G.Ll. (eds.), *After the Australopithecines. Stratigraphy, ecology, and culture change in the Middle Pleistocene*, p. 495-542. Mouton Publishers, the Hague.

Isaac G.Ll., 1981: Stone Age visiting cards: approaches to the study of early land-use patterns. In: Hodder I., Isaac G. and Hammond N. (eds.), *Pattern of the Past*, p. 131-155. Cambridge University Press, Cambridge.

Isaac G.Ll., 1984: The Archaeology of Human Origins. Studies of the Lower Pleistocene in east Africa, 1971-1981. *Advances in World Archaeology* 3, 1-87.

Isaac G.Ll. and Isaac B. (eds.), 1997: *Koobi Fora research project Volume 5: Plio-Pleistocene archaeology*. Clarendon Press, Oxford.

Isaac G.Ll., Harris J.W.K. and Marshall F., 1981: Small is informative: the application of the study of mini-sites and least-effort criteria in the interpretation of the Early Pleistocene archaeological record at Koobi Fora, Kenya. In: Clark J.D. and Isaac G. (eds.), *Las Industrias mas Antiguas (X Congresso Union International de Ciencias Prehistoricas y Protohistoricas)*. Mexico City.

Itihara M., Kadar D. and Watanabe N., 1985a: Concluding remarks. In: Watanabe N. and Kadar D. (eds.), *Quaternary geology of the hominid fossil bearing Formations in Java. Report of the Indonesia-Japan Joint Research Project CTA-41, 1976-1979*, p. 367-378. Geological Research and Development Centre special publication no. 4, Bandung.

Itihara M., Wikarno and Kagemori Y., 1985b: Tektites from the Sangiran Area. In: Watanabe N. and Kadar D. (eds.), *Quaternary geology of the hominid fossil bearing Formations in Java. Report of the Indonesia-Japan Joint Research Project CTA-41, 1976-1979*, p. 125-128. Geological Research and Development Centre special publication no. 4, Bandung.

Itihara M., Sudijono, Kadar D., Shibasaki T., Kumai H., Yoshikawa S., Aziz F., Soeradi T., Wikarno, Kadar A.P., Hasibuan F. and Kagemori Y., 1985c: Geology and Stratigraphy of the Sangiran Area. In: Watanabe N. and Kadar D. (eds.), *Quaternary geology of the hominid fossil bearing Formations in Java. Report of the Indonesia-Japan Joint Research Project CTA-41, 1976-1979*, p. 7-27. Geological Research and Development Centre special publication no. 4, Bandung.

Itihara M., Watanabe N., Kadar D. and Kumai H., 1994: Quaternary Stratigraphy of the Hominid Fossil Bearing Formations in the Sangiran Area, central Java. *Courier Forschungs-Institut Senckenberg* 171, 123-128.

Izett G.A. and Obradovich J.D., 1992: Laser-fusion ^{40}Ar/^{39}Ar ages of Australasian tektites. *Lunar Planet. Sci.* 23, 593-594.

Jacob T., 1973: Palaeoanthropological Discoveries in Indonesia With Special Reference to the Finds of the Last two decades. *Journal of Human Evolution* 2, 473-485.

Jones P.R., 1980: Experimental butchery with modern stone tools and its relevance for palaeolithic archaeology. *World Archaeology* 12, 153-165.

117

Jones P.R., 1994: Results of experimental work in relation to the stone industries of Olduvai Gorge. In Leakey M.D. and Roe D.A. (eds.), *Olduvai Gorge volume 5, excavations in Beds III, IV and the Masek Beds, 1968-1971*, p. 254-298. Cambridge University Press, Cambridge.

Kadar D., 1985: Upper Cenozoic foraminiferal biostratigraphy of the kalibeng and Pucangan Formations in the Sangiran Dome area, central Java. In: Watanabe N. and Kadar D. (eds.), *Quaternary geology of the hominid fossil bearing Formations in Java. Report of the Indonesia-Japan Joint Research Project CTA-41, 1976-1979*, p. 219-229. Geological Research and Development Centre special publication no. 4, Bandung.

Keates S.G., 1994: Archaeological Evidence of Hominid Behaviour in Pleistocene China and Southeast Asia. *Courier Forschungs-Institut Senckenberg* 171, 141-150.

Keates S., 2000: Tektites and the Age Paradox in Mid-Pleistocene China. *Science* 289, 507a.

Keeley L.H., 1993: The Utilization of Lithic Artifacts. In: Singer R., Gladfelter B.G. and Wymer J.J. (eds.), *The Lower Paleolithic Site at Hoxne, England*, p. 129-149. University of Chicago Press, Chicago.

Keeley L.H. and Toth N., 1981: Microwear polishes on early stone tools from Koobi Fora, Kenya. *Nature* 293, 464-465.

Kibunjia M., 1994: Pliocene archaeological occurrences in the Lake Turkana basin. *Journal of Human Evolution* 27, 159-171

Kibunjia M., Roche H., Brown F.H. and Leakey R.E., 1992: Pliocene and Pleistocene archaeological sites west of Lake Turkana, Kenya. *Journal of Human Evolution* 23, 431-438.

Kingston J.D., Marino B.D. and Hill A., 1994: Isotopic Evidence for neogene Hominid Paleoenvironments in the Kenya Rift Valley. *Science* 264, 955-959.

Koeberl C. and Glass B.P., 2000: Tektites and the Age Paradox in Mid-Pleistocene China. *Science* 289, 507a.

Kolen J., 1999: Hominids without homes. On the nature of Middle Palaeolithic settlement in Europe. In Roebroeks W. and Gamble C. (eds.), *The Middle Palaeolithic occupation of Europe*, p. 139-175. University of Leiden, Leiden.

Kumai H. Itihara M., Sudijono, Shibasaki T., Aziz F., Yoshikawa S., Akahane S. Soeradi T., Hayashi T. and Furuyama K., 1985: Geology and stratigraphy of the Mojokerto area. In: Watanabe N. and Kadar D. (eds.), *Quaternary geology of the hominid fossil bearing Formations in Java. Report of the Indonesia-Japan Joint Research Project CTA-41, 1976-1979*, p. 55-61. Geological Research and Development Centre special publication no. 4, Bandung.

Langbroek M., 1998: *Maastricht-Belvédère site H. Techno-typologische analyse van een Midden-Paleolitische vuursteenscatter*. Universiteit Leiden, unpublished report.

Langbroek M., 2001: The trouble with Neandertals. *Archaeological Dialogues* 8, 123-151.

Langbroek M. and Roebroeks W., 2000: Extraterrestrial evidence on the age of the hominids from Java. *Journal of Human Evolution* 38, 595-600.

Larick R. and Ciochon R.L., 1996: The African Emergence and early Asian Dispersals of the Genus *Homo*. *American Scientist* 84, 538-551.

Larick R., Ciochon R.L., Ziam Y., Sudijono, Suminto, Rizal Y. and Aziz F., 2000: Lithostratigraphic Context for Kln-1993.05-SNJ, a Fossil Colobine Maxilla from Jokotingkir, Sangiran Dome. *International Journal of Primatology* 21, 731-759.

Larick R., Ciochon R.L., Zaim Y., Sudijono, Suminto, Rizal Y., Aziz F., Reagan M. and Heizler M., 2001: Early Pleistocene ^{40}Ar/^{39}Ar ages for Bapang Formation hominins, Central Jawa, Indonesia. *Proc. National Acad. Sciences, USA* 98, 4866-4871.

Leakey M.D., 1971: *Olduvai Gorge. Volume 3: excavations in Beds I and II, 1960-1963*. Cambridge University Press, Cambridge.

Leakey M.D., 1975: Cultural Patterns in the Olduvai Sequence. In: Butzer K.W. and Isaac G.Ll. (eds.), *After the Australopithecines. Stratigraphy, ecology, and culture change in the Middle Pleistocene*, p. 477-493. Mouton Publishers, the Hague.

Leakey M.G., Feibel C.S., McDougall I. and Walker A., 1995: New four million-year-old hominid species from Kanapoi and Allia Bay, Kenya. *Nature* 376, 565-571.

Leakey M.G., Spoor F., Brown F.H., Gathogo P.N., Kiarie C., Leakey L.N. and McDougall I., 2001: New hominin genus from eastern Africa shows diverse middle Pliocene lineages. Nature 410, 433-440.

Leakey M.D., 1975: Cultural Patterns in the Olduvai Sequence. In: Butzer K.W. and Isaac G. Ll. (eds.), *After the Australopithecines: stratigraphy, ecology, and culture change in the Middle Pleistocene*, p. 477-493. Mouton Publishers, The Hague.

Lee M. and Wei K., 2000: Australasian microtektites in the South China Sea and the West Philippine Sea: Implications for age, size, and location of the impact crater. *Meteoritics and Planetary Science* 35, 1151-1155.

Lee-Thorp J., Thackeray J.F. and Van der Merwe N., 2000: The hunters and the hunted revisited. *Journal of Human Evolution* 39, 565-576.

Leinders J.J.M., Aziz F., Sondaar P.Y. and De Vos J., 1985: The age of the hominid-bearing deposits of Java: state of the art. *Geologie en Mijnbouw* 64, 167-173.

Leone G., Bonadonna F. and Zanchetta G., 2000: Stable isotope record in mollusca and pedogenic carbonate from Late Pliocene soils of central Italy. *Palaeogeography, Palaeoclimatology, Palaeoecology* 163, 115-131.

Ljubin V.P. and Bosinksi G., 1995: The earliest occupation of the caucasus region. In: Roebroeks W. and Van Kolfschoten T. (eds.), *The earliest occupation of Europe, Proceedings of the ESF workshop at Tautavel (France), 1993*, p. 207-254. Leiden University Press, Leiden.

Lu H., Liu X., Zhang F., An Z. and Dodson J., 1999: Astronomical calibration of loess-paleosol deposits at Luochuan, central Chinese Loess Plateau. *Palaeogeography, Palaeoclimatology, Palaeoecology* 154, 237-246.

Manzi G., Mallegni F. and Ascenzi A., 2001: A cranium for the earliest Europeans: Phylogenetic position of the hominid from Ceprano, Italy. *Proc. Nat. Acad. Sci. USA* 98, 10011-10016.

Marean C.W., 1997: Hunter-Gatherer Foraging Strategies in Tropical Grasslands: Model Building and Testing in the East African Middle and Later Stone Age. *Journal of Anthropological Archaeology* 16, 189-225.

Matsu'ura S., 1982: A Chronological Framing for the Sangiran Hominids. Fundamental Study by the Fluorine Dating Method. *Bulletin of the National Science Museum, Tokyo, series D* 8, 1-53.

Matsu'ura S., 1985: A consideration of the stratigraphic horizons of hominid finds from Sangiran by the Fluorine method. In: Watanabe N. and Kadar D. (eds.), *Quaternary geology of the hominid fossil bearing Formations in Java. Report of the Indonesia-Japan Joint Research Project CTA-41, 1976-1979*, p. 359-366. Geological Research and Development Centre special publication no. 4, Bandung.

Matsu'ura S., 1986: Fluorine and Phosphate Analysis of Fossil Bones from the Kabuh Formation of Trinil. *Bulletin of the national Science Museum, Tokyo, series D* 12, 1-9.

McDougall I., Brown F. H., Cerling T. E. and Hillhouse J. W., 1992: A reappraisal of the geomagnetic polarity time scale to 4 Ma using data from the Turkana Basin, East Africa. *Geophysical Research Letters* 19, 2349-2352.

McGrew W.C., 1992: *Chimpanzee material Culture: implications for Human evolution*. Cambridge University Press, Cambridge.

Mercader J., Panger M. and Boesch C., 2002: Excavation of a Chimpanzee Stone Tool Site in the African Rainforest. *Science* 296, 1452-1455.

Mishra S., 1992: The Age of the Acheulian in India. New Evidence. *Current Anthropology* 33, 325-328.

Mishra S., 1999: Developing an Indian stone age chronology. In: Murray T. (ed.), *Time and Archaeology*, p. 80-87. Routledge, London.

Mishra S., Venkatesan T.R., Rajaguru S.N. and Somayajulu B.L.K., 1995: Earliest Acheulean Industry from Peninsular India. *Current Anthropology* 36, 847-851.

Misra V.N., 1987: Middle Pleistocene Adaptations in India. In: Soffer O. (ed.), *The Pleistocene Old World, regional perspectives*, p. 99-119. Plenum Press, New York.

Morwood M.J., Aziz F., Van den Bergh G.D., Sondaar P.Y. and de Vos J., 1997: Stone artefacts from the 1994 exacavation at Mata Menge, West Central Flores, Indonesia. *Australian Archaeology* 44, 26-34.

Morwood M.J., O'Sullivan P.B., Aziz F. and Raza A., 1998: Fission-track ages of stone tools and fossils on the east Indonesian island of Flores. *Nature* 392, 173-176.

Morwood M.J., Aziz F., O'Sullivan P., Nasruddin, Hobbs D.R. and Raza A., 1999: Archaeological and palaeontological research in central Flores, east Indonesia: results of fieldwork 1997-98. *Antiquity* 73, 273-286.

Movius H., 1944: *Early man and Pleistocene stratigraphy in southern and eastern Asia.* Peabody Museum of Archaeology and Ethnology Papers 19, Harvard.

Movius H., 1948: The Lower palaeolithic cultures of southern and eastern Asia. *Trans. Am. Phil. Soc.* 38, 329-420.

Moyà-Solà S. and Köhler M., 1997: The Orce skull, anatomy of a mistake. *Journal of Human Evolution* 33, 91-97.

Mussi M., 1995: The earliest occupation of Europe: Italy. In: Roebroeks W. and Van Kolfschoten T. (eds.), *The earliest occupation of Europe, Proceedings of the ESF workshop at Tautavel (France), 1993*, p. 27-49. Leiden University Press, Leiden.

Mussi M., 2001: *Earliest Italy. An Overview of the Italian Paleolithic and Mesolithic.* Kluwer Academic Publishers, Dordrecht.

Navarro B.M., Turq A., Ballester J.A. and Oms O., 1997: Fuente Nueva-3 (Orce, Granada, Spain) and the first human occupation of Europe. *Journal of Human Evolution* 33, 611-620.

Oakley K.P., Andrews P., Keeley L.H. and Clark J.D., 1977: A Reappraisal of the Clacton Spearpoint. *Proc. Prehist. Soc.* 43, 13-30.

Obradovich J.D., Naeser C.W., Izett G.A., Pasini G. and Bigazzi G., 1982: Age constraints on the proposed Plio-Pleistocene boundary stratotype at Vrica, Italy. *Nature* 298, 55-59.

Olsen J.W. and Ciochon R.L., 1990: A review of evidence for postulated Middle Pleistocene occupations in Viet Nam. *Journal of Human Evolution* 19, 761-788.

Oms O., Parés J.M., Martínez-Navarro B., Agusti J., Toto I., Martínez-Fernández G. and Turq A., 2000: Early human occupation of Western Europe: paleomagnetic dates for two paleolithic sites in Spain. *Proc. Nat. Acad. Sci. USA* 97, 10666-10670.

Orchiston D.W. and Siesser W.G., 1982: Chronostratigraphy of the Plio-Pleistocene fossil hominids of Java. *Mod. Quat. Res. SE Asia* 7, 131-149.

Paine M., 2001: Source of Australasian Tektites? *Meteorite!* 7, 34-37.

Palmqvist P., 1997: A critical re-evaluation of the evidence for the presence of hominids in Lower Pleistocene times at Venta Micena, Southern Spain. *Journal of Human Evolution* 33, 83-89.

Parés J.M. and Pérez-Gonzáles A., 1995: Palaeomagnetic Age for Hominid Fossils at Atapuerca Archaeological Site, Spain. *Science* 269, 830-832.

Parés J.M. and Pérez-González A., 1999: Magnetochronology and stratigraphy at Gran Dolina section, Atapuerca (Burgos, Spain). *Journal of Human Evolution* 37, 325-342.

Peretto C. (ed.), 1992: *I primi abitanti della Valle Padana: Monte Poggiolo. Nel quadro delle conoscenze Europee.* Jaca Books spa, Milano.

Peters C.R., and Blumenschine R.J., 1995: Landscape perspectives on possible land-use patterns for early Pleistocene hominids in the Olduvai Basin, Tanzania. *Journal of Human Evolution* 29, 321-362.

Petraglia M.D., 2003: The Lower Paleolithic of the Arabian Peninsula: Occupations, Adaptations, and Dispersals. *Journal of World Prehistory* 17, 141-179

Pitts M. and Roberts M., 1997: *Fairweather Eden: life in Britain half a million years ago as revealed by the excavations at Boxgrove.* Century, London.

Pope G.G., 1985: Taxonomy, Dating and Palaeoenvironment. The palaeoecology of the early Far Eastern hominids. *Mod. Quat. Res. SE Asia* 9, 65-80.

Pope G.G. and Cronin J.E., 1984: The Asian *Hominidae. Journal of Human Evolution* 13, 377-396.

Pope G.G. and Keates S.G., 1994: The Evolution of Human Cognition and Cultural Capacity: a view from the Far East. In: Corruccini R.S. and Ciochon R.L. (eds.), *Integrative Paths to the Past, Palaeoanthropological Advances in Honor of F. Clark Howell*, p. 531-567. Prentice Hall, New Jersey.

Pope G.G., Barr S., Macdonald A. and Nakabanlang S., 1986: Earliest Radiometrically Dated Artifacts from Southeast Asia. *Current Anthropology* 27, 275-279.

Potts R., 1998: Variability Selection in Hominid Evolution. *Evolutionary Anthropology* 7, 81-96.

Potts R., Huang W., Hou Y., Deino A., Yuan B., Guo Z. and Clark J., 2000: reply to: Tektites and the Age Paradox in Mid-Pleistocene China. *Science* 289, 507a-508a.

Qiu Z. and Qiu Z, 1995: Chronological sequence and subdivision of Chinese Neogene mammalian faunas. *Palaeogeography, Palaeoclimatology, Palaeoecology* 116, 41-70.

Quade J. and Cerling T.E., 1995: Expansion of C_4 grasses in the Late Miocene of Northern Pakistan: evidence from stable isotopes in paleosols. *Palaeogeography, Palaeoclimatology, Palaeoecology* 115, 91-116.

Ranov V.A., 1991: Les sites très anciens de l'age de la pierre en U.R.S.S. In: Bonifay E. and Vandermeersch B. (eds.), *Les premiers Européens*, p. 209-216. Editions CTHS, Paris.

Ranov V.A., Carbonell E. and Rodriguez X.D., 1995: Kuldara, earliest human occupation in central Asia in its Afro-Asian context. *Current Anthropology* 36, 337-346.

Raynal J.P. and Texier J.P., 1989: Découverte d'Acheuléen ancien dans la carrière Thomas 1 à Casablanca et problème de l'ancienneté de la presence humaine au Maroc. *C. R. Acad. Sci. Paris* 308-II, 1743-1749.

Raynal J.P., Magoga L. and Bindon P., 1995a: Tephrofacts and the first human occupation of the French Massif central. In: Roebroeks W. and Van Kolfschoten T. (eds.), *The earliest occupation of Europe, Proceedings of the ESF workshop at tautavel (France), 1993*, p. 129-146. Leiden University, Leiden.

Raynal J.P., Magoga L., Sbihi-Alaoui F. and Geraads D., 1995b: The earliest occupation of Atlantic Morocco. The Casablanca evidence. In: Roebroeks W. and Van Kolfschoten T. (eds.), *The earliest occupation of Europe, Proceedings of the ESF workshop at tautavel (France), 1993*, p. 255-262. Leiden University, Leiden.

Raynal J.P., Sbihi-Alaoui F.Z., Geraads D., Magoga L. and Mohi A., 2001: The earliest occupation of North-Africa: the Moroccan perspective. *Quaternary International* 75, 65-75.

Reed K.E., 1997: Early hominid evolution and ecological change through the African Plio-Pleistocene. *Journal of Human Evolution* 32, 289-322.

Rendell H. and Dennell R.W., 1985: Dated Lower Palaeolithic Artefacts from Northern Pakistan. *Current Anthropology* 26, 393.

Retallack G.J. (2001): Cenozoic Expansion of Grasslands and Climatic Cooling. *Journal of Geology* 109, 407-426.

Reynolds T.E.G., 1993: Problems in the stone age of South-East Asia. *Proc. Prehist. Soc.* 59, 1-15.

Rhodes E.J., Raynal J.P., Geraads D. and Sbihi-Alaoui F., 1994: Premières dates RPE pour l'Acheléen du Maroc Atlantique (Grotte des Rhinocéros, Casablanca). *C. R. Acad. Sci. Paris* 319-II, 1109-1115.

Richards M.P., Pettitt P.B., Trinkaus E., Smith F.H., Paunovic M. and Karavanic I., 2000: Neandertal diet at Vindija and Neandertal predation. The evidence from stable isotopes. *Proc. Nat. Acad. Sci. USA* 97, 7663-7666.

Roberts M.B. and Parfitt S.A., 1999: *Boxgrove, A Middle Pleistocene hominid site at Eartham Quarry, Boxgrove, West Sussex*. English Heritage archaeological report 17, London.

Roberts M.B., Gamble C.S. and Bridgland D.R., 1995: The earliest Occupation of Europe: the British Isles. In: Roebroeks W. and Van Kolfschoten T. (eds.), *The earliest occupation of Europe, Proceedings of the ESF workshop at Tautavel (France), 1993*, p. 165-182. Leiden University, Leiden.

Roberts M.B., Parfitt S.A., Pope M.I. and Wenban-Smith F.F., 1997: Boxgrove, West Sussex: Rescue Excavations of a Lower Palaeolithic landsurface (Boxgrove Project B, 1989-91). *Proc. Prehist. Soc.* 63, 303-358.

Roberts R., Bird M., Olley J., Galbraith R., Lawson E., Laslett G., Yoshida H., Jones R., Fullagar R., Jacobsen G. and Hua Q., 1998: Optical and radiocarbon dating at Jinmium rock shelter in northern Australia. *Nature* 393, 358-362.

Roche H., Delagnes A., Brugal J-P., Feibel C., Kibunjia M., Mourre V. and Texier J-P., 1999: Early hominid stone tool production and technical skill 2.34 Myr ago in West Turkana, Kenya. *Nature* 399, 57-60.

Roe D.A., 1995: The Orce Basin (Andalucia, Spain) and the initial palaeolithic of Europe. *Oxford Journal of Archaeology* 14, 1-12.

Roebroeks W., 1986: On the "Lower Paleolithic" Site La belle Roche: An Alternative Interpretation. *Current Anthropology* 27, 369-370.

Roebroeks W., 1988: *From Find Scatters to early Hominid Behaviour. A study of Middle Palaeolithic river side setllements at Maastricht-Belvédère (The Netherlands)*. PhD dissertation, Leiden University (*Analecta Praehistorica Leidensia* 21).

Roebroeks W., 1994: Updating the Earliest Occupation of Europe. *Current Anthropology* 35, 301-305.

Roebroeks W., 1996: The English Palaeolithic record: absence of evidence, evidence of absence and the first occupation of Europe. In: Gamble C. and Lawson A. (eds.), *The English Palaeolithic Reviewed: papers from a day conference held at the Society of Antiquaries of London, 28 October 1994*, p. 57-62. Trust for Wessex Archaeology, Salisbury.

Roebroeks W., 2001: Hominid behaviour and the earliest occupation of Europe: an exploration. *Journal of Human Evolution* 41, 437-461.

Roebroeks W. and Van Kolfschoten T., 1994: The earliest occupation of Europe, a short Chronology. *Antiquity* 68, 489-503.

Roebroeks W. and Van Kolfschoten T. (eds.), 1995: *The earliest occupation of Europe, Proceedings of the ESF workshop at Tautavel (France), 1993*. Leiden University, Leiden.

Roebroeks W., Kolen J. and Rensink E., 1988: Planning depth, anticipation and the organization of Middle paleolithic technology: the "archaic natives" meet Eve's descendants. *Helinium* 28, 17-34.

Roebroeks W., De Loecker D., Hennekens P. and van Ieperen M., 1995: "A veil of stones": on the interpretation of an early Middle Palaeolithic low density scatter at Maastricht-Belvédère (The Netherlands). *Analecta Praehistorica Leidensia* 25, 1-16.

Rogers M.J., Harris J.W.K. and feibel C.S., 1994: Changing patterns of land use by Plio-Pleistocene hominids in the Lake Turkana Basin. *Journal of Human Evolution* 27, 139-158.

Ronen A., 1991: The Yiron-gravel lithic assemblage. Artifacts older than 2.4 My in Israel. *Archäologisches Korrespondenzblatt* 21, 159-164.

Sahnouni M., 1998: *The Lower Palaeolithic of the Maghreb: excavations and analyses at Ain Hanech, Algeria*. BAR International Series 698.

Sahnouni M. and De Heinzelin J., 1998: The Site of Ain Hanech Revisited: New Investigations at this Lower Pleistocene Site in Northern Algeria. *Journal of Archaeological Science* 25, 1083-1101.

Sahnouni M., De Heinzelin J., Brown F. and Saoudi Y., 1996: Récentes Recherches dans le gisement Oldowayen d'Ain Hanceh, Algérie. *C. R. Acad. Sci. Paris* 323-II, 639-644.

Sahnouni M., Schick K. and Toth N., 1997: An Experimental Investigation into the Nature of Faceted Limestone "Spheroids" in the Early Palaeolithic. *Journal of Archaeological Science* 24, 701-713.

Saragusti I. and Goren-Inbar N., 2001: The biface assemblage from Gesher Benot Ya'agov, Israel: illuminating patterns in "Out of Africa" dispersal. *Quaternary International* 75, 85-89.

Sartono S., Sémah F., Astadiredja K.A.S., Sukendarmono M. and Djubiantono T., 1981: The age of *Homo modjokertensis*. *Mod. Quat. Res. SE Asia* 6, 91-102.

Schick K.D., 1994: The Movius Line Reconsidered. Perspectives on the Earlier Palaeolithic of Eastern Asia. In: Corruccini R.S. and Ciochon R.L. (eds*.), Integrative Paths to the Past, Palaeoanthropological Advances in Honor of F. Clark Howell*, p. 569-596. Prentice Hall, New Jersey.

Schick K.D. and Dong Z., 1993: Early Palaeolithic of China and Eastern Asia. *Evolutionary Anthropology* 2, 22-35.

Schick K.D., Toth N., Wei Q., Clark J.D. and Etler D., 1991: Archaeological perspectives in the Nihewan Basin, China. *Journal of Human Evolution* 21, 13-26.

Schick K.D. and Toth N., 1994: Early Stone Age technology in Africa: a review and case study into the nature and function of spheroids and subspheroids. In: Corruccini R.S. and Ciochon R.L. (eds*.), Integrative Paths to the Past, Palaeoanthropological Advances in Honor of F. Clark Howell*, p. 429-449. Prentice Hall, New Jersey.

Schmidt G. and Wasson J.T., 1993: Masses of the impactor, the Australasian tektites, and size estimates of the main source crater. *Meteoritics* 28, 430-431.

Schneider D.A., Kent D.V. and Mello G.A., 1992: A detailed chronology of the Australasian impact event, the Brunhes-Matuyama geomagnetic polarity reversal, and global climate change. *Earth Planet. Sci. Let.* 111, 395-405.

Schnetzler C.C. and McHone J.F., 1996: Source of Australasian tektites: investigating possible impact sites in Laos. *Meteoritics & Planetary Science* 31, 73-76.

123

Schwartz J.H. and Tattersall I, 1996: Whose teeth? *Nature* 381, 201-202.

Segre A. and Ascenzi A., 1984: Italy's Earliest Middle Pleistocene Hominid Site. *Current Anthropology* 25, 230-233.

Sémah F., 1982: Pliocene and Pleistocene geomagnetic reversals recorded in the Gemolong and Sangiran domes (central Java). *Mod. Quat. Res. SE Asia* 7, 151-164.

Sémah F., Sémah A., Djubiantono T. and Simunjuntak H.T., 1992 : Did they also make stone tools? *Journal of Human Evolution* 23, 439-446.

Sémah F., Falguères C., Yokoyama Y., Féraud G., Saleki H. and Djubiantono T., 1997: Arrivée et disparition des *Homo erectus* a Java, les données actuelles. Paper presented at the *Third meeting of the European Association of Archaeologists, Ravenna (Italy), September 1997*, p. 24-28 (abstract).

Sémah F., Saleki H. and Falguères C., 2000: Did Early Man reach Java during the Late Pliocene? *Journal of Archaeological Science* 27, 763-769.

Semaw S., 2000: The World's Oldest Stone Artefacts from Gona, Ethiopia: Their Implications for Understanding Stone Technology and patterns of Human Evolution Between 2.6-1.5 Million Years Ago. *Journal of Archaeological Science* 27, 1197-1214.

Semaw S., Renne P., Harris J.W.K., Feibel C.S., Bernor R.L., Fesseha N. and Mowbray K., 1997: 2.5-million-year-old stone tools from Gona, Ethiopia. *Nature* 385, 333-336.

Sept J.M., 1986: Plant Foods and Early Hominids at site FxJj50, Koobi Fora, Kenya. *Journal of Human Evolution* 15, 751-770.

Sept J.M., 1994: Beyond bones: archaeological sites, early hominid subsistence, and the costs and benefits of exploiting wild plant foods in east African riverine landscapes. *Journal of Human Evolution* 27, 295-320.

Shackley M., 1984: Palaeolithic archaeology in the Mongolian People's Republic. A report on the state of the art. *Proc. Prehist. Soc.* 50, 23-34.

Shipman P., 1986: Scavenging or hunting in early hominids: theoretical frameworks and tests. *American Anthropology* 88, 27-43.

Shipman P., 2001: *The Man Who Found the Missing Link. The extraordinary life of Eugene Dubois.* Weidenfeld & Nicolson, London.

Sillen A., Hall G., Richardson S. and Armstrong R., 1998: $^{87}Sr/^{86}Sr$ in modern and fossil foodwebs of the Sterkfontein Valley: implications for early hominid habitat preference. *Geochimica et Cosmochimica Acta* 162, 2463-2473.

Sondaar P.Y., Van den Bergh G.D., Mubroto B., Aziz F., De Vos J. and Batu U.L., 1994: Middle Pleistocene faunal turnover and colonization of Flores (Indonesia) by *Homo erectus*. *C.R. Acad. Sci. Paris* 319-II, 1255-1262.

Spencer L.M., 1997: Dietary adaptations of Plio-Pleistocene Bovidae: implications for hominid habitat use. *Journal of Human Evolution* 32, 201-228.

Speth J.D., 1987: Early Hominid Subsistence Strategies in Seasonal Habitats. *Journal of Archaeological Science* 14, 13-29.

Speth J.D. and Spielmann K.A., 1983: Energy Source, Protein Metabolism, and Hunter-Gatherer Subsistence Strategies. *Journal of Anthropological Archaeology* 2, 1-31.

Spooner N.A., 1998: Human occupation of Jinmium, northern Australia: 116,000 years ago or much less? *Antiquity* 72, 173-178.

Stern N., 1993: The Structure of the Lower Pleistocene Archaeological Record. *Current Anthropology* 34, 201-225.

Stern N., 1994: The implications of time-averaging for reconstructing the land-use patterns of early tool-using hominids. *Journal of Human Evolution* 27, 89-105.

Stringer C., 1990: The Asian Connection. *New Scientist*, 17 November 1990, 33-37.

Stringer C. and Gamble C., 1993: *In Search of the Neanderthals. Solving the puzzle of Human origins*. Thames and Hudson, London.

Susman R.L., 1991: Who made the Oldowan tools? Fossil evidence for tool behavior on Plio-Pleistocene hominids. *J. Anthr. Res.* 47, 129-151.

Svoboda J., 1987: Lithic Industreis of the Arago, Vértesszöllös, and Blizingsleben Hominids: Comparison and Evolutionary Interpretation. *Current Anthropology* 28, 219-227.

Swisher C.C., 1994: Reply to 'Dating Hominid Sites in Indonesia'. *Science* 266, 1727.

Swisher C.C., 1997: A revised geochronology for the Plio-Pleistocene hominid-bearing strata of Sangiran Java, Indonesia. *Abstracts of the Palaeoanthropology Society Meetings, 1-2 April 1997 (Journal of Human Evolution 32, A23)*.

Swisher C.C., Curtiss G.H., Jacob T., Getty A.G., Suprijo A. and Widiasmoro, 1994: Age of the Earliest Known Hominids in Java, Indonesia. *Science* 263, 1118-1121.

Swisher C.C., Rink W.J., Antón S.C., Schwarcz H.P., Curtiss G.H., Suprijo A. and Widiasmoro, 1996: latest *Homo erectus* of Java, Potential Contemporaneity with *Homo sapiens* in Southeast Asia. *Science* 274, 1870-1874.

Tappen M., 1995: Savanna Ecology and Natural Bone Deposition. Implications for Early Hominid Site Formation, Hunting, and Scavenging. *Current Anthropology* 36, 223-260.

Tappen M., Adler D.S., Ferring C.R., Gabunia M., Vekua A. and Swisher C.C., 2002: Akhlakalaki: The Taphonomy of an Early Pleistocene locality in the Republic of Georgia. *Journal of Archaeological Science* 29, 1367-1391.

Tauxe L., Herbert T., Shackleton N.J. and Kok Y.S., 1996: Astronomical calibration of the Matuyama-Brunhes boundary: Consequences for magnetic remanence acquisition in marine carbonates and the Asian loess sequence. *Earth Planet. Sci. Let.* 140, 133-146.

Tchernov E., 1989: The age of the Ubeidiya Formation. *Israeli Journal of Earth Sciences* 36, 3-30.

Tchernov E., 1992: Eurasian-African biotic exchanges through the Levantine corridor during the Neogene and Quaternary. *Courier Forschungs-Institut Senckenberg* 153, 103-123.

Templeton A.R., 2002: Out of Africa again and again. *Nature* 416, 45-51.

Theunissen L.T.G., 1985: *Eugène Dubois en de aapmens van Java*. Rodopi, Amsterdam.

Theunissen B., De Vos J., Sondaar P.Y. en Aziz F., 1990 : The stablishment of a chronological framework for the hominid-bearing deposits of Java: a historical survey. In: Laporte L.F. (ed.), *Establishment of a geologic framework for Palaeoanthropology*, p. 39-54. Geological Society of America Special Paper 242.

Thieme H., 1996: Altpaläolitische wurfspeere aus Schöningen, Niedersachsen –ein vorbericht. *Archäologisches Korrespondenzblatt* 26, 377-393.

Thieme H., 1997: Lower Palaeolithic hunting spears from Germany. *Nature* 385, 807-810.

Thieme H., 1999: Altpaläolithische Holtzgeräte aus Schöningen, Lkr. Helmstedt. Bedeutsame Funde zur Kulturentwicklung des Frühen Menschen. *Germania* 77, 451-487.

Thomas H., Geraads D., Janjou D., Vaslet D., Memesh A., Billiou D., Bocherens H., Dobigny G., Eisenmann V., Gayet M., De Lapparent de Broin F., Petter G. and Halawani M., 1998: First Pleistocene faunas from the Arabian Peninsula: An Nafud desert, Saudi Arabia. *C. R. Acad. Sci. Paris* 326, 145-152.

Thorne A., Grün R., Mortimer G., Spooner N.A., Simpson J.J., McCulloch M., Taylor L. and Curnoe D., 1999: Australia's oldest human remains. Age of the Lake Mungo 3 skeleton. *Journal of Human Evolution* 36, 591-612.

Tiemei C. and Yunping H., 1988: Chronological study of Chinese palaeolithic archaeology and palaeoanthropology. *Jahrbuch des Römisch-Germanischen Zentralmuseums Mainz* 35, 97-109.

Tixier J., Roe D., Turq A., Gibert J., Martinez B., Arribas A., Gibert L., Maillo A. and Iglesias A., 1995: Présence d'industries lithiques dans le Pléistocène inférieur de la région d'Orce (Grenade, Espagne): quel est l'état de la question? *C. R. Acad. Sci. Paris* 321-II, 71-78.

Tobias P.V., 1966: *A Member of the Genus Homo from 'Ubeidiya*. The Israel Academy of Sciences and Humanities, Jerusalem.

Toth N., 1987: Behavioural inferences from early stone artifact assemblages: an experimental model. *Journal of Human Evolution* 16, 763-787.

Toth N. and Schick K.D., 1986: The First Million Years: the archaeology of protohuman culture. *Advances in Archaeological Method and Theory* 9, 1-96.

Toth N. and Schick K.D., 1993: Early stone industries and inferences regarding language and cognition. In: Gibson K.R. and Ingold T. (eds.), *Tools, Language and Cognition in Human Evolution*, p. 346-362. Cambridge University Press, Cambridge.

Toth N., Schick K.D., Savage-Rumbaugh E.S., Sevcik R.A. and Rumbaugh D.M., 1993: Pan the Tool-Maker: Investigations into the Stone Tool-Making and Tool-Using Capabilities of a Bonobo (*Pan paniscus*). *Journal of Archaeological Science* 20, 81-91.

Tougard C., Chaimanee Y., Suteethorn V., Triamwichanon S. and Jaeger J., 1996: Extension of the geographic distribution of the giant Panda (*Ailuropoda*) and search for the reasons for its progressive disappearance in Southeast Asia during the latest Middle Pleistocene. *C. R. Acad. Sci. Paris* 323-II, 973-979.

Trinkaus E. and Shipman P., 1993: *The Neandertals. Changing the image of mankind*. Alfred A. Knopf, New York.

Tuffreau A. and Antoine P, 1995: The earliest occupation of Europe: Continental Northwestern Europe. In: Roebroeks W. and Van Kolfschoten T. (eds.), *The earliest occupation of Europe, Proceedings of the ESF workshop at Tautavel (France), 1993*, p. 147-163. Leiden University, Leiden.

Tuffreau A., Lamotte A. and Marcy J-L., 1997a: Land-use and site function in Acheulean complexes of the Somme Valley. *World Archaeology* 29, 225-241.

Tuffreau A., Lamotte A., Antoine P. and Marcy J-L., 1997b : Le Gisement Acheuleen de la Ferme de l'Epinette a Cagny (Somme, France). *Archäologisches Korrespondenzblatt* 27, 513-530.

Turner A., 1992 : Large carnivores and earliest European hominids : changing determinants of resource availibility during the Lower and Middle Pleistocene. *Journal of Human Evolution* 22, 109-126.

Turq A., Martínez-Navarro B., Palmqvist P., Arribas A., Agusti J. and Rodríguez Vidal J., 1996: Le Plio-Pleistocene de la Région d'Orce, province de Grenade, Espagne: bilan et perspectives de recherche. *Paleo* 8, 161-204.

Urabe A., Nakaya H., Muto T., Katoh S., Hyodo M. and Xue S., 2001: Lithostratigraphy and depositional history of the Late Cenozoic hominid-bearing successions in the Yuanmou Basin, southwest China. *Quaternary Science Reviews* 20, 1671-1681.

Valet J-P. and Meynadier L., 1993: Geomagnetic field intensity and reversals during the past four million years. *Nature* 366, 234-238.

Van Kolfschoten T., 1998: Biostratigraphical evidence of the earliest occupation of Europe. In: Carbonell E., Bermúdez de Castro J.M., Arsuaga J.L., Rodriguez X.P. (eds.), *Los primeros pobladores de Europa: Ultimos descrubimientos y debate actual*, p. 101-115. Burgos, Diario de Burgos.

Vekua A., Lordkipanidze D., Rightmire G.P., Agusti J., Ferring R., Maisuradze G., Mouskelishvili A., Nioradze M., Pnce de Leon M., Tappen M., Tvalchrelidze M. and Zollikofer C., 2002: A New Skull of Early *Homo* from Dmanisi, Georgia. *Science* 297, 85-89.

Verosub K.L., 1983: Geomagnetic excursions, a critical assessment of the evidence as recorded in sediments of the Brunhes Epoch. *Phil. Trans. Roy. Soc. London* A 306, 161-168.

Verosub K.L. and Tchernov E., 1991: Résultats préliminaires de l'etude magnétostratigraphique d'une séquence sédimentaire à industrie humaine en Israèl. In: Bonifay E. and Vandermeersch B. (eds.), *Les premiers Europeéns*, p. 237-242. Editions CTHS, Paris.

Verpoorte A., 2001: *Places of art, traces of fire. A contextual approach to anthropomorphic figurines in the Pavlovian (central Europe, 29-24 kyr BP)*. Archaeological Studies Leiden University 8 / Dolnověstonické Studie 6, Leiden/Brno.

Villa P., 2001: Early Italy and the colonization of Western Europe. *Quaternary International* 75, 113-130.

Vincent A.S., 1984: Plant foods in savanna environments: a preliminary report of tubers eaten by the Hadza of northern Tanzania. *World Archaeology* 17, 131-148.

Von Koenigswald W., 1992: Various aspects of migrations in terrestrial mammals in relation to Pleistocene faunas of Central Europe. *Courier Forschungs-Institut Senckenberg* 153, 39-47.

Walker D. and Sieveking A.G., 1962: The Palaeolithic Industry of Kota Tampan, Perak, Malaya. *Proc. Prehist. Soc.* 28, 103-139.

Walker A. and Shipman P., 1996: *The Wisdom of Bones. In Search of Human Origins*. London.

Ward C., Leakey M. and Walker A., 1999: The New Hominid Species *Australopithecus anamensis*. *Evolutionary Anthropology* 7, 197-205.

Watanabe H., 1985: The Chopper-Chopping Tool Complex of eastern Asia: An Ethnoarchaeological-Ecological Reexamination. *Journal of Anthropological Archaeology* 4, 1-18.

Watanabe N. and Kadar D., 1985 (eds.): *Quaternary geology of the hominid fossil bearing Formations in Java. Report of the Indonesia-Japan Joint Research Project CTA-41, 1976-1979*. Geological Research and Development Centre special publication no. 4, Bandung.

Werker E. and Goren-Inbar N., 2001: reconstruction of the Woody vegetation at the Acheulian Site of Gesher Benot Ya'aqov, Dead Sea Rift, Israel. In: Purdy B.A. (ed.), *Enduring records. The environmental and cultural heritage of wetlands*, p. 206-213. Oxbow books, Oxford.

Whalen N.M. and Pease D.W., 1992: Early mankind in Arabia. *Aramco World* 43(2), 16-23.

White M.J., 2000: The Clactonian Question: On the Interpretation of Core-and-Flake Assemblages in the British Lower Palaeolithic. *Journal of World Prehistory* 14, 1-63.

White T.D., Suwa G. and Asfaw B., 1994: *Australopithecus ramidus*, a new species of early hominid from Aramis, Ethiopia. *Nature* 371, 306-312.

White T.D., Suwa G. and Asfaw B., 1995: Corrigendum: *Australopithecus ramidus*, a new species of early hominid from Aramis, Ethiopia. *Nature* 375, 88.

Williams M.A.J., Williams F.M., Gasse F., Curtiss G.H. and Adamson D.A., 1979: Plio-Pleistocene environments at Gadeb prehistoric site, Ethiopia. *Nature* 282, 29-33.

WoldeGabriel G., White T.D., Suwa G., Renne P., De Heinzelin J., Hart W.K. and Heiken G., 1994: Ecological and temporal placement of early Pliocene hominids at Aramis, Ethiopia. *Nature* 371, 330-333.

WoldeGabriel G., Haile-Selassie Y., Renne P.R., Hart W.K., Ambrose S.H., Asfaw B., Heiken G. and White T., 2001: Geology and palaeontology of the Late Miocene Middle Awash valley, Afar rift, Ethiopia. *Nature* 412, 175-178.

Woo J., 1964: Mandible of *Sinanthropus lantianensis. Current Anthropology* 5, 98-101.

Woo J., 1966: The skull of Lantian Man. *Current Anthropology* 7, 83-86.

Wood B., 1997: The oldest whodunnit in the World. *Nature* 385, 292-293.

Wood B. and Turner A., 1995: Out of Africa and into Asia. *Nature* 378, 239-240.

Wynn T. and Tierson F., 1990: Regional Comparison of the Shapes of Later Acheulean Handaxes. *American Anthropologist* 92, 73-84.

Yi S. and Clark G.A., 1983: Observations on the Lower Palaeolithic of Northeast Asia. *Current Anthropology* 24, 181-202.

Yokoyama Y., Bahain J.J., Falguères C. and Gaignepain J., 1992: Tentative de datation par la méthode de la résonance de spin électronique (ESR) de sédiments quaternaires de la région de Forlì (Italie). In: Peretto C.(ed.), *I primi abitanti della Valle Padana: Monte Poggiolo. Nel quadro delle conoscenze Europee*, p. 337-346. Jaca Books spa, Milano.

Yoshikawa S. and Suminto, 1985: Tuff layers and pumice tuff beds of the Pliocene and Pleistocene sediments in the Sangiran area.In: Watanabe N. and Kadar D. (eds.), *Quaternary geology of the hominid fossil bearing Formations in Java. Report of the Indonesia-Japan Joint Research Project CTA-41, 1976-1979*, p. 97-106. Geological Research and Development Centre special publication no. 4, Bandung.

Zhu R.X., Hoffman K.A., Potts R., Deng C.L., Pan Y.X., Guo B., Shi C.D., Guo Z.T., Yuan B.Y., Hou Y.M. and Huang W.W., 2001: Earliest presence of humans in northeast Asia. *Nature* 413, 413-417.

www.ingramcontent.com/pod-product-compliance
Lightning Source LLC
Chambersburg PA
CBHW061001030426
42334CB00033B/3319